T0321427

SCOTLAND'S STORIES

HISTORIC TALES FOR INCREDIBLE PLACES

GRAEME JOHNCOCK

First published 2023

The History Press
97 St George's Place, Cheltenham,
Gloucestershire, GL50 3QB
www.thehistorypress.co.uk

© Graeme Johncock, 2023

The right of Graeme Johncock to be identified as the Author
of this work has been asserted in accordance with the
Copyright, Designs and Patents Act 1988.

All rights reserved. No part of this book may be reprinted
or reproduced or utilised in any form or by any electronic,
mechanical or other means, now known or hereafter invented,
including photocopying and recording, or in any information
storage or retrieval system, without the permission in writing
from the Publishers.

British Library Cataloguing in Publication Data.
A catalogue record for this book is available from the British Library.

ISBN 978 1 8039 9266 2

Typesetting and origination by The History Press.
Printed and bound in Great Britain by TJ Books Limited, Padstow, Cornwall.

Trees for Life

CONTENTS

To the ever-patient Emma and the ever-youthful Molly.
I doubt I would have written this were it not for both of you.

FOREWORD

Scotland is rich in stories. Under every rock and in every stream lie tales of fact, fiction or something in between. Trees whisper stories of Celts and Picts, while the seas roar with Viking lore. Clansmen passed them down. Victorians romanticised them. And now, Graeme shares them with the world.

The very land whets our imaginations; littered with dark, expansive forests, towering ruins and solitary standing stones, it is hardly surprising that there is a story in all that we see. Our stories bring us together around the fire, and they let us reach out our hands to the past.

From fairies in their green hills to real-life stories of clansmen and war heroes, Graeme has left no stone unturned in capturing Scotland's vibrant history and folklore. Having worked with Graeme since our early days as a charity, we have had plenty of opportunities to discuss the allure of these tales and their relevance today. At Folklore Scotland we have always been fascinated with the real-life places that lie behind these stories – there is something uncanny and magical about the boundary where the intangible meets the tangible and stories spring to life.

As you explore Scotland, listen for the ancient folk, embrace a wanderer's lust, and let Graeme be your guide through Scotland's stories.

Rebecca and David White
Co-Founders of Folklore Scotland

INTRODUCTION

Everybody loves a good story – young and old alike.

The medium may have changed over the generations, with most people now watching TV shows instead of sitting around a fire, but the essence is the same. Stories can get your heart pumping a little bit faster, make the hair on the back of your neck stand up or even bring you to tears.

Most importantly, stories bring places to life. They can transform a pile of stones into the scene of a daring escape or a dark cave into the lair of a supernatural creature.

That's what makes Scotland's stories so incredible. This small country is absolutely packed full of history, myths and legends, with very few of them set in a land far far away. Most are tied to a specific castle, glen, loch or rock that is still recognisable today.

This book is your guide to those places, so you can stand in the same spot where something incredible once happened and imagine it playing out before your eyes. There are stories of real-life heroes, accounts of brutal battles, legends of folklore and plenty of ghostly goings-on.

Some of Scotland's stories are world-famous like the legendary Loch Ness Monster. Others are lesser-known, local tales of mysterious curses, supernatural creatures and incredible bravery. All of them deserve to be told and every place deserves to be seen.

From the unique folklore of the Northern Isles to Borders Ballads, from the castles of Aberdeenshire to the clans of the west coast, Scotland has an incredible variety of stories to enjoy.

Wherever or whenever you're planning to visit, or if reading is your way of travelling virtually, I hope you find that this book and these stories help to make Scotland even more enjoyable.

ABERDEENSHIRE

THE GIANT TRAPPED UNDER BENNACHIE

The iconic shape of Bennachie makes it one of Aberdeenshire's most iconic hills. It's nowhere near the highest mountain in Scotland, but there may be more to this landmark than meets the eye.

It was once home to a fearsome giant called Jock O' Bennachie, as ancient as he was enormous. Jock wasn't alone in the Aberdeenshire hills: his biggest rival, also named Jock, lived nearby at the Tap O' Noth.

These two giants hated each other and, to make things worse, were competing for the attention of a beautiful giantess called Lady Anne. Unfortunately for Jock O' Bennachie, Anne had taken a shine to his rival and wasn't very subtle about it. One day, poor Jock gazed across to Tap O' Noth and spotted the giant couple canoodling in view of all Aberdeenshire.

Enraged, he picked up a boulder and launched it at them. The other Jock saw it coming a mile away and booted it right back, knocking a chunk out the top of Bennachie that can still be seen today. Boulders were flying back and forward, but Lady Anne wasn't going to have them destroying half of Aberdeenshire on her behalf.

She pushed in front of Jock O' Noth, pleading for him to stop, when a boulder hit her square on, crushing her to death. Jock O' Bennachie was even more devastated now, and to make matters worse, he was terrified his rival would come looking for revenge. He fled down from his hilltop, hiding out of shame and expecting to meet his end at any moment.

That night, Jock suddenly awoke with an uneasy sense that somebody else was moving in the darkness. The shape of a giant face loomed in front of him as a familiar, soft voice whispered his name. In the faint moonlight, he could see it was the beautiful Lady Anne!

He was overjoyed, his guilt was gone and the pair embraced. Maybe it had all just been a horrible nightmare!

However, something wasn't right. Jock couldn't hear the wind blowing or animals scurrying any more. As he looked around in confusion, Lady Anne had transformed into an old cackling fairy woman, pulling an enormous door closed and shrouding Jock in darkness.

'You did kill that poor giantess and now you're going to pay for your crime.' And with a last laugh, she sealed Jock deep beneath Bennachie. The words of her curse were passed around Aberdeenshire. Jock would be trapped in the darkness until a one-eyed only son found the keys to that doorway, hidden under a juniper tree.

As far as I know, he's still in there.

THE CURSE OF FYVIE CASTLE

Fyvie Castle is one of the grandest homes in Aberdeenshire, large and lavish but also cursed. Legendary prophet Thomas the Rhymer visited soon after the castle was built in the thirteenth century, but became furious when the gates were slammed in his face. He declared that the fate of the castle would be tied to three stones that had been stolen from a nearby church.

The grand Fyvie Castle – cursed by Thomas the Rhymer and haunted by Lilias Drummond.

One was in the highest tower, one in the lady's bower and one below the water gate. Until all three were brought back together, the owner of Fyvie Castle would have a difficult succession and all who lived there would suffer.

Only one of the stones has ever been found, now on display inside and said to occasionally become damp, weeping at being apart from the others. The curse has held true and has probably contributed to the number of spirits haunting Fyvie's halls.

Known as the head ghost, the Green Lady was Lilias Drummond when alive and married to the cruel Alexander Seton. He cared about nothing other than producing an heir, so after several daughters but no sons, he lost patience, placing the blame on his wife.

Alexander locked Lilias away inside Fyvie, where she sadly died and her cruel husband wasted no time in replacing her. On his wedding night, instead of the happy couple consummating their marriage, they were kept awake by a strange scratching and wailing from outside the walls.

In the morning, an exhausted Alexander looked through the window to find something terrifying on the ledge outside.

The name D. Lilias Drummond was found etched into the stone, far too high for any human to have reached. It's still there for Fyvie's visitors to see and so is Dame Lilias, her presence given away by the faint scent of rose petal perfume.

KILDRUMMY CASTLE'S BRAVE DEFENDERS

Guarding a passage through the Cairngorms, the vast ruin of Kildrummy Castle still lives up to its title as the Noblest of Northern Castles. Built in the thirteenth century, the soaring towers and enormous walls made this one of Scotland's most impressive fortresses.

That's why Robert the Bruce sent his wife, sisters and daughter here for protection in 1306. Defeated in battle and now on the run, the King ordered his brother Neil to guard his family at Kildrummy, deep in the heart of Scotland.

Unfortunately, it didn't take long for Edward, the Prince of Wales to discover where the King's family were hiding and set out to capture some crucial hostages. He would have to take Kildrummy Castle first though, and under the care of Neil Bruce that was no easy task.

As the days passed, the numbers outside the castle grew bigger and the defenders' odds of survival grew smaller. While they still had the chance, the women slipped out of the castle to flee further north, although their efforts only led to English prisons. Neil remained behind, holding Kildrummy for six weeks until the castle finally fell. Not by brute force or even tactical genius, but by treachery.

The castle blacksmith had been bribed to start a fire inside the walls. While the blaze spread, a fresh attack began on the walls and the defenders were fighting on two fronts. By morning, the garrison had no choice but to surrender and Neil was hanged by Edward as a traitor.

The treacherous blacksmith got his reward, but not as he was expecting. Legend says that a large sum of gold was delivered as promised – molten and poured down his throat.

OLD ABERDEEN'S HISTORIC BRIDGE

Walk over the Brig O' Balgownie in Old Aberdeen and you're crossing one of the oldest standing bridges in Britain. For around 500 years, this was the only thing connecting Aberdeen to the north, which is an impressively long history considering the bridge carries a curse.

The bridge is thought to have been started around 1290, pausing construction for the First War of Independence, and finally finished on the orders of Robert the Bruce around 1320. The current structure was repaired and strengthened in the seventeenth century but at the core it's the same bridge.

The following prophecy has been attributed to the prophet Thomas the Rhymer:

Brig O' Balgownie, black's yer wa';
Wi' a wife's ae son, and a meer's ae foal,
Doon ye shall fa'.

That means the bridge is just waiting for an only son, riding a horse that was an only foal, to cross before collapsing.

The poet Lord Byron wrote that when the time came for him to ride over the bridge, he paused. Familiar with the rhyme after growing up in Aberdeenshire and being an only child, he was a bit worried since he didn't know much about his horse. Fortunately, he made it safely across the Don, so we can assume that his steed had siblings.

THE LEGEND OF THE MAIDEN STONE

Not far outside Inverurie, in the shadow of Bennachie, looms the enormous 3m-tall Maiden Stone. It displays Pictish images on one side, a Christian cross on the reverse and archaeologists will tell you it was carved by the Picts around AD 700. Storytellers, on the other hand, have a very different explanation.

The 3m-tall Maiden Stone, with a chunk missing where the Devil grabbed the girl's shoulder.

Not far from here lived a laird and his beautiful daughter, with an incredible view of Bennachie from their window. The laird's daughter had been courted by every young man for 100 miles and there was a collective disappointment when she eventually agreed to settle down with one lucky suitor.

Most had accepted their loss by her wedding day, but as the maiden baked bannocks that morning, somebody new came calling. The stranger struck up a conversation, even attempting to convince her to call off the wedding! He was charming, handsome and witty, but she wasn't going to change her mind that easily.

With a cunning smile on his face, the visitor offered the maiden a bet. If he could build a path to the top of Bennachie before she had finished baking her bannocks, would she marry him then?

It was an impossible task, so to get rid of him the maiden said, 'Aye right then' with a roll of her eyes.

Within the hour, her bannocks were almost ready and she peered out the window. To her shock, there was a gleaming new path leading up the hill, still known as the Maiden Causeway today. The handsome stranger was running down it towards her and she realised now that it was the Devil in disguise.

Sprinting out the door, the maiden could see her pursuer was catching up fast. Praying with all her might, she declared that it would be better to be turned to stone than married to the Devil!

Her prayer was answered, transforming her into the Maiden Stone just as the Devil caught her shoulder, which explains the large chunk missing from the monument. She's stood here quietly ever since.

CRAIGIEVAR CASTLE'S NAKED GHOST

Craigievar Castle is maybe better known simply as the pink castle. While it might look like something out of a fairy tale, not all of its stories are child friendly, especially its naked ghost.

The castle was once home to Red Sir John Forbes, his nickname coming from both his bright hair and fiery temper. One day, believing he was alone in Craigievar, he heard light footsteps and giggling coming from a bedroom upstairs.

Sword in hand, Red John burst in to find his daughter in bed with a son of his sworn enemies, the Gordons. Without even the chance to put his clothes on, the young Gordon found himself fighting for his life. No match for Red John, the boy was backed up against the window and given two choices:

1. Be run through by John's sword.
2. Jump from the window.

If he survived the fall, then he would be free to limp back naked to his father. Unfortunately, that 50ft drop onto granite slabs proved to be a death sentence.

Today, the window he jumped from is covered over by a huge panel behind a bed, built in an attempt to stop the ghost of that young Gordon from getting back in. It didn't work and visitors, often men, sometimes find their clothes being tugged by an unseen hand.

Clearly, the ghost is still naked and wants a bit of decency in the afterlife.

SECURING THE HONOURS OF SCOTLAND AT DUNNOTTAR CASTLE

Dunnottar is one of the most instantly recognised castles in Scotland, it's also one of the oldest! This headland has been fortified for well over 1,000 years and Donald II, one the earliest Kings of Scots, was killed here in battle.

Fast forward to the mid-seventeenth century and Oliver Cromwell had taken control of England, before destroying their crown jewels as a symbol of the monarchy. Instead of following suit, Scotland declared Charles II their new king and crowned him at Scone Palace.

In response, Cromwell invaded and Edinburgh quickly fell, so the crown, sword and sceptre that make up the Honours of Scotland had to be taken somewhere safer. Dunnottar Castle, home to William Keith, was the obvious choice and to avoid any prying eyes, each piece was brought into the castle by Katherine Drummond, hidden inside sacks of wool.

Regardless of the deception, Cromwell's army eventually arrived on the Aberdeenshire coast to capture Dunnottar. The castle held out for months, but it was clear they couldn't last forever. It was time to get the Honours back out again.

There are two stories about how that happened. Christine Fletcher, the wife of a local minister, claimed that she smuggled each piece out in three trips, right under the nose of the besieging army. A later story said that Fletcher lowered them from a window to the beach, where her servant hid them in a creel.

Either way, they were taken to her husband's church at Kinneff and buried beneath the floorboards. Every few months, the floor was prised up and the Honours aired out to save them from damage.

Once Cromwell's army had stormed Dunnottar Castle, they were told that the treasure they were looking for had been sent overseas and far out of their reach. Nine years later, with Charles II now back in charge, the Honours were dug up and put back in their rightful place.

DRUM CASTLE'S LOYAL LAIRDS

Drum Castle looks like a different building from every angle with a medieval tower, Jacobean wing and Victorian extension. While it's grown throughout the centuries and adapted to new styles, one thing that has never changed is the loyalty of the Irvines of Drum.

The castle was gifted to William de Irwyn in 1323 by Robert the Bruce as a reward for supporting him to secure the Scottish throne. William played a particularly special role, guarding the King as he slept under a holly bush, which is where the leaves on the Irvine crest come from.

Drum Castle would remain the seat of Clan Irvine for the next 650 years, throughout the many ups and downs of Scottish history.

They were called to defend the Scottish crown once again during the Red Battle of Harlaw in 1411. During the fight, Alexander Irvine the 3rd Laird of

Drum Castle with its medieval tower – home to the Irvines for 650 years.

Drum saw himself facing the legendary MacLean Chief, Red Hector of the Battles. Left to fight one on one and matching each other blow for blow, the pair ended up falling side by side.

When the Jacobite risings started, the Irvines stayed true to the Stuart regime and supported Bonnie Prince Charlie in 1745. Like everybody else who opposed the government, once the dust had settled the 17th Laird of Drum was a hunted fugitive. Unlike most others, this Alexander Irvine refused to flee the country and stayed a little closer to home.

It was a dangerous choice, but for three years the Laird hid right under the nose of the authorities. Every time the soldiers arrived unannounced, Alexander hid in a secret room inside Drum Castle while his sister Mary covered for him. They did unfortunately make off with the family silver though.

It was a popular story, but without knowing where that secret room was, it could have just been another far-fetched legend. Then, in 2013, archaeologists discovered a secret room which may have been the loyal Laird's hiding place, covered over and forgotten for generations!

THE LADY GHOSTS OF CRATHES CASTLE

Castles don't come much more picturesque than Crathes, but underneath the beauty lie tragic stories of ghostly figures.

The most famous is the Green Lady, spotted by many people over the years including Queen Victoria. She appears either as a young woman carrying a baby or a green orb, gliding across the room before disappearing into the fireplace.

Said to have been a servant girl who became pregnant by one of the Burnett lairds, she disappeared mysteriously shortly after giving birth and the scandal was covered up. Whatever the truth behind the legend, when the castle was undergoing renovations in the 1800s, the skeleton of a baby was discovered underneath the fireplace of the Green Lady's room.

Often forgotten, the story of the White Lady is much older, from before the present sixteenth-century castle was built. Back then the Burnett family lived on an artificial island in a nearby loch and that was where the young Laird Alexander Burnett was preparing for his upcoming wedding.

His blushing bride Bertha was staying with the family in the lead-up to the big day, but like many ambitious mothers, Lady Agnes didn't think Bertha was good enough for her only son. Alexander was smitten though, so there was nothing she could do.

That was until the Laird rode off to deal with some business, just days before the wedding. Agnes took her opportunity to strike, poisoning the lovely Bertha during dinner and when Alexander returned, he was crushed with the news. Even though he strongly suspected his mother, there was no way to prove it.

On the day of the wedding, Bertha's parents arrived to find their daughter wrapped in a white shroud instead of a white dress. As they came face to face with Lady Agnes, a look of terror came over her. Pointing behind the grieving couple, Agnes cried, 'She comes! She comes!' before dropping dead at their feet.

It's said that every year, on the anniversary of Bertha's death, the White Lady appears, walking from the old island to Crathes Castle. Even after they moved, she didn't ever want the Burnetts to forget about her fate.

THE WIZARD LAIRD OF LOCH SKENE

On a bright sunny day, the Loch of Skene is a lovely place to wander but visit during an icy winter and there's more than just the temperature to make you shiver.

In the late seventeenth century, the local laird was the cruel Alexander Seaton, known better to his tenants as the Wizard of Skene. He learned his evil trade from the Devil himself and had the power to freeze his enemies where they stood or make them dance until their feet bled. Luckily, you knew he was coming by the noise of all the crows following his every move.

One dark, frosty winter's night, the Wizard instructed his coachman Kilgour to meet him and another passenger near the Loch of Skene. Before he left, Alexander stared the coachman dead in the eyes and offered a grave warning. Don't look at the guest's face under any circumstances.

Following his orders, Kilgour sat up front and gazed straight ahead as he drove. The weather was cold enough that the Loch of Skene was entirely frozen over, so the trio slowly journeyed straight across the ice. However, the coachman overheard some disturbing whispers behind him.

His curiosity got the better of him, and he turned in his seat to have a quick peek at who the visitor was. At that moment, the hooded figure snapped his head round and Kilgour found himself staring into the eyes of the Devil. He panicked and lost control of the reins, causing his coach to veer wildly to the side, tip over and smash through the ice.

While the Devil and Wizard both survived unscathed, the poor coachman was never found. Sometimes, when the Loch of Skene freezes over, it's said that two parallel grooves, like the ruts from a carriage, can still be seen today. If that's not enough, take a short trip to Skene Church and find the grave of Alexander Seaton himself – an odd place to find a servant of the Devil!

THE BATTLE OF RED HARLAW NEAR INVERURIE

Not every great Scottish battle was a patriotic fight against invading English or Vikings. There have always been plenty of internal power struggles to keep fighting men well practised and the Harlaw Monument above Inverurie commemorates one of the bloodiest.

At the start of the fifteenth century, Scotland had been stuck with the weak King Robert III, followed by the young King James growing up in English captivity. Into that power vacuum stepped the Duke of Albany, already the most powerful man in Scotland, but now deciding to add the Earldom of Ross to his vast lands.

One man who wasn't happy about the situation was Donald of Islay, the Chief of Clan Donald, who had his own claim to Ross. Calling together the west coast clans, Donald sailed around the north of Scotland and promptly captured Dingwall to prove his point.

After coercing the locals into joining them, his army swelled to 10,000 men and they began marching to Aberdeen. This seemingly unstoppable horde was met near Inverurie by the Earl of Mar and 2,000 men. They might have been outnumbered, but these were heavily armoured warriors, the best that the north-east could offer.

The Battle of Harlaw was intensely fierce. Those lightly armoured Islanders swarmed against their enemy but struggled to break through. Hundreds were chopped down just to be replaced by a fresh wave of warriors and the Lowland nobility were decimated; between a quarter and a half lay slain.

The dwindling Aberdeenshire army camped that night assuming the next

The Battle of Harlaw Monument, standing high above Inverurie with Bennachie in the distance.

day would be their last but when they woke up, they were alone. Donald had retreated back home, giving up his claim to Ross. Both sides claimed victory and the bloody conflict would become famous as the Red Battle of Harlaw!

A CHILLING GHOST STORY FROM HUNTLY CASTLE

The Gordon Earls of Huntly were rarely a quiet bunch, some of them so boisterous that they kicked up a fuss even after death. Recorded immediately after the event, the death of the 5th Earl remains one of the most chilling tales from Aberdeenshire.

In 1578, the Earl suddenly collapsed during a game of football in the grounds of Huntly Castle. After being carried inside, vomiting black blood, he didn't survive for long and his corpse was left in his chamber until burial.

People began complaining of an icy chill in the neighbouring rooms, even shivering in front of a roaring fire, before mysteriously dropping down as if dead. When they awoke, all anybody could remember was a strangely cold, dark feeling before they passed out.

A surgeon from Aberdeen failed to determine the cause of the Earl's death, so the body was taken to the chapel. To the surprise of Huntly's brother, shuffling and scraping noises began coming from the Earl's locked and now empty bedroom.

Together, the group plucked up the courage to peer into the dark room. It was as empty as they expected. As the Earl's brother crept inside, the noises started again all around him. Bolting out of the room, he bravely returned, armed with plenty of candles this time for one last look.

Before he stepped foot through the doorway, the candles started flickering and the shuffling was heard louder than ever. Whatever was hiding in the Earl's bedroom clearly didn't want to be disturbed and that was all the warning they needed to leave it well alone.

THE WORLD'S GREATEST ATHLETE AT POTARCH BRIDGE

Right outside the door of the Old Potarch Hotel sit two enormous stones fitted with iron rings, daring visitors to try and lift them. It's obvious that these are no ordinary rocks, but what makes the Dinnie Stones truly special is their connection with the world's greatest athlete.

Donald Dinnie was the son of a local stonemason and had been winning local competitions and Highland Games since the tender age of 16. In 1860, while working on the Potarch Bridge, he decided to prove his strength by lifting these two stones being used as scaffolding counterweights.

Donald successfully carried all 332kg across the 17ft width of the bridge with his bare hands, a feat that has only ever been matched by a handful of people, including his father.

This Aberdeenshire strongman would become a worldwide sensation, labelled the greatest athlete of the nineteenth century. During his career he won over 10,000 competitions, amassing prize money that would reach into the millions today. His victories included being crowned champion of the Highland Games twenty-one years in a row between 1856 and 1876.

By that point Donald was travelling the world, defeating professional wrestlers along with anything else thrown his way. The most impressive thing about his stone-carrying feat is that he wasn't an enormous, hulking brute. Measuring 6ft 1in and weighing 15st, Donald was an all-round athlete, just as capable a sprinter and jumper as he was a strongman.

No doubt he would be proud that these stones named after him are still in use today for those who arrange it in advance. He'll be even more proud to know that most challengers struggle to get them off the ground, never mind across the Potarch Bridge!

GHASTLY GIGHT CASTLE

Well off the usual tourist trail, Gight Castle seems a sinister location, being slowly reclaimed by nature. Maybe that's for the best, as this ruin seems to be a favourite haunt of the Devil.

Gight was built by the Gordons high on a hill above the winding Ythan River, but its position was of little reassurance to the 7th Laird when a small army came knocking. Knowing that he couldn't defend his home, he hid any wealth that he couldn't carry off in a deep pool in the river.

Once the coast was clear again, it was time to collect it, but a man of his stature wouldn't dive into the river himself. His servant was forced down into the depths before suddenly bursting back to the surface in a panic. White as a sheet, he screamed that the Devil was down there guarding the hoard!

The Laird of Gight wasn't somebody to be refused and the diver was forced back in at the point of a sword. As the seconds passed, the Laird began to get a little concerned, before his servant finally reappeared, floating to the surface in four separate pieces.

That's not the only legend surrounding Gight Castle though, and when Thomas the Rhymer visited the area he prophesied:

At Gight three men by sudden death shall dee,
After that the land shall lie in lea.

When the Earl of Aberdeen bought Gight as a home for his son Lord Haddo, it had been 500 years since the prophecy and the words were almost forgotten. Then Haddo fell from his horse, followed a short time later by his close servant. People began to whisper about the two sudden deaths.

Years passed and two estate workers were discussing the local legend of the unfulfilled prophecy. One joked to the other that Thomas the Rhymer couldn't have been a very good prophet after all! The next day, the wall of the farmhouse collapsed on top of him.

ANGUS & DUNDEE

THE HIDDEN CAMUS CROSS

It's not easy to find, but hidden deep in Camustane Wood, not far from Monikie, is the beautiful Camus Cross. This freestanding stone cross is around 1,000 years old and elaborately carved on both sides. It might look like just a work of art, but local tradition claims that the mound it's sitting on is the burial cairn of Camus, an important Viking warlord.

Camus is said to have been killed at the Battle of Barry, a story that's been passed down through the centuries although nobody knows its source. The battle supposedly took place where Carnoustie stands today and until recently, was widely accepted as fact.

At the start of the eleventh century, Malcolm II was King of Scots, ruling in an incredibly turbulent time. He spent his entire reign dealing with local uprisings, seaborne invasions and devastating raids across the southern border.

After Malcolm had won a few small victories, a huge force of Danes under the leadership of Camus landed at Lunan Bay to teach the King of Scots a lesson. They marched along the coast, burning towns to provoke a reaction, while the Scots gathered in Dundee.

It all culminated in the Battle of Barry, where the Scots managed to get the better of the invaders once again. When Camus saw that the day was lost, he fled into the hills with Robert de Keith hot on his heels and this carved cross is said to be erected where he was struck dead.

There's even a theory that the name Carnoustie comes from 'Craws Nestie', due to all the crows that came to peck at the fallen warriors. Huge burial sites were uncovered in the area, once thought to prove the story of the battle, but modern historians now believe the Battle of Barry and even Camus himself, could be entirely fictional.

The Camus Cross standing on a mound in the middle of an avenue of trees in Camustane Woods.

True or not, walking down the wooded avenue towards the Camus Cross makes your imagination run wild. With crows screeching above you, it's hard not to keep checking over your shoulder for the ghosts of long-dead Viking warriors!

THE KELPIE OF ST VIGEANS

St Vigeans might just look like a regular church on a hill, but legend says it sits on an artificial mound on thick iron bars above a deep loch. Built with the help of a kelpie, these supernatural creatures live in water, take the form of horses on land and usually prey on unsuspecting travellers.

The builder of St Vigeans managed to capture a kelpie's bridle, which enslaved it to his will. With the strength of ten regular horses, it was a great help when it came to constructing the church, right above its home.

Using the kelpie's strength to drag the heavy blocks of stone wasn't the smartest move since it was a proud creature. Once released, it uttered a terrible curse that one day a minister would kill himself and on the very next Communion, the church would tumble into the loch below.

The story was passed down, with local people taking pride in the unique legend of their little church. Then one day in the 1720s, tragedy struck. Very sadly, the first half of the curse came true and the congregation refused to take Communion there for almost forty years in case the second part followed.

Eventually, a new minister found somebody brave enough to take the risk. Just before Communion, the entire congregation ran outside to watch from a safe distance, fully expecting the church to collapse.

Fortunately, that didn't happen and St Vigeans still stands. Maybe something broke the curse or maybe the kelpie finally decided to forgive and forget.

THE WHITE LADY OF EDZELL CASTLE

The stunning red Edzell Castle with its ornate garden is a pleasure to visit on a sunny day. It's not quite as inviting late at night though, with the walls haunted by the crying ghost of the White Lady.

This lady is believed to be the spirit of Katherine Campbell, wife of the 9th Earl of Crawford. After the Earl died, Katherine stayed at Edzell with her son until she sadly passed away in the winter of 1578 and was laid to rest in the nearby Lindsay burial aisle.

She had been a wealthy woman and there were rumours that she had been buried with a hoard of jewellery. A couple of locals decided that a dead body didn't need any riches, they were going to steal it before anybody else had a chance, breaking into the crypt the same night Katherine was laid to rest.

They didn't find the treasure they had expected, but there were a few bits and pieces worth selling on. The biggest prize were the golden rings, but no matter how hard they pulled or twisted, they weren't coming off. Since she was already dead, one of the robbers just took a knife to Katherine's finger.

To their horror, the corpse sat bolt upright and let out a high-pitched scream! Katherine wasn't dead after all, but the terrified men ran for their lives at the sight of a walking corpse.

A very confused Katherine stumbled from the burial aisle to Edzell Castle in the depth of winter, having lost a lot of blood. It was the castle guards' turn to run screaming when a lady dressed in white, covered in blood and wailing appeared in the dead of night. Instead of letting their mistress inside the gates, the guards just hid indoors.

The unfortunate Katherine died outside the walls and it seems as if her spirit is still there, trying to get safely inside the castle.

THE REEKIE LINN'S DEVILISH VISITOR

Not far from the border where Perthshire and Angus meet, the River Isla crashes down over the Reekie Linn waterfall. Its name means Smoky Pool and when the river is in spate, a fine mist rises out of the deep gorge. If you've got good eyes, then through the spray you might spot a large cave down far below.

That's the Black Dub, a cavern once used by a man on the run. Some stories say he was a local laird, others call him a notorious, cattle-rustling outlaw. Either way, this character had just killed a man and now he was on the run.

Well hidden by the smoky roar of the Reekie Linn, the killer was dealing with a heavy conscience when he saw something that changed his life. A big, black growling dog was padding slowly towards him out of the gloom. One thing about hiding next to a waterfall this powerful – nobody can hear you scream.

The man was in no doubt that this was the Devil visiting him because of his crimes. He was so terrified that he immediately clambered out of the cave, up the gorge and straight to the authorities to hand himself in.

While the cave can be seen from across the gorge, it's not accessible by any path and is far too dangerous to attempt a visit. You never know what would be waiting inside anyway!

The Reekie Linn Waterfall in full spate, hiding a dark cave to the bottom left that's haunted by the Devil.

THE BROWNIE OF FERN DEN

The hamlet of Fern is a tiny place, with a few scattered homes and a quaint but perfectly situated old church. Deep in the Angus countryside and surrounded by well-tended fields, this quiet spot was once home to the brownie of Fern Den.

He wasn't like most brownies who make their home in grand houses, farms or mills though, this rough-looking little creature lived out among the trees and streams. In some old accounts of the story, he's referred to as a 'ghaist', meaning something supernatural, but from his description and habits, we can be sure of his true identity.

This brownie might not have lived on a farm, but he was a regular visitor to the farmhouse near Fern Den. Arriving after the sun had set, he would clean the byre, thresh the harvested crops and carry out any other tasks that needed finished. If he needed any milk or food, he was more than welcome to help himself.

While the farmer and his wife loved the brownie for his help, the other farm workers hated him for making them look lazy. They whispered rumours that he was a dangerous beast and people began to fear passing through Fern Den in case they bumped into him!

Then one day, the farmer's wife fell ill. She was so sick that it didn't look like she was going to make it through to morning without help from a healer in the next village over. He couldn't risk leaving his wife, so somebody else would have to ride out into the darkness to fetch help.

All the servants argued about who would go, none willing to risk the creature in Fern Den or anything else lurking in the night. The brownie was listening behind a door, furious at the lot of them for wasting time while their mistress suffered. Grabbing a big coat and floppy hat off the peg, he jumped on the farmer's horse to do yet another task by himself.

Knocking on the healer's door, the brownie explained the urgency of the situation and swept the old lady up onto the mare in front of him. She looked at this little figure curiously but had no time to argue before they were racing away back towards the farmhouse.

It was clear the healer was getting nervous when they approached the darkness of Fern Den.

'What if we meet the terrifying brownie?!' she asked.

Her companion replied, 'I can assure you madam; you won't meet any creature more dangerous than I tonight.'

Once they arrived, the brownie helped his passenger down and knocked his hat off in the process. The healer looked shocked, gasping at his odd appearance and asked what kind of creature he was!

He replied, 'Just you go and see to my mistress, but if anybody should ask, tell them that you rode in the company of the brownie of Fern Den!'

THE REBEL LAIRD IN THE ANGUS GLENS

Glen Esk is a sleepy place, with a long road that stops near the Old Kirk at Loch Lee and travellers are faced with hours of walking through mountain passes to get any further. It might be quiet today, but in the mid-eighteenth century this area was swarming with government soldiers, hunting for the Laird of Balnamoon.

As a loyal Jacobite, James Carnegy was one of many forced on the run after the Battle of Culloden. He had survived that carnage but was a wanted man and knew his home was no longer safe. Instead, James lay low in the isolated hills and small glens at the head of Glen Esk, becoming known as the Rebel Laird.

Hidden in Glen Mark near the Queen's Well, the tiny Balnamoon's cave is where the Laird sheltered whenever the soldiers came looking. The good people of the Angus Glens kept James well fed and watered, protecting him from prying eyes for months. That was until the local Presbyterian minister discovered what had been going on.

He betrayed James's position and the Rebel Laird was dragged down Glen Esk all the way to London for trial, but for once British bureaucracy worked in his favour.

In order to inherit his wife's family land, he had been forced to take her name and designation, becoming James Carnegy-Arbuthnott of Findowrie. The arrest warrant was clearly for James Carnegy of Balnamoon, so obviously they had the wrong person and were forced to let him go!

The Laird of Balnamoon was allowed to return home and live the rest of his days in comfort, but maybe he still visited his cave from time to time, just for a bit of peace and quiet.

KIRRIEMUIR'S PROTECTIVE STANDING STONE

Kirriemuir is a fantastic small town, home to Scotland's oldest sweet shop and the childhood home of *Peter Pan* author J.M. Barrie. Up the hill where Barrie used to play cricket, you can find a monolith that's literally half the stone it used to be.

A long time ago, on a busy market day in Kirriemuir, three outlaws were on the prowl. They targeted a farmer who had done well selling his stock that day, preparing an ambush on his road home. That poor farmer was beaten and robbed before the outlaws fled the scene, taking their ill-gotten gains up to a quiet spot on Kirriemuir Hill.

Hiding behind the standing stone, they were splitting their loot into three shares when they heard a loud crack. Gazing up, the last thing they saw was half a slab of rock falling on top of them as the standing stone split in two.

That fallen half was said to have lain there for years. The townsfolk knew the outlaws' haul of coins was buried underneath, but they were too afraid to dig it up. Maybe the standing stone was the guardian of the town or maybe for some reason those coins were cursed. After all, one man had been beaten senseless and three others killed over it.

However, the fallen half of the stone isn't there any more, just the smaller upright section acting as a headstone for the robbers. Supposedly, the removed part is now built into a nearby field wall, but there's no mention of the buried money. It might still be there, unless whoever reused the stone found it and maybe picked up a curse at the same time.

THE BATTLE OF ARBROATH ABBEY

Arbroath Abbey is famous for the signing of the Declaration of Arbroath in 1320, however, there's another less well-known story there that deserves to be told. Just over 100 years after the declaration was signed, the peace and tranquillity of Arbroath Abbey would be shattered.

The monks had employed Alexander Lindsay as their Baillie of Regality, responsible for upholding local law. He was the son of the powerful Earl of Crawford, so should have been a reassuring protector, but instead turned out to be an irresponsible lout. Lindsay abused his power, while his men caused mayhem within the abbey walls.

Eventually, the monks couldn't handle it any longer and replaced him with Alexander Ogilvy, the Lindsay family's biggest rival. In response, the furious, ousted noble raised an army of 1,000 men and marched them to the doors of Arbroath Abbey.

Ogilvy and his allies were badly outnumbered, but they bravely squared off against Lindsay's troops. Insults flew back and forward while the two sides worked up the courage to attack. All the while Lindsay's father, the Earl of Crawford, was racing from Dundee to stop the madness.

He reached Arbroath just in time, galloping in between the lines of armed men to try and keep the peace. One of Ogilvy's men mistook Crawford's calls for diplomacy as a call to attack and launched a spear, snatching him from the horse and killing him instantly.

That dramatic act broke the stalemate and the Battle of Arbroath had begun. The fighting lasted for hours as the outnumbered Ogilvy side was chased across the Angus countryside. By the time it was over, Ogilvy himself was dead and Lindsay was victorious, letting his army loose to wreak even more havoc now that Arbroath Abbey was now back in his control.

ABERLEMNO'S PICTISH STONES

There are few better places to find Pictish stones than in Angus and they don't come much more fascinating than in Aberlemno. Along the roadside by the village hall stand three of varying ages, but the most remarkable is found by the church.

Not only is the craftsmanship of the Aberlemno Kirkyard Stone extraordinary, but unlike most Pictish stones, we might know what story it's telling. It's impossible to be certain and there will always be different theories, but it's clear that there's a battle scene unfolding.

Following the lines, long-haired figures are facing off against helmeted foes, with spears and swords, both on foot and horseback. It's been suggested that the stone was carved to commemorate the Battle of Dun Nechtain in AD 685, a conflict that helped shape Scotland.

In the seventh century, the powerful Kingdom of Northumbria was stretching its control north, deep into Pictish territory. They already ruled the Lothians, were pushing through Fife into Angus and if things carried on, most of eastern Scotland would be under Northumbrian rule. The Picts weren't just going to roll over and let that happen.

They regathered and carried out numerous raids on Northumbrian territory. Like a swarm of angry wasps, the Picts succeeded in poking the bear and King Ecgfrith gathered his mighty army to march north and deal with them properly.

King Bridei led the Picts, but at the sight of the Northumbrian host, his men retreated further and further into Pictland. Seeing his enemy on the run, Ecgfrith followed in haste, not realising he was marching into a trap.

Now deep in Pictish territory, at a narrow pass, Bridei put his plan into action and destroyed the Northumbrian Army at the Battle of Dun Nechtain. In the bottom right of the Aberlemno Kirkyard Stone, a figure being pecked is suggested to be King Ecgfrith himself, the bird symbolising his death on the battlefield.

There are other suggestions for the location of the battle but its importance in preserving the independence of the Picts can't be overstated. While all of the

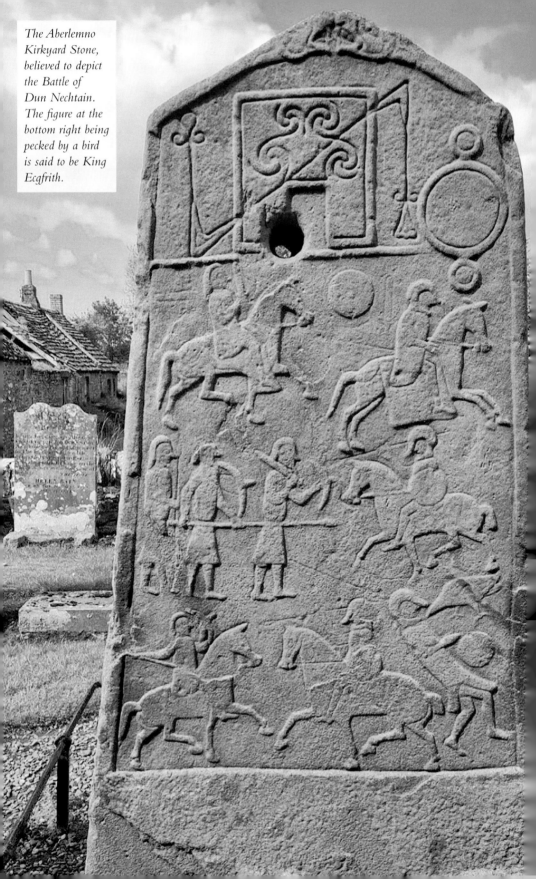

The Aberlemno Kirkyard Stone, believed to depict the Battle of Dun Nechtain. The figure at the bottom right being pecked by a bird is said to be King Ecgfrith.

Aberlemno Pictish stones are worth seeing, it's worth remembering that they're protected by insulated boxes during the frosty winter months.

THE ETERNAL CARD GAME IN GLAMIS CASTLE

The impressive Glamis Castle might have sprawled into an enormous building now, but there's no mistaking the old stone keep at its heart. Among all the stories these walls have to tell, that's where to find the very best of them.

One Saturday night in the fifteenth century, a raucous group were drinking and playing cards in the lower levels of Glamis Castle. As the hour was reaching midnight, people began to get twitchy and disappear off to bed. They knew it was a terrible sin to gamble on the Sabbath.

There was one man who didn't care. Sometimes it's said to be Earl Beardie of Crawford, other times it's Alexander Lyon of Glamis. Either way, in his drunken state this fool roared that he didn't care what the others thought. He would play cards on the Sabbath. He would play until doomsday. He would even play with the Devil himself.

Suddenly, a heavy knock came at the door. It was a tall, dark stranger seeking warmth and shelter, maybe even a wee game of cards, too. Common sense was out the window and he was welcomed to the table.

Once midnight passed and it was now early on Sunday morning, the stranger revealed himself to be the Devil, here to grant the man's wish. The little room they had been sitting in had somehow been blocked up and the fool was now trapped inside, playing cards with the Devil for eternity.

There's a strange feeling in that lower hall, and there's a clear space in the wall where that alcove for playing cards should be. Stand on the lawn outside Glamis Castle, look up towards the old keep and you can even see an extra window, with nothing but wall on the other side.

THE DRAGON OF DUNDEE

Over 1,000 years ago, a shadow fell across the countryside around Dundee. Nobody knew exactly what had changed, but they could feel it in the air. Livestock started disappearing and strange, distant noises were heard in the night.

One morning, a farmer from Pitempton sent the eldest of his nine daughters to fetch water from a nearby well. Impatient at how long she was taking, the farmer sent another daughter after her. Neither returned, so one by one the girls disappeared, searching for their sisters.

Eventually, the farmer realised something was wrong and went after his nine daughters to the well himself. He was met with a horrific sight. His daughters had all been killed by a terrifying dragon and the farmer was lucky to escape with his own life.

Sprinting into town, he screamed the news to everybody he passed and Martin, the town's blacksmith, was heartbroken. He was betrothed to the farmer's eldest daughter, but he wasn't the kind of man who ran away from danger.

Picking up a freshly forged sword, the angry smith jumped on his horse and sped off towards the dragon's lair. Martin fought the beast with all the fury you can imagine, and it was clear that the dragon had met its match. The beast tried to flee across the hills, but the young man refused to let it escape.

A crowd had gathered to watch the spectacle and as he battled with the monster, they shouted, 'Strike Martin!' With a final, great thrust of his sword, Martin pierced the dragon's heart and it staggered a few paces before toppling over, laying its head on a rock to die.

In its dying moments, the dragon lamented:

Tempted at Pitempton,
Draigled at Baldragon,
Stricken at Strathmartin,
And kill'd at Martin's Stane.

Legend claims their battlefield was named Strike Martin, which developed into Strathmartine and on the outskirts of Dundee you can still find Pitempton Road and Baldragon Wood. A metal dragon statue in the centre of Dundee High Street reminds shoppers of the story, but much more interesting is Martin's Stone. Standing in the middle of a field to the north of Dundee, this is where the monster was said to have been killed and shows a man on horseback with the serpent/dragon below!

ARGYLL

HOW THE DOG STONE GOT ITS SHAPE

A short walk along the shore between Oban and Dunollie Castle stands a peculiar-looking pillar of rock known as the Dog Stone. This was where the legendary hero Fingal would tie up his dog Bran anytime the hound couldn't accompany him on an adventure.

Naturally, Bran wasn't just any old dog. He was an enormous Scottish Deerhound as tall as Fingal's shoulder, multicoloured with a belly of white and fierce eyes. Instead of a rope, Bran had to be chained to the base of this rock. Impatient for his master's return, he would pace round and round the Dog Stone and as the chain slowly wore away the bottom, the unusual shape was formed!

Bran wasn't always left behind though and features in plenty of Fingal's legends, often saving his neck. Any time Fingal's warriors were hungry, the big dog would head off into the forest alone and come back with something delicious. This loyal friend even saved his master after Fingal was captured by the Irish King Cormac.

The ransom for Fingal's return was a delivery of several pairs of animals from a long list and Bran wasted no time in getting to work. Deer, rabbits and tiny mice were no problem and either out of fear or respect, they marched past the Irish King on Bran's command.

Cormac must have been laughing to himself when all but the final animal had arrived. Surely even Bran couldn't manage a feat this impossible. To Cormac's surprise, he heard a loud bark before two large whales, painfully and unsteadily walked on past, followed by the ever-faithful Bran!

The Dog Stone, worn away at its base by the giant dog Bran pacing in circles while chained here

CASTLE STALKER & DONALD OF THE HAMMERS

Perched on an island in a sea loch, Castle Stalker has a story equally as dramatic as its location. While originally built by the MacDougalls to guard the route along Loch Linnhe, it was the Stewarts of Appin who made Castle Stalker into what we see today.

In 1520 disaster struck when their Chief, Alexander Stewart, was caught by their rivals the Campbells while fishing in the loch alone. Those in the castle could only stand and watch as Alexander was killed, terrified that their enemy would press the advantage and attack Castle Stalker next!

The Chief's son, Donald, was only a baby at the time and his nurse decided that the castle was no longer a safe place for him. She took the child to a local blacksmith to raise him in secret, well protected from the Campbells. Working in the forge gave the boy legendary strength, able to wield a huge blacksmith's hammer in each hand, becoming known as 'Donald nan Ord', or Donald of the Hammers.

Eventually, the day came when his true identity was revealed and the young Chief decided to put those hammers to work. In 1544, Donald gathered the Stewarts together and attacked the Campbells at Dunstaffnage Castle. He avenged his father's death, killing nine Campbells in the process, before taking his rightful place in Castle Stalker.

Eventually the castle was lost by the Stewarts to their old enemy in 1620, not through battle but after a drunken wager. The Stewarts tried to reclaim it several times, even bombarding their former home during the 1745 Jacobite Rising, but they didn't have cannon nearly powerful enough.

In the end, it was abandoned and left to ruin. Fortunately, the tower was purchased, firstly by Charles Stewart of Achara in 1908 and then by Lt Col Stewart Allward. Luckily, the Stewarts were playing the long game and Castle Stalker has now been restored to its former glory.

CROSSING THE ATLANTIC AT THE CLACHAN BRIDGE

There aren't many places where you can cross the Atlantic Ocean in seconds, but the Clachan Bridge is one of them! Also known as the Bridge Over the Atlantic, it joins the island of Seil to the Scottish mainland and with ocean found on either side, technically that's what flows through its arch.

Once you're safely over the Atlantic and on Seil, the first place you come to is an inn called the Tigh an Truish. This translates as the House of Trousers, explained in a story that harks back to the post-Jacobite era.

In the mid-eighteenth century, the British government attempted to suppress Highland culture by passing the Act of Proscription. One of the main parts of this law was prohibiting most men from wearing what they called 'Highland clothes' including kilts, plaid and even tartan coats.

The islanders of Seil weren't particularly worried about government inspections at home. However, they did have to travel onto the mainland occasionally for things like driving cattle to lowland markets. When they arrived at Tigh an Truish, they would get changed into regular trousers to travel on the mainland, putting their kilts back on when they returned!

DUNSTAFFNAGE CASTLE'S WEDDING CRASHERS

Dunstaffnage means 'fort of the headland' and this formidable, thirteenth-century castle once allowed the MacDougalls to control the entrance to Loch Etive, access to Loch Awe and therefore a large part of Argyll. It was a privileged and very tactical position to hold.

When John MacDougall died without a legitimate son, Dunstaffnage Castle along with the Lordship of Lorn passed to the husband of his eldest daughter, John Stewart. Not everybody was happy with the line of succession and the MacDougalls were merely biding their time to strike back.

John Stewart ended up with exactly the same problem as his predecessor – his only male son Dugald was illegitimate and didn't stand to inherit. In 1463, with John not getting any younger, he decided to marry his mistress and solidify his son's succession.

An illegitimate MacDougall descendent called Alan saw his chance to strike. If he could just stop that wedding from going ahead, then maybe he could put forward his own claim to be named Lord of Lorn.

It's a short walk from Dunstaffnage Castle to the little chapel that still stands in the woods, but the Stewarts weren't expecting a small group of MacDougalls to be lying in wait. The wedding party were ambushed, with Alan rushing straight for his goal, viciously stabbing the groom. While the uninvited guests were chased off, they did manage to slip inside the castle's open door, barring it behind them.

John Stewart was bleeding heavily, but his men managed to get him to the chapel in time to say his vows. He died believing he had a legitimate heir, not knowing that he had lost Dunstaffnage Castle in the process. It would be a year before a royal army managed to evict the MacDougalls from the fortress.

After all of that, the Lordship of Lorn and Dunstaffnage Castle wasn't granted to either the Stewarts or the MacDougalls. It passed to Colin Campbell instead, who had married John's legitimate daughter. The Stewarts were granted the lands of Appin instead and while the feud with the MacDougalls was over, generations of fighting the Campbells had just begun.

THE ANCIENT CORONATION SITE ON DUNADD HILL

Rising out of the Great Moss in Kilmartin Glen, Dunadd isn't just any old hill. This easily defended fort was once the beating heart of the Kingdom of Dàl Riata. It's one of the few sites mentioned by name in early histories and the Gaelic Scots ruled a kingdom from here that stretched across the Irish Sea.

Dunadd Hill's footprint, a possible coronation site for the Kings of Dàl Riata.

Standing on top of Dunadd Fort, there are 800 prehistoric monuments within just a few miles; from rock art to burial cairns to huge standing stones. While they're all fascinating, nothing gets the imagination going quite like the human footprint carved into the rock atop Dunadd.

We don't know much about any coronation ceremonies from that time, but the footprint is thought to be an inauguration place for the Kings of Dàl Riata. Their descendants would eventually become the kings and queens of Scotland and it's an interesting feeling to place your foot in that same spot.

Imagine a new king climbing his way up Dunadd, before ceremoniously standing in the carving like those who came before, connecting him both with his ancestors and the land they ruled over.

Where the footprint came from has its own story. When Ossian, the son of the hero Fingal, was hunting around Kilmartin Glen he was strangely attacked by his own dogs. In his desperation to flee, he leapt all the way to the top of Dunadd and this deep footprint was where he landed!

THE GLAISTIG OF DUNOLLIE CASTLE

There has been a fortress keeping watch over the crossing between modern Oban and Kerrera for at least 1,300 years. Where the imposing stone tower of Dunollie Castle stands now, ancient Kings of Lorne once ruled.

While never quite as important as Dunadd, this important defensive spot lasted much longer, making its way to Clan MacDougall. They would go on to control much of Argyll, but they weren't alone here. Dunollie Castle was also home to a very mischievous glaistig.

These supernatural creatures could be dangerously disruptive or incredibly useful. For all the violence that the castle saw, this glaistig appeared to be a calming, hard-working presence. She would arrive every evening at dusk before spending the night sweeping and cleaning the castle. Any clothes or shoes left outside a room would be washed and dried by morning.

Just like the brownies found in southern Scotland, glaistigs worked hard but could be fickle beings. When she wanted to let the MacDougalls know that she wasn't happy, the family would find dust sprinkled over their meal. Fortunately, this glaistig had a sense of humour and the one person she always left alone was the castle's fool.

When the MacDougalls left the castle and moved into the mansion house next door, sightings appear to have stopped. That must have been one decision too far for the glaistig and she disappeared for good.

THE FAIRIES OF KINTRAW

Standing in a field beside the road heading south into Kilmartin Glen, the Kintraw Standing Stone isn't the biggest in Scotland but at 13ft high it's still humbling to stand next to. The 4,000-year-old stone, surrounded by burial cairns, stands near a small fairy hill and they might all be connected with this story.

One day, a farmer's wife from the area passed away, leaving behind her husband and two young children. Even with that recent tragedy, the farmer went off to church on Sunday, leaving the children behind to look after themselves.

When he returned, the brother and sister enthusiastically told him that their mother had come to comfort them. The grieving widower got angry with them, shouting that they needed to stop the silly games and let their mother go.

Every Sunday, the children would say the same thing and their father would get upset. Eventually, he told them that the next time they saw their mother, they should ask how her visit was possible.

The children did as they were told and it turned out she wasn't dead after all! Their mother had been taken by the fairies under the hill and was only able to escape for a short while every Sunday. If her coffin was opened, they would only find a withered leaf inside.

They told their father, who immediately went to the minister to ask his advice about checking his wife's coffin. The man of God scoffed at the idea. Nobody was going to be dug up from his churchyard because of a silly, superstitious belief. Fairies didn't exist!

It wasn't long before the minister was found dead on the road running past the Kintraw Standing Stone. If you didn't know by now, never mock the fairies.

SAILING ACROSS LAND AT TARBERT

From its lofty vantage point, the Royal Castle of Tarbert once guarded an important crossing. Not in the sea loch where the modern ferry runs, but in the other direction, across the dry land behind the castle.

The clue is in the name – Tarbert comes from Old Irish meaning an isthmus narrow enough to portage a boat across. It translates literally as 'drag boat' and there are at least a dozen similar place names around Scotland with various alternate spellings.

Crossing the mile-long strip of land at Tarbert saved sailors a very long, treacherous journey around the length of Kintyre. Robert the Bruce is said to have made the trip in 1306 while running to safety on the west coast and experiencing its importance at first-hand convinced him to strengthen the crumbling castle here.

At the end of the eleventh century, long before the royal castle existed, Tarbert played a little-known but crucial role in Scottish history. The Norwegian King Magnus Barelegs had successfully beaten Edgar King of Scots into agreeing to an embarrassing treaty, signing over all the islands on Scotland's west coast.

A stickler for the fine print, Magnus asked Edgar to confirm exactly what the definition of an island was. The unhappy King of Scots huffed that an island is obviously a piece of land that you can sail a boat all the way around. With that description, the Norwegian must have smirked.

That's because Magnus wasn't happy with just the Hebridean Islands, he wanted control of Kintyre as well. His ship sailed around the long peninsula until he came to Tarbert, where his men hauled it out of the water and dragged it across to the loch on the other side while he stayed at the helm 'sailing'.

Using Edgar's own interpretation, Kintyre was declared an island and claimed as part of the Norwegian treaty!

KILMORY KNAP CHAPEL & THE MACMILLAN CROSS

Argyll is spoilt for choice when it comes to fantastic little chapels, full of historic grave slabs carved with claymores and warriors. You could visit Kirkton or Keills for a peaceful wander, but only Kilmory Knap Chapel has the MacMillan Cross.

For a long time, this was Clan MacMillan territory, granted the lands of Knapdale as loyal supporters of the MacDonalds and keepers of nearby Castle Sween.

They even carved into a rock on the beach:

MacMillan's right to Knap shall be
As long's this rock withstands the sea.

Originally, the MacMillans were strongly based in Lochaber, allied with the Camerons and feuding regularly with the Mackintoshes. Then on Palm Sunday in 1430, both of these traditions would mark disaster for them.

The MacMillan Cross inside Kilmory Knap Chapel with a warrior's sword below a depiction of the crucifixion.

While they were worshipping in a Cameron church, the Mackintoshes stormed in and ambushed the congregation. Unprepared for battle, they never stood a chance, but Alexander MacMillan escaped, fleeing all the way south to the safety of Knapdale.

He was most likely the man who erected the incredible MacMillan Cross, it even has his name on it. Maybe it was a memorial to those who were lost that fateful Sunday.

As the power of the west coast clans suffered under royal attack, the lands of Knapdale were taken from the MacMillans and granted to the Campbells. The prophetic charter that had been inscribed into the rock was apparently smashed to pieces and allowed to wash out to sea.

The MacMillans who had called this place home drifted away to other areas. Some of them were welcomed by Clan Cameron in return for sword service, but also no doubt in remembrance of the tragedy they had shared in that church all those years before.

ESCAPE FROM INNIS CHONNEL CASTLE

Hidden away among the trees on the quiet side of Loch Awe, few people make the effort to visit Innis Chonnel Castle. This island fortress is the older and less visited sibling of the popular Kilchurn and Inveraray Castles, but in some ways it's much more impressive.

This historic stronghold was where the vast empire of Clan Campbell likely began, but as their power increased, they left it behind. The safety of Loch Awe was seemingly less important than the easy access to the sea offered by Loch Fyne, so the Clan Chief moved to Inveraray.

Instead of a comfortable home, the old castle at Innis Chonnel became a secure prison. In the fifteenth century, Donald Dubh Macdonald, heir to the Lordship of the Isles but with a Campbell mother, was captured as a baby and imprisoned here. His father and grandfather had both continually rebelled against the Scottish Crown and now Donald was the one paying for it.

The boy grew into a man while locked in his island prison until a daring rescue by his clansmen whisked him away to the Isle of Lewis. Donald made his ancestors proud by immediately rebelling against the King, only to end up captured once more and held in Edinburgh Castle for almost forty years.

Old Donald was finally released in 1543, but if it was for good behaviour then that didn't last long. He declared yet another rebellion, signing a pact with the English King Henry VIII and pledging to raise 8,000 men to support his invasion of Scotland.

Even though the islanders were angry at the way they and their chiefs had been treated, Donald Dubh struggled to gather the army he had promised. Instead, he retired to the safety of Ireland to plan his next expedition, where he soon died of a fever.

Poor Donald had spent fewer than ten years of his entire life as a free man, but at least he spent his teenage years in as picturesque a spot as Innis Chonnel Castle.

HOW LOCH AWE WAS FORMED

Legend says that Scotland was created by the mysterious, ancient entity known as the Cailleach. This giant, blue-skinned hag shaped the mountains and the glens with the use of her enormous hammer, using the peaks as stepping stones. She formed the numerous islands by dropping great chunks of earth and rock from a creel that she carried on her back.

Some of the Cailleach's creations weren't quite so intentional though.

One of her favourite haunts was the mighty Ben Cruachan, the highest mountain in Argyll. There she would lift a huge rock, releasing the crystal-clear waters of a well to refresh herself, before securely dropping the stopper back in place. The views and the water were unbeatable.

Then, after a particularly long day herding her beloved deer, the Cailleach was far more tired than normal. She lifted the protective stone on the mountain, drank deeply to quench her thirst and began to relax. The relief of finally taking the weight off her feet accompanied by the gentle sound of trickling water was enough to send this ancient goddess off to sleep.

However, she had forgotten to cover the well again and the trickling water became a flowing river that ended up as a raging torrent pouring down the slopes of Ben Cruachan. By the time the Cailleach had awoken, it was too late and all of that water had formed into Loch Awe – the longest freshwater loch in Scotland.

THE LAIRD OF OLD CASTLE LACHLAN

On the quiet side of Loch Fyne, known as Argyll's Secret Coast, you'll find the ruined shell of Old Castle Lachlan. Once the bustling home of the Chief of Clan MacLachlan, it's a serene spot today, peaceful until the castle's unusual ghost turns up.

The MacLachlans had been loyal to the Stuart monarchs during the early Jacobite risings and, like many others, had suffered badly for it. When Bonnie Prince Charlie landed in 1745 and sent word for his supporters to gather once more, Lachlan MacLachlan had his doubts.

Old Castle Lachlan had an ancient inhabitant called a brownie living in its depths, known as Master Harry. One day, he approached the Chief in distress after seeing a vision of a stranger arriving in the north who would spell doom for Lachlan MacLachlan.

Regardless of his own fate, the Chief knew he had a duty to his clan, who were eager to fight for their cause. As he left the castle at the head of 100 men, Lachlan stopped to pray at the small chapel of Kilmorie, where almost every chief before him lay buried. Remounting his horse, it turned three times anticlockwise – a terrible omen for what was to come.

Sadly, for Lachlan, he was plucked from his saddle by a cannonball while leading his men at Culloden. The horse survived and somehow found its own way home to Loch Fyne. Watching the riderless horse swim across the narrow strip of water to Old Castle Lachlan, the inhabitants knew their Chief was gone.

The horse was inconsolable, refusing to leave the stables, even when a warship sailed up the loch and bombarded the castle into pieces. Its spirit is thought to still be there and the sound of its whinny echoes around the ruined walls while invisible hooves crunch through the rubble. Let's just hope Master Harry has stuck around as well, so they can keep each other company.

THE HARP-PLAYING GHOST OF INVERARY CASTLE

When the Campbell Duke of Argyll decided that the original Inveraray Castle wasn't appropriate for his status, he commissioned today's symmetrical replacement, moving the whole town of Inveraray a little further away in the process. While this version of the castle is barely 250 years old, it seems that one of its ghosts is even older.

In 1644, the Marquis of Montrose, commander of the Royalist forces, attacked the old Castle of Inveraray, forcing Argyll to flee his home. Most of the servants were simply left behind to fend for themselves and that included a young Irish harpist.

Unfortunately, Montrose's army had a large Irish contingent and they were furious that one of their own worked for Argyll. With their blood up, they didn't just murder the lad, they left his dismembered body on the bed. Once the Campbells returned to Inveraray, it was clear they weren't alone by the faint harp music coming from the room where the boy was killed.

Inveraray Castle – still home to the Duke of Argyll and haunted by a ghostly harp player.

Many years later, that bed was moved to the present Inveraray Castle, into what's known as the MacArthur Room. If the Campbells thought that escaping the old castle would remove the memory of what had happened, they were wrong. It seems that the harpist has followed the bed.

A strong feeling of dread fills the space and furniture has been known to move around of its own accord. The ghost isn't violent or aggressive in any way but has become a portent of death for the Campbells along with a phantom galley ship that sails along Loch Fyne. When a member of the family is about to pass away, harp music can be heard floating along the corridors of Inveraray Castle.

DUNCAN BAN MACINTYRE – A GREAT GAELIC POET

Look up from the banks of Loch Awe and you might spot the impressive Duncan Ban Macintyre monument. He was an influential Gaelic poet from the eighteenth century, sometimes called the Robert Burns of the Highlands.

Duncan Ban or Fair Duncan was born near Loch Awe in the days when Gaelic was still the dominant language in Argyll. Even without formal education, he turned out to be a gifted poet with razor-sharp wit. Working the land around the loch as a forester and gamekeeper, his poetry gives a rare insight into the life of everyday people in this part of Scotland.

Duncan wrote about the things important to his life, like windswept, rugged mountains and his favourite gun, Nic Còiseim. While those were what he loved, he also included the things he hated, like sheep.

After years of working in the Edinburgh City Guard, he returned to visit Loch Awe and was distraught at what he saw. The land that he had loved and cared for was almost empty apart from hundreds of sheep, inspiring the satirical 'Song to the Foxes'. Duncan wished a long, healthy life and good luck to foxes because of their skill in hunting the sheep that he despised.

During the 1745 Jacobite Rising, being from Argyll, Duncan fought on the government side, although we don't know where his true sympathies lay. The only reason he was in the army was that an old landowner called Fletcher had hired him to fight in his place.

Unfortunately, he lost his employer's antique sword during the Battle of Falkirk Muir and returned to Loch Awe before Culloden. Furious at the missing family heirloom, Fletcher refused to pay the agreed fee, so of course Duncan wrote a scathing poem about it.

Judging by his description of how the rubbish, dented old sword badly bruised his hip while walking, it wouldn't be a surprise if he had thrown it away to save carrying it back!

KILCHURN CASTLE & THE BLACK KNIGHT OF RHODES

Kilchurn Castle rises out of the waters of Loch Awe as one of the most atmospheric ruins in Scotland, with a story to match. It surrounds the fifteenth-century castle's builder, Colin Campbell of Glenorchy, a famous Crusader nicknamed the Black Knight of Rhodes.

While Colin was away fighting in the Holy Land, he had a strange dream that troubled him deeply. He consulted a priest to put his mind at ease, but the man looked at him gravely. The Crusader was told to race home to Kilchurn Castle immediately to avert disaster for both him and his family.

Colin had been away from Scotland for seven years but had been sending regular letters home to update his wife, Lady Margaret. Unfortunately, his rival, the Baron MacCorquodale, had intercepted the messengers and convinced Margaret that her husband had died in the fighting.

It was a dangerous time for a widow to hold on to the newly built Kilchurn Castle and the Baron offered Margaret protection through marriage. Reluctantly she conceded.

Colin arrived home the same day the wedding was to be held, but in his rush, he hadn't brought any fine clothes or cleaned himself up. Nobody would believe it if he just strolled in like this and besides, the Baron's soldiers outside would surely drag him off to kill him if they knew his real identity!

Instead, Colin played the part of a beggar and was allowed to join the feast as an act of charity to celebrate the special day. Now inside, he noticed more than enough of his clansmen scattered around the room to take care of the Baron's troops. He just had to make sure that they would all recognise him in his unkempt state.

Colin ate the food offered but declared he would only be served his drink by the lady of the house. Bemused, Lady Margaret agreed and handed this hooded stranger a goblet. Draining it in one, he passed it back with a ring dropped inside.

This talisman had been a gift from Margaret to keep him safe and she gasped when she realised who was standing in front of her. Throwing back his cloak, Colin stood tall and his wife declared her husband had returned.

The Campbell clansmen cheered, then sprang to action, chasing the Baron and his men out of Kilchurn Castle and putting the wedding feast to better use, celebrating their Laird's return.

AYRSHIRE & ARRAN

THE GIANT PENCIL OF LARGS

In the thirteenth century, Scotland looked a little different, with much of the west coast and Hebrides belonging to the Kingdom of Norway. There's plenty of evidence of that Scandinavian influence to be found either in local place names or in a giant pencil beside the town of Largs.

The peculiar monument marks an attempt by King Alexander III to claim this part of Scotland back in 1263. Unsurprisingly, King Haakon of Norway wasn't happy to let it go without a fight and as the descendants of Vikings, these men really knew how to fight.

Haakon's enormous fleet sailed up the Firth of Clyde in a clear show of force. There, just off the Ayrshire coast, the Norwegians waited to see what the King of Scots would throw at them.

It was clear that Alexander didn't have enough men to fight and was in no position to bargain for the islands either. Instead, the King of Scots dragged the talks out, delaying any agreements and giving time for more men to gather further inland. It was getting late in the year, so if he could hold them off long enough, then the weather might turn to the Scots' advantage.

King Haakon had finally had enough time-wasting and looked ready to send his vast army to trample their way across the Scottish mainland. Then Alexander got what he had been praying for, a fierce storm whipped across the water one evening. By morning, a host of Norwegian ships had been washed up on the beach at Largs, torn from their anchors and smashed to pieces.

When a small force landed to try and repair the damaged ships, the Scots suddenly attacked, swarming across the beach to meet the Scandinavians. The Battle of Largs was intense, with both sides fighting to a standstill and neither able to gain the upper hand.

There was no clear winner, but enough damage had been done to force Haakon to retreat to Orkney, where he died that winter. His hopes of holding on to western Scotland died with him and his successor signed any claim he had to the Hebrides over to the King of Scots.

The Battle of Largs was no overwhelming victory, but it changed the course of Scottish history. When the time came to build the memorial in 1912 on the Largs coast, it was designed as a smaller replica of the Brechin Cathedral Round Tower. It seemed fitting as it was believed at the time that the tower was built as protection from Viking raiders!

THE FAIRY CAVES UNDER CULZEAN CASTLE

The lavish Culzean Castle doesn't look like your typical Scottish fortress but look a little closer and you'll find that it's full of surprises. At the castle's core are the thick walls of the original tower and beneath its polished floors are a series of mysterious caves.

Accessed from the beach, these caverns hold an abundance of legends. They were such an important feature that the family living in the castle were named after them, becoming known as the Lairds of Co'.

Legend says that in the sixteenth century, a small boy carrying a little wooden mug saw the Laird of Co' outside the castle and begged him for some ale to help his sick mother. The Laird was a kind man and had no hesitation in sending the child inside for ale from his personal store.

There was a barrel already open, so the Laird's servant started to pour into the mug. The barrel got emptier and emptier, but the mug wasn't getting fuller. Even when the cask was drained, the boy insisted that he had been promised a full mug and it clearly wasn't full yet.

The servant knew magic when he saw it, this was obviously one of the fairies who lived below the castle. He was loath to open a new barrel just to lose that as well. However, the Laird insisted that he must stick to his word even if it took all the ale in Culzean's cellar. To the servant's surprise, it only took one drop before the mug was full.

Years later, when the Laird of Co' was fighting in Flanders, he was captured and sentenced to death. There was no chance of escape from his prison and the night before his execution, the Laird was dreaming of home when his mind wandered to that peculiar day with the mysterious child.

At that very moment, the door to his cell swung open and in walked the little boy. He hadn't aged a day and the Laird was now convinced he was one of Culzean's fairies. His rescuer grinned and commanded, 'Laird of Co', rise and go.' The Laird followed the fairy boy out of the dungeon, hopped onto his back and was flown back to Culzean Castle in no time at all.

Before the fairy boy disappeared back to his home in the caves, the Laird asked why he had rescued him. The fairy replied that every good turn deserves another and the nobleman had cared enough to help his poor old mother.

WHERE THE MACHRIE MOOR STONES CAME FROM

The Machrie Moor Standing Stones are one of the most incredible sights on the Isle of Arran. It's much more than just the handful of iconic, tall monoliths usually seen on postcards, there are the remains of six stone circles spread across the moor, in a landscape dotted with other ancient remains.

The most famous of the Machrie Moor Standing Stones in the Isle of Arran's most sacred spot.

This part of Arran was clearly considered sacred for a very long time. Around 6,500 years ago there were simple timber circles here, replaced with stones between 1,000 and 3,000 years later. The iconic red sandstone pillars were originally part of circles and stand around 4 or 5m tall. One of those lies on the ground in pieces after somebody once tried to carve it into a millstone.

Whoever began that process got reasonably far, but something must have stopped them. It might have been their conscience but then again, maybe it was the fairies of Arran. Some believe that they were the ones responsible for creating the stone circles. Sitting on the hills surrounding the moor, they would flick boulders down in competition with each other.

One small double-ringed stone circle near the ruined farmhouse is known as Fingal's Cauldron Seat. The inside circle has large granite blocks with smaller stones surrounding the outside. Legend says that Fingal used the central stones to support a great big cauldron for cooking his dinner.

His enormous dog, Bran, was so bad for stealing food that Fingal had to tie the hound up through a small hole in one of the stones. That hole is still there, worn smooth over time and offerings of milk were once poured through it as an offering to keep the Arran fairies happy!

DUNURE CASTLE & THE ROASTING OF THE COMMENDATOR

Dunure Castle was once home to the powerful Kennedy family, each generation seemingly more ambitious than the last. When it came to Gilbert Kennedy, the 4th Earl of Cassilis, he took things to a much darker level.

Described as a greedy man who cared little about how he obtained land, Gilbert grew so powerful that he became known as the King of Carrick. In one of his audacious acts, he bribed a monk to forge documents granting him the lands of Glenluce Abbey. To cover his tracks, Gilbert paid a peasant to kill the monk and then had the peasant hanged for theft.

That had worked so well that the Earl soon set his sights on Crossraguel Abbey, but found the Commendator Allan Stewart a much tougher character to bargain with. To change his mind, Gilbert captured Allan, bringing him to Dunure Castle in as peaceful a manner as possible.

He flattered and honoured him, trying to woo his forced guest into donating Crossraguel's rich lands to the Kennedy cause. The Commendator saw right through the charade. It was clear that determined Allan wasn't going to comply and the Earl wanted this over and done with.

It was time to be a little more persuasive, so poor Allan was dragged down to the Black Vault of Dunure. In the depths of the castle, a great fire was stoked while the prisoner was stripped and bound, slathered with oil and tied to the chimney.

The Commendator was slowly roasted over the flames and, unsurprisingly, soon gave in to the Earl's demands. Finally happy, Gilbert left Dunure Castle behind to spread the good news, no doubt leaving orders to quietly dispose of the evidence. Thankfully, the Laird of Bargany had heard about the roasting and stormed the castle to rescue him.

It's a wild story, but a true one and the reason we know so much is that the Commendator made it safely to the Privy Council in Edinburgh to report the Earl's actions. Even though Gilbert was forced to apologise and pay Allan annual compensation, he was still allowed to keep the Crossraguel Abbey's lands!

Who said that crime doesn't pay?

WHO BUILT DUNDONALD CASTLE

With incredible views from its hilltop location, it's a surprise that the ruins of Dundonald Castle don't get more attention. The great, vaulted rooms contain a wealth of history, including being where King Robert II died in 1390, but it's the name of the castle that holds the most curious story.

Dundonald simply means 'the Fort of Donald' and local legend claims that the first castle here was built by a very fortunate man called Donald Din. There's even a rhyme that was already considered old almost 200 years ago that tells us that the castle was built entirely of stone:

Donald Din, Built his house without a pin.

As well as the slightly more elaborate:

There stands a castle in the west, they call it Donald Din
There's no a nail in all its roof, nor yet a wooden pin.

Both of these are involved in the story of Donald Din, who started out as nothing more than a poor man with a tiny patch of land to farm. He had the same dream three times in the same night, that he must travel down to London Bridge to discover a great treasure. It was a long journey for somebody without means, but Donald was sure his dream meant something.

After weeks of travelling, the Ayrshire man arrived on London Bridge and waited for something to happen. Time passed as did hundreds of people, but there was no great treasure to be found.

Dejected, Donald leant on the parapet of the bridge and sighed loudly as he wondered why he had been such an idiot. A stranger standing next to him looked over and asked what was wrong, nodding in understanding at the reply.

It turned out, he had once had a similar dream about a hoard of gold buried in a distant place, but even after years of searching, was no closer to finding it. After a detailed description, Donald realised that treasure was buried in his very own vegetable patch!

Rushing back home to Ayrshire, the formerly poor man found a huge pot of gold beneath his cabbages and used it to fund the construction of the very first Dundonald Castle!

KING ROBERT THE BRUCE'S ARRAN HIDEOUT

The west coast of Arran is littered with fascinating caves, but one entrance is just a little more impressive than the rest. An elaborate gate guards King's Cave, one of the many locations that lay claim to the story of Robert Bruce and the Spider.

In the winter of 1306, King Robert was on the run and nobody knows for sure where he went, but Arran is a strong candidate. His dream of uniting Scotland was hanging by a thread and a famous story tells that while sitting in a cave, the King took inspiration from a spider trying to build a web.

A dozen times the spider missed its jump and fell to the floor, only to climb back up and start again. Then eventually, the leap was successful and the rest of the spider's web was easily completed.

It reminded Robert of his own struggle; just because he had failed several times, it only took one victory to get a foothold and begin to build momentum. The lesson learned was that if, at first, you don't succeed, try and try again.

In truth, the earliest written example of the spider legend didn't appear until long after Robert the Bruce had died. The original version had Sir James Douglas watching the spider and sharing the lesson with the sombre King.

Robert the Bruce certainly wasn't the first person to use this cave; it's full of much older carvings and was originally known as Fionn's Cave until the nineteenth century. Fingal and his warriors are said to have used Arran as a hunting ground and would spend their nights in this cave.

Among the collection of carvings along the walls, you can find holes chipped into the back of the cave, where legend says the warriors placed beams for cooking their fresh boar or venison.

King's Cave on the Isle of Arran's west coast, one contender for Robert the Bruce's hiding place.

THE SAILOR'S GRAVE OF ARRAN

The Sailor's Grave can be found on the north-west coast of Arran, next to a layby between Lochranza and Catacol. It dates from 1854 when a ship anchored off Lochranza and sent a pleading request to the local islanders.

One of their crew, John McLean, had come down with a mysterious illness and had passed away on board. They were looking for the nearest consecrated ground to bury him.

The folk of Lochranza point blank refused to take the body. They were too worried that whatever plague had taken the sailor would then spread, so the ship was pointed 2 miles down the coast to try their luck at Catacol instead.

Unfortunately, the Catacol residents felt exactly the same way, the fear of disease was just too strong. Poor John had nowhere to go and the ship couldn't keep his body on board much longer.

Instead, the crew were forced to bury him beside the road, in a lonely spot halfway between the two settlements. Over the years, as people passed by, they began to drop pebbles from the beach on John's grave. It may have just been a token of respect, or it may have been an attempt to ease their guilty conscience after stopping this poor sailor from being buried in a churchyard.

THE BATTLE OF LOUDON HILL

Visit the big lump of Loudon Hill and you'll come face to face with the Spirit of Scotland, a metal monument showing the outline of William Wallace, who supposedly won a skirmish here against an English convoy. However, the story that really made Loudon Hill famous is attributed to another Scottish hero.

In 1307, Robert the Bruce was slowly clawing his way back into control of Scotland with his guerrilla tactics. Small victories were welcome, but the day was approaching when he would need to win a fixed battle and that show-down would come at Loudon Hill.

Robert's small army was badly outnumbered, 600 Scots facing 3,000 Englishmen led by the Earl of Pembroke. That was the same man who had defeated Bruce at Methven only a year earlier, but the King had learned a tough lesson that day.

He picked the perfect battlefield, using local knowledge to his advantage. Loudon Hill was surrounded by a boggy marsh, with only one narrow high-way through the middle and the Scots created deep trenches to funnel their opponents even closer together, negating their advantage of numbers.

Pembroke and his heavy cavalry took the easy route, doing exactly what Robert had expected and charging straight towards his waiting spears. It was a big mistake. Deep pits filled with sharp spikes had been camouflaged, right in front of the Scottish line. As the front rank of riders fell straight in, those pushing from behind only added to the chaos.

As the Scots pressed forward with their spears, the disorganised mass of men and horses panicked and ran. It had been a battle of wits against sheer power and Robert's tactical genius had won the day. He had got his revenge against the man who had embarrassed him and proved himself as a worthy King of Scots.

BORDERS

THE WORM OF LINTON KIRK

The tiny Linton Kirk sits in a peaceful area of the Borders, but things weren't so quiet when the area was terrorised by the Linton Worm. This wasn't what we think of as a worm today, it was a vicious serpent that hid in a hollow under Linton Hill, living off the local livestock.

With huge, powerful jaws and rank, poisonous breath that could kill anybody who came near, nobody was brave enough to even try. The locals could only look on from a distance as the beast picked off their animals one by one before retreating again under the hill.

Linton Kirk with a carved stone above the entrance depicting the death of the Worm of Linton.

The legend reached the ears of John de Somerville, a man who was desperate to prove himself a hero. Riding over to challenge the beast, he was warned that it was impossible to get within sword distance and no arrow could penetrate the monster's hide. The locals assured him that there was no way to defeat it, but Somerville wouldn't listen.

He sat quietly on his horse outside the worm's lair as it slowly crept out to meet him. The worm opened its jaws wide, but it couldn't stretch quite far enough to swallow both man and horse together. This problem had never occurred before, so the beast just stood still in confusion. As long as Somerville stayed out of range of its poisonous breath, he should be safe and that gave him an idea.

After a visit to the nearest blacksmith, he came back with a specially made lance, twice as long as normal with a spinning spike on the end. Adding burning peat to the spike, he mounted his horse again and rode off to wait for the beast. Once again it slowly crept out and opened its jaws wide.

Somerville took his chance, charging forward and ramming the burning peat down its throat on the end of the lance. The creature was slain and Somerville was knighted by the King in thanks, becoming the first Baron of Linton.

A very old carved stone can still be found above the door of Linton Kirk to commemorate the story, showing a hero on horseback lancing a monster.

THE REDCAP OF HERMITAGE CASTLE

With Hermitage Castle being known as the 'guardhouse of the bloodiest valley in Britain', it's no surprise that it has a dark story to tell. These oppressive walls have long been left to ruin, but legend says the castle is still home to one sinister creature.

The early inhabitants were the de Soulis family, butlers to the King of Scots and Lords of Liddesdale. One particularly nasty Lord Soulis loved nothing more than death and destruction. He had even found a like-minded assistant, who was the only creature that enjoyed bloodshed as much as he did.

This small beast was called a redcap, a little goblin with a hat that needed to be soaked in blood regularly to maintain its vibrant colour. There was no better place to provide a steady supply than right in the often-contested border country.

In return for what the redcap required, it granted Soulis a magical ability. He could neither be harmed by steel nor bound by rope and his behaviour grew ever more despicable, thinking himself invincible. Eventually, the locals hatched a plan to rid themselves of this monstrous figure forever.

Together, they stormed Hermitage Castle to seize Soulis, wrapping him in lead and boiling him in a cauldron. The redcap couldn't be dealt with quite so easily though and even without the cruelty of Soulis, there was plenty of fighting around Hermitage Castle to satisfy its thirst.

Things are much calmer in the area today, but if you see a flash of red inside Hermitage then beware. That redcap must be getting desperate.

THE WIZARD WHO CLEAVED THE EILDON HILLS

One of Scotland's most fascinating, but underappreciated, characters is Michael Scott, a wizard who was so notorious that he was mentioned by name in Dante's *Inferno*. Many of his acts are remembered in Borders legends, including cleaving the Eildon Hills in three, but the most interesting is where his power came from.

As a young man, Michael loved hiking across the hills and while travelling with his friends one day, they heard an angry hiss behind them. A great white serpent was about to attack. Michael's friends turned and ran, but he stood his ground, striking it twice with all his strength and splitting it into three pieces.

Catching up with his companions, they all walked a little bit faster than before, eventually coming to a cottage, where they paid for a night's rest. When they retold the tale of their strange encounter, their host looked shocked. She exclaimed that their ordeal wasn't yet over!

That snake had attacked before and been mortally wounded, only to heal itself in a nearby burn. It relentlessly hunted down its attacker for revenge, so if they didn't rush back out and retrieve the middle section now then it would be too late!

Michael was the only one brave enough to head into the darkness, finding that the snake's head was gone but successfully returning with the middle as instructed. The woman was clearly delighted, exclaiming that the only way to destroy it for good was to cook it. Michael was feeling the chill in his bones from the midnight trip, so offered to stay by the fire and watch the pot.

He was to wake his host as soon as the meal was ready but otherwise not to taste any of it. However, as time wore on, the smell was irresistible and Michael's stomach was rumbling loud enough to wake the rest of the house. What harm could a little taste really do?

He dipped his finger in the juice and as soon as it touched his lips, he let out a cry. Suddenly, he could feel immense power coursing through him as he gained the knowledge of everything that had ever been or ever would be.

Stobo Kirk, believed to be founded by St Mungo and the location of the baptism of 'Merlin the Wizard'.

His host ran through in despair, knowing that the magic of the white snake was now lost to her. She was disappointed but knew that Michael had been the one to earn the gift and could only hope that he would use it wisely.

MERLIN THE WIZARD'S BAPTISM AT STOBO KIRK

Dating back to the 1100s, Stobo Kirk is one of the oldest functioning churches in Scotland. The slightly more modern building incorporates part of an older chapel that has connections to a man called Myrddin Wyllt. Somebody often known better as Merlin the Wizard.

The Merlin most people know from the Arthurian legends was created by Geoffrey of Monmouth for his semi-fictional *History of the Kings of Britain*. However, he was based on real historical characters and one of those was the sixth-century Myrddin of the Wild, also known as Merlinus of Caledonia.

It might sound like a strange name for a Scottish character, but Myrddin came from the Kingdom of Strathclyde, where the language and culture were closer to Welsh than Gaelic. It's said that Myrddin either saw a distressing omen or witnessed horrendous slaughter during a battle and fled into the depths of the Caledonian Forest for solitude.

There he wandered the Borders as a wild man of the woods until stumbling upon the small chapel at Stobo. It had recently been established by St Kentigern, the man affectionately known as Mungo and more famous as the patron saint of Glasgow. Somehow, Mungo connected with the babbling Myrddin and successfully converted and baptised him here.

Although he may have found some spiritual peace, Myrddin was still haunted by the vision of his own triple death. Eventually, he was chased off a high cliff by an angry mob, landing on a fisherman's spike in the river, where his head fell under the water. After suffering these three deaths in one, Myrddin was buried at Drumelzier, near a spot known ever since as Merlindale.

TROJAN COWS AT ROXBURGH CASTLE

There's practically nothing left of either the town or castle of Roxburgh, just a pile of stones on a mound across the river from Floors Castle. It's hard to believe that this was once one of the most important trading hubs in Scotland, with a seemingly impregnable castle. Nothing is impossible though, sometimes you just have to think outside the box.

In 1314, Robert the Bruce and his lieutenants were working their way around Scotland, capturing castles from supporters of King Edward of England. They didn't have the numbers, time or siege equipment to face these strongholds head on though, and they were forced to rely on cunning and speed instead.

Roxburgh Castle was a daunting place and even with a large army, a traditional assault would have been madness. That's why the King entrusted its capture to his right-hand man Sir James Douglas, known for his tactical brilliance and ruthless attitude.

His small band of warriors waited until the feast of Shrovetide, right before Lent, when most of the garrison would be drunkenly distracted with celebrations. Disguising themselves with cloaks, they slowly crept on their hands and knees ever closer to the walls. In the darkness, the few soldiers on watch saw nothing more than a herd of cows grazing outside the walls.

They had no idea what was happening until it was too late. Rope ladders had already reached the ramparts and the Scots were swarming over the top. The governor tried his best to rally the defenders in the main tower, surrendering after receiving an arrow through the cheek.

The Douglas Cows had won this important castle, but rather than wasting men defending the walls, they destroyed as much as they could. Roxburgh Castle was eventually rebuilt, just to be captured by the English once more.

Unfortunately, King James II didn't take inspiration from this story in 1460 when he was blown up by one of his own cannon trying to retake it!

THE GHOST THAT DANCED AT JEDBURGH ABBEY

The grand ruin at Jedburgh Abbey is probably the most impressive in the Borders. Founded by King David I right on the border with England, this was his way of showing off Scotland's place on the world stage.

While the abbey's construction may have been a statement of confidence for David, it wasn't ideal for his descendants. Jedburgh was far too tempting for passing English armies and was pillaged regularly as they travelled further north.

Time and time again, the Augustinian monks would rebuild and regroup. Almost every Scottish king had to deal with trouble at Jedburgh Abbey, but the experience of Alexander III tops them all.

The King married his second wife Yolande de Dreux there in 1285 and initially, it was a joyous celebration. Alexander was especially pleased as he had no surviving children and was desperate to secure an heir with his new wife. Then the mood changed halfway through the afterparty when a strange figure appeared in the hall.

The dancing stopped and the music faded away as a spectral skeleton moved towards the happy couple. This horrific wedding crasher didn't say a word, it just slowly raised a finger and pointed towards the King. Everybody agreed this was a terrible omen for the royal wedding night, but nobody could have imagined what it truly meant.

Just a year later, Alexander was killed falling from his horse at Kinghorn while trying to reach Yolande on a stormy night. He had died without that heir he craved and Scotland was soon plunged into the succession crisis that led to the Wars of Independence.

A terrible omen indeed.

THE BEAR GATES OF TRAQUAIR HOUSE

Dating back to at least 1107, visited by twenty-seven kings and queens and still lived in today, Traquair is the oldest inhabited house in Scotland. It began as a small hunting lodge, grew into a defensive peel tower, finally transforming into what we have today in the seventeenth century and hasn't been changed since!

Traquair House's famous Bear Gates – locked since 1745 until a Stuart sits on the throne once more.

Inside you can find a hoard of relics, from an early 1500s hunting mural to a crib used by Mary, Queen of Scots to hold the infant James VI. Despite the dangers, the family at Traquair remained staunchly Catholic after the Scottish Reformation. A secret chamber for Mass was built into the top floor, connected to a hidden staircase should the priest need to escape quickly.

That devotion to their faith was one reason that the Lairds of Traquair were such strong supporters of the Jacobite cause. Bonnie Prince Charlie found a warm bed there and a loyal friend in the 5th Earl of Traquair during his campaign in 1745.

As the army left to march south to Derby, the Earl closed his impressive new gates topped with bears behind the Prince. He vowed they would never be opened again until a Stuart king was back on the throne and the Bear Gates have remained locked ever since!

THOMAS THE RHYMER'S STONE

Just outside of Melrose, at the foot of the Eildon Hills, Rhmyer's Stone marks where the Eildon Tree once stood. This is where the prophet Thomas the Rhymer is said to have gained his power of second sight.

While snoozing under its branches, the young man woke to find himself in the shadow of the most beautiful woman he had ever seen. He immediately jumped to his feet and bowed low, declaring that he must be in the presence of the Queen of Heaven.

The smiling woman replied that she was in fact Queen of the Fairies and had been looking for him. Asking for a kiss, Thomas readily complied and immediately became trapped by her spell. The Queen ordered him up behind her on a majestic white horse to start the journey to the Fairy Kingdom, where he would serve for seven years.

In time, they reached a mysterious crossroads with a neat path lined with flowers leading to hell and another rough track full of thorns leading to heaven. They took a third, thick with ferns and greener than Thomas could have imagined. When they came to a bountiful garden, Thomas was handed a strange fruit to eat.

Unsure if it was payment or punishment, the fruit granted him a tongue that could never lie. He would need to wait to test it out though. The Queen warned her companion that if he ever wanted to return home then he couldn't speak a single word inside the Fairy Kingdom. Astounded by the day's events, Thomas could only nod.

The young man settled in for seven long years of silent servitude, but only a few days passed when the Queen released him from his bond. Time passed differently here, and he was already free to return to the Eildon Tree where they had first met.

Back in the Borders, it became apparent that not only could Thomas not lie but anything he said would come to pass. By the time he was an old man, Thomas the Rhymer was a living legend.

Then one day a servant brought him news that a pure white deer had been seen walking near the Eildon Tree. Thomas knew that this was a sign from the fairies and without another word he walked outside, never to be seen again.

One of his many prophecies claimed:

At Eildon Tree, if yon shall be,
a brig ower Tweed yon there may se.

That once seemed impossible, but the Leaderfoot Viaduct that opened in 1863 is high enough that if you visit Rhymer's Stone you can just make it out from where the tree once stood.

DEFENDING KELSO ABBEY

The last remains of Kelso Abbey tower over the rest of the town, a shadow of its former self but with plenty of stories to bring it to life. This was once the richest monastic house in the Borders, the coronation site of James III and even the first line of defence for Kelso.

The abbey bells would toll in warning at the sign of approaching trouble and they were in near constant use. Allegedly some monks didn't like the idea of an army carrying off their expensive bells, so they hid them in the River Tweed. Sadly, they didn't live long enough to retrieve them and somewhere beneath the dark water, a ringing sound can still be heard when danger approaches Kelso.

During one particularly fierce attack by an English army in the 1540s, this religious building was transformed into a makeshift castle. Kelso town was easily secured by the invaders, but a small garrison of townsfolk had barricaded themselves inside the abbey. Putting up a good fight, they were eventually forced right into the highest tower by cannon fire, where they could make their last stand.

It was clearly a lost cause and the wisest abseiled down the walls to escape as best they could while the bravest stayed to fight on, just to be killed the next day. Kelso Abbey was destroyed and after the Reformation in 1560 it wasn't worth rebuilding. Most of the stone was recycled throughout the town, apart from a few soaring walls to remind us of this once impressive building.

THE MYSTERY OF FATLIPS CASTLE

There are dozens of small towers dotted around the Borders, but none have a name as fascinating as Fatlips Castle, perched up on Minto Crags. Nobody knows for sure what the true story behind the odd name is, but there are a few different theories.

One claims that this was once home to a special goat called Fatlips. Every time a raiding party approached, it would scream out in warning, giving the defenders a chance to defend themselves. Another explanation is that one resident laird was a little over-friendly, demanding that everybody receive a sloppy kiss from him on entry!

The tower was originally built by Turnbull of Barnhill, a famous Border reiver. These reivers operated on both sides of the border, carrying out light-

ning raids on small, nimble horses that could easily pick their way over poor terrain. They would return with somebody else's cattle before another group of reivers would do the same thing to them.

Just like Fatlips, the Turnbulls have a legend about where their name came from. A man called William of Rule was accompanying Robert the Bruce on a hunt one day when a wild bull suddenly attacked. Fortunately, William was a giant of a man and immediately jumped into action, charging in front of the King.

He grabbed the bull by the horns, turned its head to the side and, with immense strength, held it long enough for the others to finish it off. Robert rewarded William with these lands in the Borders, the symbol of a bull's head on his coat of arms and the new surname 'Turn-e-bull'.

The curiously named Fatlips Castle, a typical peel tower for Border reivers.

HUME CASTLE'S FALSE ALARM

The fancifully restored Hume Castle was once known as the Watchdog of the Eastern Border, part of a series of towers ready to spread word of any approaching invasion. There had been a simple fortification on this small outcrop as early as the twelfth century, both as an early warning system and a meeting point for local militia to gather before joining any Scottish armies marching south.

It might seem to be in a strong spot, but it was practically obsolete after the introduction of cannon. The castle would surely have become just a pile of rubble if it hadn't been for the 3rd Earl Marchmont, who built the romantic folly around the ruin that we have today. It even proved useful during the Napoleonic Wars as an early warning beacon system for spreading news of a French invasion on the coast and was vital to Britain's defence!

Unfortunately, things didn't always go to plan.

On 4 January 1804, during a long winter's night, a recently transferred sergeant of the Berwickshire volunteers spotted something in the darkness. It looked like embers and as he strained his eyes, that small glow turned into unmistakable flames. The beacons were being lit, the French were coming!

Setting fire to his beacon at Hume Castle, the message was picked up further along the line and before long the Borders were ablaze and 3,000 men roused from their beds for action.

Unfortunately, all the overeager sergeant had spotted were the fires of charcoal burners on nearby Dirrington Law. The panic that this now unpopular figure had spread became known as the Great Alarm.

THE BRAVE HEART BURIED IN MELROSE ABBEY

There's something very special about Melrose Abbey. That's not just down to its beautiful setting, the charming town or even the bagpipe-playing pig found among the high stonework. It's because of one very special burial.

Melrose has plenty of interesting residents, including King Alexander II and Michael Scott the Wizard, who was killed here by falling masonry and is supposedly buried with his magic books, although we don't know exactly where that is. However, the most famous burial in the grounds of Melrose Abbey is undoubtedly the heart of King Robert the Bruce.

Robert did a lot of impressive things, spending his surprisingly long reign in an almost constant battle to secure his throne and protect his country. Barely a year before his death in 1329, the King of England finally agreed to recognise Bruce as the rightful King of Scots by signing the Treaty of Edinburgh–Northampton.

Scotland was now secure, but Robert had run out of time to fulfil his ambition of going on a Crusade. Since he couldn't make it to the Holy Land himself, on his deathbed he made James Douglas promise to take the most important part of him there instead. The King's heart was placed in a casket, hung around his friend's neck and taken in search of a Crusade.

Douglas and a small group of Scottish knights ended up joining King Alfonso of Castile in a campaign in southern Spain, although not many survived the fierce fighting. One account claims that the Scots led an attack so fierce that they became isolated and surrounded by the enemy. Douglas launched Robert's heart at the enemy in a last act of defiance, shouting, 'Lead on Brave Heart and I will follow thee'.

Robert's heart was returned to Scotland and believed to be buried in Melrose Abbey, but nobody knew where. Then in 1996, a mysterious lead casket was dug up with a little note inside that said it had already been opened in 1921 and contained a mummified heart.

Modern science dated it to the correct period and that was all the evidence needed. Robert the Bruce's heart was reburied with a memorial stone in place for all to pay respect to the most famous King of Scots!

CAITHNESS

A LONG CLIMB DOWN THE WHALIGOE STEPS

An outdoor staircase might not sound like an obvious tourist attraction, but the Whaligoe Steps are much more than just that. Over 300 steps descend the exposed cliff face, winding down to a natural, rocky harbour below. On a stretch of coastline dominated by high cliffs, any protected inlet like this was a godsend.

Whaligoe had been known as a safe haven for centuries, with a rough track available for the few fishermen brave enough to make their way down. The engineer Thomas Telford declared it an awful place for a harbour, but David Brodie disagreed. In the late 1700s, he saw enough potential to fund the construction of the Whaligoe Steps.

The harbour supported the herring boats that were once a common sight around Caithness. Small vessels could be dragged up onto the rocks by hand and larger schooners anchored to the cliff face. Later, an artificial dock was built, complete with a salt house, tar fire and winches for pulling boats up and their remains can all be seen today.

Getting down the steps is one thing but spare a thought for the tough women who once climbed up daily while carrying enormous baskets of fish!

When the fishing stopped, volunteers including Iain Sutherland kept the steps tidy as a labour of love. When a terrible landslide covered the Whaligoe Steps with several tonnes of rock in 1975, Iain figured it would take four men several days to clear it, so definitely a job for better weather. When spring came, they arrived to find the steps as good as new.

Iain checked with Etta Juhle, who also helped look after the steps, and it turned out that she was responsible. Remarkably, Etta had spent her winter shifting the whole lot on her own, with nothing more than a small shovel and bucket. You'll find a little monument stone to this incredible woman at the top of the steps.

Remember, these aren't just steps. They're a reminder of a harder time when people had to work against the odds just to survive. The next time the internet goes down or a meeting runs late, take a moment to reflect on those who lived and worked at the Whaligoe Steps.

THE SELKIE'S GRAVE AT OLRIG KIRK

If you didn't know it was there, you would be unlikely to stumble upon Old Olrig Kirk or find the Selkie's Grave. Also known as St Trothan's, this ruined church is just outside Castletown, between Thurso and Dunnet Head, isolated from the main road and smothered by trees.

It's said that one day in the distant past, an old fisherman found a baby girl wrapped up in a sealskin abandoned on Castletown beach. He and his wife had no children of their own so it seemed like a blessing to them. They happily took the baby in and raised it as their own.

However, rumours surrounded the child all her life. The locals believed that she was a selkie, a supernatural creature that looks just like a seal but with the power to remove its skin and take on human form. It didn't help matters that as she grew older, the girl began to see things that others couldn't.

Some consider what's known as second sight to be a blessing, but when the girl claimed to see the Devil in the rafters of Olrig Kirk, she was banished from its walls. People don't need many excuses to avoid somebody who they think is different and it must have been a hard upbringing for the selkie girl.

The Selkie's Grave, with offerings of shells and seaweed.

One man saw past the rumours though, since the girl tragically died in childbirth. Right up the back of the oldest graveyard, behind the old church building and almost against the wall, you can find her grave. It's a small stone with a hollow inside that's said to never dry out even during times of drought.

It's a small consolation that the girl was accepted enough to be buried within the graveyard and today people like to leave gifts at the selkie's grave. Stop by the beach before you visit and remember to bring some shells or seaweed to leave behind.

THE ORIGIN OF JOHN O' GROATS

Many people are familiar with John O' Groats as the end of the length of Britain walk from Land's End in Cornwall. Thousands of people get their picture next to the signpost there every year without realising who John was or why he built an octagonal house.

At the end of the fifteenth century, King James IV granted a Dutchman called Jan de Groot the right to run a ferry from Caithness to Orkney. With the Northern Isles only recently becoming part of Scotland, Jan was making good money with his ferry.

Unfortunately, that meant each of his children wanted to take over once their father retired. All seven would bitterly fight and the whole de Groot family was close to being torn apart.

The biggest argument was about who would sit next to the head of the table closest to the door since that was the traditional place of honour. Jan wasn't even close to retiring and his children were already squabbling, so he came up with a temporary solution.

By the time the family had their next big gathering, Jan had built himself a house with eight sides, each with its own door, leading to an octagonal table inside. Nobody would be sitting at the head of the table, everybody was equal. The children might still squabble over who took over the family business, but at least they could have a meal in peace now.

When Jan was laid to rest at Canisbay Church, a local legend claimed that the fortune he made from his ferry business was buried with him. Time after time, unscrupulous graverobbers would hear the rumour and dig him up to hunt for gold, although there was nothing to find.

It's said that things became so bad that Jan's gravestone had to be moved inside the church and his body left unmarked to ensure that he could finally rest in peace!

A VISIT FROM THE VALKYRIES AT SYSA HILL

It's not hard to find evidence of Scandinavian occupation around the north and west of Scotland, in both the culture and the place names. Some areas have a much deeper connection than others, but none can claim a story quite like the small hill of Sysa.

While he was Earl of Orkney, a man called Sigurd the Stout was gifted an enchanted raven banner by his mother. Any army that carried the banner before it was ensured victory in battle, but whoever physically held it was doomed to die. Sigurd barely needed any help as he conquered Caithness and the Hebrides, but the real test was when he began to fight in Ireland.

During the Battle of Clontarf, soldier after soldier carrying the banner was cut down. The tide was turning against him, so Sigurd was forced to bend down and pick up the flagpole himself. Even a warrior of his skill couldn't avoid the curse and the Earl was soon run through with a spear.

Back in Caithness, at that exact moment, a man called Dorrad witnessed a surprising scene. A dozen Valkyries flew past him, riding their mounts right into the hillside of Sysa. These mythological figures aren't usually spotted in Scotland and the curious man couldn't resist finding out what they were up to.

Creeping up to Sysa and peeking into the mound, he discovered an unimaginably gruesome sight. The Valkyries were singing a haunting song while weaving on a grotesque loom comprised of human entrails, heads, bloody swords and spears. As the creatures snipped threads and wove their blood-soaked pattern, they were deciding the fate of each warrior during the Battle of Clontarf.

Once the Valkyries had finished, they tore their artwork into a dozen pieces, six sections carried south and the other six north. Dorrad might have been traumatised, but he was fortunate to make it away from the grisly spectacle of Sysa Hill in one piece.

FAMILY MISFORTUNES AT CASTLE SINCLAIR GIRNIGOE

Precariously perched on the cliffs north of Wick, Castle Sinclair Girnigoe is still clinging on after being battered by the sea for hundreds of years. The Sinclairs were Earls of Caithness, one of the strongest families in Scotland, but they didn't always get along with their neighbours or with each other.

In the sixteenth century, the 4th Earl George Sinclair had a long-running feud with the Murrays of Aberscross. His son, John, the Master of Caithness, was sent to put an end to things and destroy the Murrays once and for all.

The Sinclairs successfully defeated their rivals in the town of Dornoch, but John realised there was a better way to handle things. He would put an end to the feud by accepting the Murrays' surrender rather than annihilating them. Without permission from his father, John took hostages to ensure good behaviour and finally made peace.

However, the Earl was furious, executing the hostages and throwing his own son into the dungeon at Castle Sinclair Girnigoe. There he stayed for seven years until his father decided he couldn't risk a traitor inheriting the Earldom. John was given no water and fed only salted beef to speed up his demise.

Castle Sinclair Girnigoe perched on a finger of land surrounded by cliffs.

It was John's son who would become the 5th Earl, named George after his murderous grandfather. Not long after taking charge, he decided to get his revenge on the two men responsible for holding his father in captivity, David and Ingram Sinclair.

George was one of the most powerful nobles in Scotland now, so he didn't bother being discreet. All three men were attending the wedding of Ingram's daughter and it proved to be the perfect occasion for the Earl to act.

First, he crossed paths with David Sinclair on his way to the celebration, calmly pulling out his sword and impaling the man. Then finding Ingram playing a friendly game of football before the wedding started, George pulled out a pistol and shot him dead.

After these two public murders in broad daylight, the Earl simply rode home to Castle Sinclair Girnigoe as if nothing had ever happened. As was often the case with the powerful, George was pardoned by the King, however, he did pick up a lasting nickname – George the Wicked.

THE OLD CAITHNESS HIGHWAY BY OUSDALE BROCH

Dotted around Caithness you'll find the remains of several drystone, Iron Age towers known as brochs. Unique to Scotland, a well-preserved example can be found at Ousdale, along with fascinating stories to keep you occupied on the walk down to the building.

Even though Ousdale Broch was abandoned well over 1,000 years ago, it didn't fade from the history books entirely. It features in the *Orkneyinga Saga* as the meeting point between a Norse army under Jarl Harald the Elder and a Scots army under King William the Lion.

This was at the start of the thirteenth century, when the notoriously cruel Harald had firmly stamped his authority on Caithness, violently dealing with any local opposition. The King of Scots wasn't happy about the Norse influence on the mainland and he gladly answered a plea for help from the Bishop of Caithness.

Jarl Harald took one look at the size of the Scottish army and decided it wasn't worth it. He agreed to submit without a single blow, giving a portion of his Caithness revenue over to William.

While descending towards Ousdale Broch, you might notice a strange series of ridges cutting across the flat landscape. This was once the main highway between Caithness and Sutherland, the only way to cross a huge granite out-crop known as the Ord. With a little imagination, you can easily envisage those who trudged along here centuries ago, just like the Sinclairs in 1513.

Their leader, William Sinclair, the 2nd Earl of Caithness, was firmly on King James's naughty list. When the King called on his nobles to gather their men for an enormous invasion of England, Sinclair saw his opportunity for redemption. Three hundred men crossed the Ord here one Monday, proudly marching to war in their green garments, ready to join up with the King's army.

Before the battle, King James agreed to pardon the Earl in thanks for his support, but with no paper to hand, he wrote his declaration on the skin of a drum. The Scots were then annihilated at the Battle of Flodden, with Sinclair and all of his men losing their lives.

Thankfully, what became known as the Drum Head Charter was taken back to the Countess of Caithness by a member of Clan Gunn. The pardon was important but had come at such a high cost that for years it was considered unlucky for Sinclairs to cross the Ord on a Monday while wearing green.

THE MERMAID OF DUNNET HEAD

Scottish mermaid stories rarely have happy endings, although often the human involved has earned any punishment they receive. One of these beautiful creatures was frequently spotted splashing around from the jagged Duncansby Stacks to the Scottish mainland's most northerly point at Dunnet Head.

When she wasn't swimming, she would sit on a rock, combing her long blonde hair. That wasn't an invitation to approach though; if anybody got too close then the mermaid would quickly slip into the water and disappear.

Then one day, a young lad turned a corner on the beach and almost bumped right into her, striking up a conversation before she could escape. Against all her instincts, the mermaid stayed to talk to the man, who turned out to be very charming indeed.

Tentatively, she agreed to meet at the same spot every day and as time went on, began bringing gifts along to impress her human companion. There are countless shipwrecks along the Caithness coast and this mermaid had a large stash of shiny artefacts. Things were going so well that she wondered why she had avoided humans for so long!

Little did she know that her human lover was using the gifts of gold and jewellery to woo the girls on shore. The boy started to forget to meet the mermaid and even when he was there, seemed more interested in what she had brought than spending any time with her.

Eventually, she discovered what her gifts were being used for and was furious. A betrayal like this deserved an extra special punishment. She waited until the next visit and, like usual, the boy was impatiently asking what presents there were today.

Instead, she sang him to sleep before dragging him through the sea to a tiny cave, hidden near Dwarwick. There, she chained him up among her hoard so that he would forever be with the gold and jewels that he craved so much.

Legend says that he's still imprisoned there and when the seas are calm and the tide is low, he can just peer out towards his old home that he'll never visit again.

DUMFRIES & GALLOWAY

THE BALLAD OF JOHNNIE ARMSTRONG OF GILNOCKIE TOWER

As the ancestral home of Clan Armstrong, Gilnockie Tower is strongly associated with Johnnie Armstrong. In the turbulent sixteenth century, the Armstrongs dominated what was known as the Debatable Lands and Johnnie could muster a small army if the need ever arose. The only person with such authority was the King himself and the 'Ballad of Johnnie Armstrong' tells of their disastrous encounter.

For centuries, kings on both sides of the border had considered these tough raiders as a necessary evil. They may have operated outside of the law, but they were the first line of defence against the nation's neighbours creeping north and when the time came for a Scots army to fight, battle-hardened men like the reivers were useful.

King James V took a very different view. He wanted peace with England and not being able to control the unruly Armstrongs was considered an insult to his royal authority. Around 1530, the King sent an invitation for Johnnie to join him on a hunt. The Armstrongs all got dressed in their best clothes to impress the King and his courtiers, but the entire thing had been a trap.

They weren't there to enjoy a hunting trip, they were there to be the prey. A royal army ambushed the Armstrongs at Carlenrig and King James was even more furious when he saw how richly these lowborn Border reivers were dressed. Nobody should ever be more impressive than their own monarch!

There would be no fair trial, even as Johnnie argued that the King had promised their safety. Declared traitors, the men were hanged from trees in the woods and a memorial to Johnnie Armstrong can be found just outside Teviothead Parish Church.

Instead of pacifying this lawless area, James's betrayal shocked and enraged communities right across southern Scotland, gaining him the reputation of a ruthless, untrustworthy king.

THE BATTLE OF GLEN TROOL

Deep in the Galloway Forest Park, on a low hill above Loch Trool, stands Bruce's Stone with its carved description in remembrance of the Battle of Glen Trool. Taking place early in 1307, shortly after Robert the Bruce had emerged from hiding, the King was battered and bruised but he wasn't beaten. All he needed was a small victory to encourage others to join him.

Bruce decided to make his comeback in the south-west of Scotland, the area he knew best. His enemies caught wind of his movements and soon patrols were scouring the area for him. Any small group that found the King was quickly defeated and with each minor victory his reputation grew.

Soon the English commander Aymer de Valence was preparing a more substantial army to crush this small group of loyal Scots. News arrived that Bruce was hiding out in Glen Trool with just a few hundred men and so an army of 2,000 rushed to stamp out the flickering flame of resistance.

That large force chased the small group of Scots they found along the banks of Loch Trool, hoping they would lead them right to Bruce himself. They didn't notice the path getting narrower, hemmed in between the loch and the steep slopes, but soon they were packed in too tightly to manoeuvre.

Bruce's Stone high above Loch Trool, directly opposite the hillside where the King's troops laid their ambush.

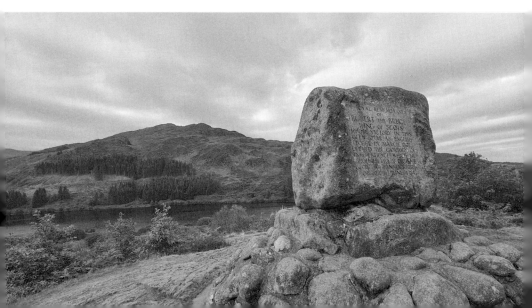

Suddenly, those fleeing Scots stopped and turned around. Their pursuers must have been confused at this small force holding their ground against impossible odds. The King had been watching from the heights marked by Bruce's Stone and now he gave the order to spring the trap.

Great, big boulders began tumbling down the hill towards the packed soldiers, who had nowhere to go. Arrows quickly followed and the English army was in turmoil. When the rest of the Scottish warriors charged down the hill, they split the long column in two.

Those who could retreat disappeared back up the path as fast as possible and the Scots had won the day. It was a small victory, but word spread fast. King Robert the Bruce was back and the flame of resistance was growing.

THE GHOST OF GALDENOCH CASTLE

Galdenoch Castle on the Rhinns of Galloway is a spooky, ruined tower with one of the strangest ghost stories in Scotland. This was once home to the Agnew family and in the seventeenth century the Laird went off to fight as a Covenanter against the Royalists. After his side was defeated in battle, Agnew began the long journey home, stopping one night at a house to seek shelter.

The owner was kind enough to let him stay but over the course of the evening it became apparent these two men had very different points of view. Instead of letting Agnew leave, the man barred the door and told him that the authorities were on their way. Seeing no other option, the desperate guest grabbed a pistol and killed his host.

He made it back home safely to Galdenoch but he was followed by the angry spirit of the murdered man. Noises were heard in the dark, with furniture scraping in empty rooms. Soon things got louder and far more violent. Eventually, the Agnews left Galdenoch Castle, some say to get away from the paranormal activity.

The ghost wasn't going anywhere though, he clearly liked his new home. Over time, it got stronger and more mischievous. One day, just when the new owners had got a fire going, a burning coal mysteriously disappeared. Minutes later, shouts came from outside that the roof of the barn was up in flames.

Not long after, the owner's old mother was sitting spinning wool when she was whisked outside, dunked in the river and left on top of a stone wall. When nobody could find her, a disembodied voice laughed and said, 'I've washed granny in the burn!'

Many ministers tried and failed to rid Galdenoch of its ghost until one particularly spiritual man called Marshall tried something different. He gathered the whole parish to stand outside and sing hymns. It didn't seem to have much effect when the ghost started singing along too and the locals had to raise their voices to drown him out.

One by one they were forced to give up as their throats ran dry, but the singing carried on all night. Come first light of dawn, only the minister and the ghost were left straining their voices. Suddenly the raspy voice of the ghost wheezed and said, 'Roar awa' Marshall, I can roar nae mair.'

He kept his word and the ghost of Galdenoch Castle has never been seen since.

THE GREY MARE'S TAIL COVENANTERS

The Grey Mare's Tail is an elegant, tumbling waterfall, cascading down 60m of rockface from Loch Skeen above. It's a breathtaking area of wilderness and its remote location was put to good use in the seventeenth century as a hiding place for Covenanters.

The King wanted to dictate affairs within the Scottish Church, declaring all unauthorised religious services as treasonous. That didn't discourage the Covenanters though, they just worshipped out in the wild, while trying to avoid the soldiers looking to violently shut them down.

The boggy ground and steep ravine that surrounded the Grey Mare's Tail were perfect for these open-air services. Mounted soldiers were useless here and the hidden crevices were too dangerous for those who didn't know the path. Lookouts high up on Watch Knowe gave plenty of warning of any government troops approaching.

It wasn't just the Covenanters who made use of the remote waterfall though. This area is famous for wild goats and two men hiding out in the ravine once heard the faint sound of hooves over the crashing water. With thoughts of a delicious supper, they quietly followed their ears to peek over a ledge.

Those hooves didn't belong to a goat, but the terrifying figure of the Devil, busy roasting one of his victims on a spit. It was a horrific sight and an even worse smell, but the pair were rooted to the spot in fear. They watched in horror as the Devil spun around and stared deep into their souls.

The Covenanters' only hope was to rely on their faith for protection, reciting as many Bible passages as they could remember at the monstrous figure. The sound was too much for the Devil to take but he had one last trick up his sleeve.

Diving into the water, he transformed into bundles of expensive, leather hides. Lesser men would have been tempted by the sight of all that wealth tumbling down the Grey Mare's Tail and followed it to their doom. Fortunately, these two weren't motivated by greed and stayed exactly where they were, living to tell the tale.

SWEETHEART ABBEY'S ROMANTIC FOUNDER

With all the doom and gloom that's often associated with Scottish historical sites, castles and cathedrals, it's a welcome change with the appropriately named Sweetheart Abbey. It's a lasting dedication of love, founded by the fascinating and incredibly wealthy Lady Devorgilla of Galloway.

Dervorgilla had inherited huge swathes of land including much of Galloway, before marrying an English noble called John Balliol, giving the family plenty of influence in both countries. Their son, also John Balliol, would become an infamous King of Scots through his mother's descent from King David I.

Devorgilla was a force to be reckoned with, so it's a good thing John Balliol Senior didn't have a fragile ego. Instead, they appear to have had a remarkably long and happy marriage of forty-five years, until John died in 1268.

He had reached a ripe old age, but his wife was still devastated by his loss. To remember her husband, Devorgilla had his heart embalmed and placed in an ivory box that she could carry around with her wherever she went. To ensure that his memory would never be lost, she spent the rest of her life and much of her fortune undertaking charitable acts in John's name.

The grandest of these was the founding of an abbey to the south of Dumfries, named Dulce Cor – Latin for Sweet Heart – in dedication to Devorgilla's love for John. When she passed away in 1290, at the ripe old age of 80 years old, this remarkable woman was buried in front of the high altar while clutching her husband's heart.

The influence and memory of this loving couple have spread further than just Sweetheart Abbey. In nearby Dumfries, the stone Devorgilla Bridge spanning the Nith replaced the wooden bridge she had funded for pilgrims on the way to Whithorn Priory. In England, you can find Balliol College, part of the University of Oxford, started by John but funded long after his death by his faithful wife.

A true couple of sweethearts!

THE DARK HISTORY OF DUNSKEY CASTLE

High on the cliffs above Portpatrick, Dunskey Castle has a dark, ominous atmosphere that might make the hair on your neck stand up. These remains are from an early sixteenth-century castle, built on top of a much older tower, which was once held by Walter de Corrie, who wasn't a very friendly man.

Walter was little better than a pirate, preying on any ships passing between Ireland and Scotland from his clifftop castle. A prisoner from one of these raids had turned out to be an excellent piper, so his captor decided to keep him as a minstrel. Slavery didn't suit this man's creativity though and he simply refused to play.

He was thrown into the dungeon at Dunskey Castle, to be starved until he learned his lesson. Looking around at his bleak situation, the piper saw a glimmer of hope. He found what looked like an opening to a secret passage that might take him down to the coast.

Dunskey Castle on the cliffs near Portpatrick with a ghostly piper hidden somewhere below.

Unfortunately, that passage only led deeper into the cliff, dropping him into a cavern with no escape. He had sealed his fate and was never seen above ground again. Guests staying in the castle used to report strange sounds like distant music from underground as the piper tried desperately to find a way out of his prison.

FINDING SOLITUDE IN ST NINIAN'S CAVE

Walk around a mile down leafy Physgill Glen to a stony beach and in the corner you'll find Ninian's Cave, named after one of Scotland's first saints. Ninian was the apostle to the southern Picts and people once thought him unusual for building his church at Whithorn out of stone, but he was just ahead of his time. Even with his cutting-edge building, he sometimes preferred to hide away for a little peace and quiet.

This seaside hideout was said to be Ninian's preferred place of solitude in the early fifth century. It was described as a cave of horrible blackness, where Ninian studied heavenly wisdom with a devoted mind. It's impossible to know if the saint truly spent any time here, but he couldn't have picked a much better spot.

People certainly believed that this was an important place for St Ninian as early as the eighth century. Around this time, the walls of the cave were carved with early Christian crosses and later excavations exposed a collection of even more loose stone crosses and carvings. These have since been moved to the museum at Whithorn Priory.

The cave would have been much bigger in Ninian's time but rockfalls over the last 1,600 years have greatly reduced its size. That means carvings that were originally inside now appear on the cave's exterior. It's still a popular pilgrimage site, with hundreds of modern offerings left behind, from twig crosses and painted rocks to photographs and toys.

PUNISHING WICKED THREATS AT CARDONESS CASTLE

Cardoness Castle is a strong and simple tower house, built by the McCullochs in the fifteenth century. These hadn't always been their lands though and the tale of how they came to inherit Cardoness is hopefully no more than a far-fetched legend.

The previous Laird of Cardoness was quick to anger and easily tempted into violence. His long-suffering wife had given birth to nine children but to the Laird's discontent, they were all girls.

When news came that the brave woman was pregnant once again, the Laird burst into her room and snarled a promise. If this child wasn't a boy, then he was going to drown his wife and all their daughters in the nearby loch. Everybody around Cardoness was relieved when a newborn son was delivered and a party was organised to celebrate the arrival of an heir.

It was deep winter, and the loch had frozen over, so a feast was organised out on the ice. The Laird, his wife and all but one sick daughter were out enjoying themselves on the frozen loch. Then disaster struck.

Just when the fun was at its highest, the ice broke. Every single person fell into the freezing cold water and perished. People claimed that the Devil was responsible, punishing the wicked Laird for making a promise so evil to his pregnant wife.

The sole, surviving daughter married Gilbert McCulloch and the family built Cardoness Castle. It seems like something from that wicked Laird may have passed down to his descendants though. These McCullochs became famous for causing trouble and fighting with their neighbours. One even robbed his own widowed mother of 1,500 animals!

So much for family values.

THE GHOST PIPER OF CLANYARD BAY

There's a common story around Scotland, found almost anywhere with a deep, dark cave, but the most famous example is at Clanyard Bay. Although the entrance is now gone, it was once thought that a network of tunnels stretched from these cliffs deep beneath the earth.

Stories spread of fairies living in the depths, although nobody was ever brave enough to go looking. Then one headstrong man decided to prove it was all nonsense. He declared there was no such thing as fairies and no matter how strongly his friends tried to persuade him not to do it, he was going inside the caves of Clanyard Bay.

To help put their minds at ease, the explorer took his bagpipes with him, playing as he walked to let them know he was safe. His faithful dog led the way and while playing a cheery jig, he disappeared from sight.

Then all of a sudden, a loud yelp echoed out of the cave and that jig switched to a sorrowful lament, sharply cut off after a few notes. Out came the dog, running at top speed, without a single hair on its body.

Nobody was foolish enough to go in after him and the brave, headstrong piper was never seen again. He isn't entirely gone though. Every so often, late at night, the faint sound of a lament on the pipes can still be heard from deep below the ground. Or is that just the sound of the wind?

EAST LOTHIAN

ST BALDRED'S BOAT AT SEACLIFF BEACH

While wandering along the sandy beach at Seacliff, you can't help but admire the unobstructed view of the mighty Bass Rock. However, things haven't always been this way. Back in the eighth century, there was one large, dangerous rock sitting among the waves here that had become the bane of local sailors.

Only visible at low tide, but dangerous no matter the hour, this rock regularly tore through fishing boats that had been caught by strong gusts of wind. St Baldred often sailed out to a sanctuary on the Bass Rock and while he was willing to face the threat himself, he became concerned for those under his care.

The preacher convinced a local fisherman to row him out to the rock one morning, stumbling and almost tumbling onto its slippery surface. His escort looked visibly worried, Baldred would surely be swept out to sea as soon as the tide rose. Nevertheless, the saint ushered him away to safety, shouting that he just had to have faith.

Once suitably far away, Baldred balanced himself, stretched out his arms, closed his eyes and began to pray. To the fisherman's surprise, the rock slowly but surely began to move. Like a giant, rocky surfboard, the saint guided the dangerous rock from the deep waves over to rest on Seacliff Beach.

A tiny, rock-cut harbour at Seacliff Beach, looking out towards Tantallon Castle.

It's still there today, marked by a little pillar topped with a cross and known as St Baldred's Boat.

CAPTURING THE BASS ROCK

The Bass Rock is a unique island sitting out in the Firth of Forth, home to huge colonies of seabirds and known as one of the wonders of the wildlife world. However, long before it became a tourist attraction, this volcanic plug was used for a much less pleasant purpose.

King Malcolm gifted it to the Lauder family and somehow they managed to build a small castle on the rocky island. It was so impressive that King James VI even tried to buy it from them!

Used alternatively as a fortress, safe haven and prison over the centuries, the most interesting period of Bass Rock's history came in the seventeenth century. The government had transformed the island into a secure prison for their political opponents and in 1691 four Jacobite inmates turned the island's impenetrability to their advantage.

The situation on that cold, hard rock must have seemed hopeless for them to begin with, but when their opportunity came, they grabbed it. Their guards were far too relaxed, believing that escape was impossible, so the prisoners were allowed to wander around at will.

Then one day, the entire garrison was helping unload a shipment of coal down at the landing dock. All the inmates had to do was walk down to the prison gate and lock them shut. The embarrassed guards had no choice but to head back to the mainland.

Using the cannon of the fortress, those Jacobite officers managed to terrorise any government ships arriving to dislodge them. Word spread of the Bass Rock's capture and the exiled King James even sent support from France. The small force on the island grew as more men arrived and they raided the East Lothian coastline using small boats.

The Jacobite force held out for three years on the Bass Rock, but without a wider rising to fight for they were at a stalemate. A meeting was arranged to discuss terms, but little did the government know that the defenders were running out of supplies.

On the day of the meeting, the cunning former prisoners put the last of their food into a lavish feast for their new guests to give the impression that they had enough to last for months. Their ruse worked! They were granted safe passage to France with a promise that their fellow supporters would be released if they would just lay down their arms and finally get off the Bass Rock!

THE ANCIENT INHABITANTS OF TRAPRAIN LAW

The low mound of Traprain Law is easily the most important hill in East Lothian. Dominating the surrounding landscape, it was occupied from as early as 1000 BC and would develop into an important hillfort for the Votadini tribe. As you climb to the summit, you can't mistake the enormous earthworks previous inhabitants left behind.

In the sixth century, the hillfort on Traprain was home to the legendary King Loth, who supposedly gave his name to the Lothians. He was a powerful figure but not a particularly nice one, even to his family.

When his daughter, Thenaw, became pregnant after an encounter with his rival, the King was furious. Her undeserving punishment was to be tied to a chariot and hurled from the top of Traprain Law. Thankfully, Thenaw survived but now everybody thought that she was a witch.

Loth decided to put her in a small coracle with no oars and cast her out into the Firth of Forth. Still pregnant, Thenaw landed in Fife at Culross, where she was taken in by the kindly St Serf. There she gave birth to a boy called Kentigern, who would one day be known as St Mungo, the founder of Glasgow.

Thenaw herself is often known as St Enoch and is a great example of a true survivor. Against all the odds and the designs of her despicable father, she managed to keep on going and start a new, better life with her son.

THE ORIGINS OF THE SALTIRE AT ATHELSTANEFORD

The small village of Athelstaneford is a tiny place, with a strange name and a big story. It's the birthplace of the Scottish flag and is now home to the National Flag Heritage Centre found in a doocot behind the church. Instead of pigeons, you'll find a video inside, explaining why Scotland proudly flies the saltire.

The year was AD 832, before Scotland was Scotland and England was England. A combined force of Picts and Scots from north of the River Forth was on a raid deep into Lothian lands, at that point controlled by Northumbrian Anglo-Saxons.

Things had gone well for the raiders, led by Angus II, the King of the Picts, and they were heading back north with an awful lot of loot. However, they were being chased down by a much larger force of Northumbrians led by a man called Athelstan.

Trapped by the Peffer Burn on ground just to the north of the present village, things weren't looking good for the combined Scot–Pict side. King Angus prayed to St Andrew, promising that if he helped them to victory they would establish him as their patron saint. When night fell, the saint came to Angus in a dream and told him to look for his sign the next day.

As the two armies lined up opposite each other, Angus looked up and saw two white clouds crossing each other on the blue sky in the shape of the saltire. He shouted to his army that it was a sign St Andrew was with them. Invigorated, they charged forward with confidence to win a vital victory.

The enemy leader Athelstan was killed while attempting to ford the river to safety and that's where the name Athelstaneford is said to come from!

It's a great story, although the exact dates and characters involved don't tie up perfectly with known historical figures. Like all good legends, it's grown arms and legs over the years, but if true, that makes the saltire the oldest national flag in the world!

DUNBAR CASTLE'S DEFIANT DAME

Dunbar Castle was once one of Scotland's strongest fortresses, a claim that was firmly put to the test in 1338. Patrick Dunbar was tied up fighting for the Scots army but left his home in the capable hands of his wife, Agnes Randolph, nicknamed Black Agnes for her dark hair and complexion.

Believing that left the castle vulnerable, William Montague, the Earl of Salisbury, arrived with a large English army to take advantage of the situation. He couldn't have been more wrong.

Black Agnes was a remarkable woman and an inspirational leader. After the English war machine arrived and blockaded Dunbar by sea, the garrison firmly declined the demand to surrender.

Salisbury responded by catapulting huge rocks at the walls, but they held strong. To mock their enemy, Agnes and her maids would end each day by dusting off the ramparts with their handkerchiefs. Those projectiles soon came in handy for the defenders, dropping them over the walls to crush the English siege engines.

The attackers turned to bribery next, paying one of the Scots to keep the gate open while they stormed the castle. The guard happily took the money but reported the plan to Agnes. When the time came, Salisbury was lucky to be hauled back and avoid capture when the portcullis slammed down shut.

Running out of options, Salisbury dragged Agnes's brother out and threatened to kill him if she didn't open the gate. Calmly, Agnes just shouted back that if her brother died then she inherited the Earldom of Moray, so that suited her fine! Thankfully, the dejected commander didn't call her bluff.

After five months and no sign of progress, Salisbury must have been hoping to starve the garrison into submission. However, a Scottish force led by Ramsay of Dalhousie managed to sneak into the castle by boat with plenty of fresh supplies.

The next day, Agnes sent a freshly baked loaf of bread and some wine out to be delivered to the English commander. Just in case he was hungry.

That was the final straw. The King of England couldn't justify the cost of a siege that wasn't going anywhere and the troops were hauled back south. It was a famous victory for Agnes Randolph, holding out against incredible odds, as well as a reminder to never underestimate a cunning Scotswoman.

All that remains of Dunbar Castle, where Black Agnes held out for months against a besieging army.

YESTER CASTLE & THE GOBLIN HA'

Buried in the woods near the village of Gifford, the remains of the once powerful Yester Castle stand quietly among the encroaching trees. This is one of the most memorable ruins in Scotland, not just for its size or location, but because of what lies below. Hidden underground, as if it was carved out of the hillside, is the mysterious Goblin Ha'.

Yester Castle was built in the thirteenth century by Sir Hugo de Giffard, secure on a small clifftop peninsula above a winding river. On the surface, Hugo was a respectable man, a powerful member of the nobility who was entrusted as one of the guardians of the young King Alexander III.

However, behind closed doors, this nobleman was rumoured to have sold his soul in return for powers of sorcery. This dark reputation spread and Giffard began to be known as the Wizard of Yester. We'll never know how much truth there is in the stories, but they were notable enough to be mentioned in the early Scottish chronicles.

Locals believed that Hugo had built his impressive new fortress using supernatural construction workers. The story claims that Yester Castle appeared in a single night with the help of an army of goblins, summoned from hell by the Wizard. The castle would remain home to his descendants for around 300 years, before eventually being abandoned for more comfortable surroundings.

Yester slowly fell into disrepair; the cut stones were pilfered for building materials and the remaining walls swallowed by nature. However, while everything else crumbled away, one part of the fortress remained secure. Safely underground and still almost perfectly intact is the vaulted Goblin Ha'.

This buried room is where the Wizard of Yester was said to perform his necromancy and arcane rituals. It's a stark contrast to the rest of the ruined castle, looking almost as strong today as it would have over 700 years ago. The only other feature of the Goblin Ha' is a single staircase in one corner, which surprisingly doesn't lead up toward the surface.

These steps lead even deeper into the hillside, although nobody knows exactly where they end. The lower section of the tunnel has been blocked by rubble and there's no obvious exit on the steep hill outside. There are theories such as access to a dungeon or castle well but it's the folklore that's stuck.

The tunnel from the Goblin Ha' is said to lead straight to hell and it's no surprise that it was filled in once the infamous Wizard was gone.

EASTER ROSS

THE FAIRIES WORKING ON THE GIZZEN BRIGGS

At the entrance to the Dornoch Firth, a dangerous sandbank known as the Gizzen Briggs stretches out into the water, sometimes clearly visible but often covered by the waves. While it might seem like a natural formation, local folklore has another explanation.

A Chief of Clan Mackay was frustrated that his sweetheart lived on the other side of the Kyle of Tongue. Any time he wanted to visit, the chief was forced to prepare his boat or undertake a long, looping journey. If only he could build a bridge across the Kyle.

Mackay visited a local wise woman, but all she could advise him to do was travel to see the witch of Tarbat Ness. That was a long journey, one that the Chief wasn't going to make himself, so he sent his trusted clansman Angus to seek the answer to his problem.

Of course, the witch already knew why Angus was there and what his Chief needed. She handed over a strange box, locked up tight, informing the clansman to take it back to Tongue, without opening it under any circumstances.

Every few steps the box was rattling and quivering, almost jumping out of Angus's hands. He hadn't gone far when curiosity got the better of him and on the shore of the Dornoch Firth, the foolish man risked a look inside.

Out jumped dozens of tiny, winged creatures that crawled all over him while yelling, 'Work! Work! Give us work!'

Angus was being assaulted from all angles, his cargo tearing chunks out of him as they begged for a task to complete. Looking around for ideas, he saw the water before him, with Dornoch on the other side, and drew inspiration from his Chief's wish.

The clansman ordered the mysterious creatures to build a bridge across the Dornoch Firth out of sand, strong enough for a human to walk across. As soon as the words left his mouth, they all whizzed off to begin their work, building bricks and ropes from the beach, clearly content with their mission.

However, as soon as the tide changed, the water washed all their hard work away. The sound of the workers wailing and crying at the destruction was too much for Angus to bear and he sailed a boat to the other side, quickly making his way back home.

The work is ongoing, with the industrious little creatures still there trying to finish the Gizzen Briggs. When the water rises and covers the sandbank, you can even hear the roaring sound of dozens of tiny voices crying at yet another failed attempt!

LADY BALCONIE AND THE BLACK ROCK GORGE

The small Allt Graad River, flowing through Glen Glass just north of Dingwall, has carved a surprisingly deep passage through the sandstone. Known as the Black Rock Gorge, these narrow depths hide small caves, dark corners and wild legends.

In the early seventeenth century, the eccentric Lady of the nearby Balconie House liked to spend her evenings wandering along the edges of the Black Rock Gorge. There were more than a few rumours circling among the locals that she had been trained in the black arts of witchcraft, so most tended to keep their distance.

She only had her servants for company and the Lady of Balconie took a shine to one maid in particular. That young girl began to accompany her mistress on those evening walks, although she was always nervous about getting too close to the edge.

Then one evening, as sunset approached, the Lady of Balconie beckoned her maid to peer over into the dark abyss of the gorge. She explained that just below was a secret path to the bottom where the views of the water were breathtaking. Try as she might, the old lady couldn't persuade the terrified girl to take even a step closer.

Suddenly, she grabbed her maid and began dragging her closer to the chasm. A tall gentleman appeared out of thin air, his deep voice halting the attempted abduction in its tracks. The Lady of Balconie was warned that if the girl wasn't willing, then the offering wasn't valid.

Standing in shock, the maid watched as her employer accepted her fate and was escorted into the depths of the Black Rock Gorge. Just before the pair disappeared, the Lady turned and threw the keys to Balconie to the girl, making a permanent impression on the rock that they landed on.

The Lady of Balconie had sold her soul to the Devil and is still trapped down there in a cave, hidden away from prying eyes and guarded by the hounds of hell. Any time a faint mist is rising from the Black Rock Gorge, that's not spray from the tumbling water but smoke from the lady baking bannocks for her master.

THE STRATHPEFFER EAGLE STONE

Along a small footpath in Strathpeffer, you can find the fenced-off Clach an Tiompain or Eagle Stone sitting on a tiny mound. It's a Class I Pictish stone, with the carving of an arch or horseshoe at the top and a bird below. This isn't

its original location, it once stood down in the valley below where it was first raised in the seventh century.

For a long time, local people believed it marked the grave of Munro clansmen, killed in a fifteenth-century battle. While it's far older than that, there's nothing to say that the Munros didn't once recycle it for their own purposes.

Another legend ties the Eagle Stone to the Brahan Seer, who declared that tragedy would strike if it fell three times. The nearby Loch Ussie would suddenly drain before the water bubbles up through a well atop Knockfarrel and pours down the hillside to create a flowing river. Ships could then sail to Strathpeffer and use the stone as an anchor.

That could be bad news for anybody who lives in between the stone and the Cromarty

Strathpeffer's Eagle Stone with a horseshoe/arch above the image of a bird.

Firth and apparently, the Eagle Stone has fallen twice already. To make sure the prophecy is never fulfilled, it's now been fixed securely in a concrete base!

WHERE THE LEGENDARY BRAHAN SEER MET HIS END

At Chanonry Point you can find a small monument dedicated to Coinneach Odhar, otherwise known as the Brahan Seer. The very existence of this fascinating character from the seventeenth century is debated, with his story blurring the lines between truth and legend. It's said that Coinneach worked as a labourer on the Earl of Seaforth's estates around Brahan Castle, gaining a reputation for wild yet accurate prophecies.

Originally born on the Isle of Lewis, Coinneach's ability came from looking through a magical, white pebble with a hole in the middle. His visions were relayed as riddles, many of which have come to pass and others that may still be to come.

Some were vague, such as black, bridleless horses belching fire that would one day charge through the glens, now attributed to steam trains. Declaring that the clans would flee before an army of sheep foretold the Highland Clearances.

Sometimes the Brahan Seer was a little more literal. Upon reaching the site of the Battle of Culloden, he exclaimed that the moor would be stained with the best blood of the Highlands and that he was thankful not to witness such a fearful period. He also announced that one day ships would sail around the back of Tomnahurich Hill, predicting the Caledonian Canal.

Unfortunately, most of Coinneach's prophecies involved doom and gloom. He claimed that the Mackenzies of Fairburn would eventually disappear, their tower fall into ruin and a cow give birth in the uppermost chamber.

Long after the Seer had died, the now-abandoned Fairburn Tower was used to store hay. One of the farmer's pregnant cows found her way into the uppermost chamber, where she couldn't be moved until after giving birth.

Sadly, this prophetic gift would be his downfall. While the Earl of Seaforth was on a trip to France, his wife begged the Brahan Seer for news on her husband. Coinneach confirmed that his master was healthy and enjoying his trip immensely. The countess began to get paranoid, begging to know why her husband was so happy!

Reluctantly, the Seer admitted that the Earl was entertaining a mistress, much fairer than herself. Unable to punish her husband, she took her rage out on Coinneach, ordering him to be placed in a spiked barrel of tar and burned at Chanonry Point.

Before his execution, the Brahan Seer had one last prophecy, foretelling the destruction of the Seaforth line. Then he threw his magical stone into a loch, where it's still waiting to be found.

NOTHING CAN STOP THE RIVER CONON KELPIE

One day, while working in a field next to the gentle River Conon, some men heard a mysterious voice boom out at midday, 'The hour has come but not the man.' There was something supernatural about the interruption and the shocked men looked around to see who was disturbing their work. It was a terrifying kelpie in the form of a powerful black stallion, waiting at a ford in the river.

Suddenly, the creature flicked its tail and disappeared into deeper water. As long as they all stayed on dry land, they should be safe enough, so nobody would be crossing the river for the next hour. Just as they began to get back to work, they heard a galloping noise behind them and thought the kelpie had already returned!

It was nothing more than a regular rider on a horse, but he was heading straight for the ford of the River Conon. The men all ran out to warn him of the kelpie's words, but he didn't care for superstitions, he had places to be.

In the end, the locals had no choice but to physically drag him from the saddle to stop him from entering the water. To keep the man safe from himself, he was locked in the old church while they went back to work.

Once the kelpie's pronounced hour had passed, the river should have been safe enough to cross again. As the workers approached the church to release their temporary prisoner, things were deathly silent. They hoped that the traveller had just given up his complaining, but even after unlocking the door, there wasn't the slightest noise from the darkness.

Peering inside they found the body of the man, face down in a low water trough. Nobody knew how or why, but the kelpie still managed to claim its victim.

THE KELPIE OF LOCH GARVE

One day, a builder living near the Black Water River opened his door to find a beautiful stallion grazing near his cottage. He thought it was his lucky day, there seemed to be no owner nearby and the horse was even beckoning him to climb aboard!

However, as soon as he jumped on its back, he realised his mistake. This wasn't a horse, but the infamous kelpie that lived far in the depths of Loch Garve. Once the creature's prey had been lured onto its back, they were stuck fast, unable to dismount and soon dragged beneath the water.

The builder found himself screaming in terror as they galloped towards the icy waters of Loch Garve. Plunging right to the bottom of the loch, his lungs were on fire from holding his breath until he submitted to his fate and took a deep gulp. To his surprise, he could still breathe!

The kelpie laughed, then told him not to be afraid, he wasn't in any danger. He had been brought here to help solve a problem and there would even be a reward in it for him.

The creature had taken a wife, but she wasn't a kelpie and while she was happy with her husband, life at the bottom of Loch Garve wasn't what she was used to. The biting cold chilled her bones and she wasn't interested in eating either people or raw fish.

What the kelpie's lair needed was a roaring fire, that was why they needed the best builder in the Highlands. His task was to construct a grand fireplace, with a chimney so enormous that it almost reached the surface of the loch.

The builder could hardly refuse and helped by the immensely strong kelpie, the fireplace and chimney were finished in no time. With a bit of kelpie magic, the fire was soon in full blaze and his wife was happy once again.

The kelpie of Loch Garve brought the relieved builder back to the surface and promised to reward him the only way he could. Any time his family needed fresh fish, they were just to leave an empty basket by the side of the loch and by morning it would be full.

It's said that the kelpie and his wife keep the fire going to this very day and even during the coldest of winters, there's one spot on Loch Garve that never freezes over. Directly above the kelpie's chimney.

EDINBURGH & MIDLOTHIAN

THE FAIRY BOY OF CALTON HILL

The view from atop Calton Hill is one of the most famous in Edinburgh, but not many realise while standing there that fairies live just beneath their feet. In the mid-seventeenth century, before this big lump was covered in monuments, an old sea captain called George Burton recorded a story of fairies in his letters written while staying in Leith.

George had been told by the hostess of his lodging house that there was an odd little drummer boy in the town with the gift of second sight. Every Thursday at midnight, the boy would slip away from Leith and into the depths of Calton Hill, where he would play his drum for the fairy folk, laughing and singing into the wee hours.

The boy wouldn't miss his weekly meeting under the hill for anything. It was said no mortal could keep him away, but this old sea captain was a curious man. He invited the boy to have dinner with him and his friends one Thursday night. They tried to distract him with question after question, on anything and everything.

Surprisingly, this young boy seemed to know more about the world than the well-travelled George. He wasn't shy about telling stories of his time with the fairies either. Entering through great golden gates that only he could see, the large host would feast on meat and wine, sometimes flying to France to enjoy the delicacies there.

Around 11 p.m., the boy managed to slip quietly out the front door, but his hosts soon caught up and coerced him back inside. He was beginning to get agitated, explaining that he really must be going as the fairies wouldn't like him to be late.

The view over Edinburgh from Calton Hill, once believed to be a home of the fairies.

Just before midnight, the men took their eyes off the boy for a second and he was gone! They rushed out to the street in time to hear him shouting as if he was being attacked and then silence.

That's where George Burton's letter ends, with no indication if the Fairy Boy of Leith was ever seen again or if he was locked up under Calton Hill for good.

THE BOND OF CRAIGMILLAR CASTLE

Craigmillar is often known as Edinburgh's 'other' castle, but it deserves much more recognition for its important part in Scotland's history. Located just outside the old city walls, it became a convenient place to escape for Scottish monarchs. James III kept political prisoners inside, young James V sheltered from the plague there and Mary, Queen of Scots was hosted a number of times.

In November 1566, the Queen escaped to Craigmillar Castle to recover after one of the most eventful and dramatic periods of her life. Earlier that year, while heavily pregnant, her husband Lord Darnley burst into her chambers at Holyrood to murder her secretary, David Rizzio. The terrified Mary even had a gun held against her unborn child to stop her from interfering.

The Queen soon gave birth to the future James VI, but it was a difficult labour and Mary fell gravely ill soon after. While recovering in Craigmillar Castle, her most loyal supporters gathered in the main hall. Something had to be done about Lord Darnley and a scheme was hatched that would become known as the Craigmillar Bond.

With or without Mary's knowledge, Darnley's death was arranged inside those walls. Three months later, the Queen's husband was suffering from his own illness at a house called Kirk O' Field in Edinburgh. In the middle of the night, an enormous explosion rocked the city as barrels of gunpowder reduced the house to rubble.

Darnley's body was discovered, not among the wreckage, but lying in the garden, half-naked and strangled along with his servant. The Craigmillar Bond had been carried out but if the plan had been to make the murder look like an accident, then it had failed badly.

THE WHITE STAG OF HOLYROOD ABBEY

Tucked away behind the palace at the foot of the Royal Mile stand the remains of the medieval Holyrood Abbey. It's one of the city's earliest buildings, constructed 900 years ago in remembrance of a legendary event.

In 1127 the area around Arthur's Seat was part of a large royal hunting forest, a popular haunt of King David I. Hunting was one of the luxuries of being King of Scots, but on the Feast of the Holy Cross, David should really have been in church. The King ignored his priest's warnings and felt suitably rewarded when his party stumbled upon a rare white stag wandering among the trees.

The King outstripped everybody in the frantic chase that followed, losing sight of his companions as well as the deer. Stopping to compose himself in a clearing, he realised that he was alone in the eerie quiet. Suddenly, the white stag burst out of the undergrowth, startling David's horse, which threw him to the ground.

He found himself lying flat on his back, nose to nose with a very angry white stag. It was even bigger close up, a dangerous beast with sharp tines on its antlers ready to run the King through. With his spear lying out of reach, all David could do was pray as the animal charged towards him.

That would have been the undignified end for the monarch had it not been for a strange light that began to shine in between the stag's antlers. It formed into the shape of the Holy Cross and, astounded by the sight, David instinctively reached out to grab it. The charging beast stopped in its tracks, panicked and then fled from the clearing.

King David had been saved and he was convinced this was a lesson from God – a warning about hunting during a sacred feast day. In thanks for his deliverance, David marked the spot where the miracle had taken place by dedicating an abbey to the Holy Cross – otherwise known as the Holy Rood.

You can find signs of the legend all around the Canongate area of Edinburgh. The image of a white stag with the Holy Cross between its antlers can be seen on the gates of Holyrood Palace, the crest of the Mercat Cross and even right on top of Canongate Kirk.

THE HISTORY AND MYSTERY OF ROSLIN CASTLE

Roslin Castle sits in a beautiful position, high on a rock above a winding river with an impressive archway that would once have been a drawbridge. At first, it looks like just a couple of pillars, one long wall and a little cottage. However, make your way underneath the arch and you'll find the rest of the castle built into the side of the cliff.

Passing through this enormous archway and turning right will take you to the hidden remains of Roslin Castle.

The Sinclair family who owned Roslin Castle are surrounded by myths and legends, from Templar Knights to the Holy Grail. During a fire in the fifteenth century, William Sinclair, the Baron of Roslin, was in such a panic about losing his library that he forced his chaplain back in to save certain documents.

While the castle burned around him, the poor man dutifully lowered baskets of books and scrolls down from a window to safety. It makes you wonder what was important enough to risk his life for.

Around 400 years later, it's said that an Italian descendant of the last provost of Rosslyn Chapel arrived at the now-ruined castle. Following instructions from his ancestor, he discovered a secret room full of ancient manuscripts, hidden in the vaults. Without revealing what he had found, they were all taken to the secure section of the Vatican library, where they remain to this day.

If you're ever lucky enough to find yourself inside Roslin Castle, there is still one legend to be fulfilled. Stand on the correct step of the correct staircase and blow a horn, then a sleeping lady will awake to guide you to a great treasure!

HALF-HANGIT MAGGIE DICKSON

The Grassmarket area of Edinburgh is famous for its collection of pubs, but Maggie Dicksons stands out for the story that it tells. Maggie was a young woman from Musselburgh who was sadly abandoned by her sailor husband in the early eighteenth century. Fortunately, she was able to find work to support herself in a Kelso inn, but things there became problematic.

Maggie had started a secret relationship with the innkeeper's son and soon became pregnant. Scared of losing her job, she kept the pregnancy hidden, even after giving birth. Sadly, the baby didn't survive and in a panic, young Maggie hid the body down by the River Tweed.

When the child was discovered, the mother was arrested and dragged to Edinburgh to stand trial. The law was firmly against women in her position. Even if she wasn't guilty of infanticide, she would be punished for concealing a pregnancy. Only 22 years old, Maggie Dickson was sentenced to be hanged at the Grassmarket.

Once a doctor had pronounced her dead, she was laid in a coffin and put in a cart bound for burial back in Musselburgh. Imagine the fright that the driver got when halfway down the road the corpse behind him began shouting and thumping inside its box. Maggie wasn't dead after all.

Back in Edinburgh, it was decided that the sentence for her crime had technically been carried out. Legally, she couldn't be punished for it again. The girl went on to live for another forty years as a local celebrity, going by the affectionate nickname Half-Hangit Maggie!

THE GRAVE OF COLONEL ANNE MACKINTOSH

In the tiny North Leith Burial Ground, one of the heroes of the 1745 Jacobite Rising lies in a forgotten grave. This isn't a broadsword-swinging, burly warrior, but Lady Anne Mackintosh, daughter of the Chief of Clan Farquharson and married to the Chief of Clan Mackintosh.

When the 1745 Jacobite Rising started, Anne was a staunch supporter like her father, but her husband was already commissioned in the government army. Regardless of her marital loyalties, at the age of 22, she rode around her lands, rallying hundreds of clansmen to fight for the Jacobite cause. Bonnie Prince Charlie gave her the nickname La Belle Rebelle, but most knew her better as Colonel Anne Mackintosh.

Colonel Anne's most heroic story took place while the Prince was visiting her home in Moy Hall, south of Inverness. Government forces soon learned that Charles was vulnerable, away from his forces with only a handful of guards. Around 1,500 soldiers marched to capture the Jacobite leader, but news of their approach reached Moy Hall first.

Charles and his guards disappeared into the dark countryside, while Anne prepared her handful of servants to defeat an army. They were ordered to hide beside the road, down among the peat stacks, with all the weapons that they could carry.

Just as the soldiers approached, the hidden defenders fired every pistol and musket, banging old swords against pans. Darting among the piles of peat, they yelled different clan battle cries at the tops of their lungs.

The government force was in disarray, they had expected a few guards, not the whole Jacobite army. Only their piper Donald MacCrimmon was killed, but the rest retreated quickly and Colonel Anne's servants had won a famous victory known as the Rout of Moy.

Her husband would later be captured by the Jacobites and placed into Anne's custody. She greeted him with, 'Your servant, Captain,' and he replied, 'Your servant, Colonel,' happily acknowledging that his wife outranked him.

Anne moved to Leith in her later years and while her exact burial spot is unknown, you can find a white Jacobite rose bush in her honour as you enter the gate.

THE WIZARD OF THE WEST BOW

The elegant, sweeping Victoria Street is modern by Edinburgh's standards, constructed in the nineteenth century to replace part of what was once the steep, cramped West Bow. It's right in the heart of the old city, home to many interesting characters over the centuries, but the most famous is undoubtedly Major Thomas Weir – the Wizard of the West Bow.

He was known as a respectable figure, so fiercely proud of his Protestant religion that people called him the Bowhead Saint. After retiring from his post in the Town Guard, Weir appeared to live a quiet life, but everything changed while the 71-year-old was lying on his sick bed.

To everybody's surprise, he began to confess to a life of crime, sin and an incestuous relationship with his sister Jean. The people of Edinburgh assumed his age had started to affect his mind but not only did Jean confirm his tales, she elaborated on them.

Apparently, they had made a pact with the Devil, who had appeared in a fiery coach, and the Major's walking stick was the source of his power. Even though the provost thought the confessions ridiculous, with the siblings constantly insisting on their guilt, he was unable to ignore them and ordered their executions.

The Wizard of the West Bow was burned in 1670, along with his walking stick that was said to turn of its own accord among the flames. When asked one last time to renounce his confession, Weir said, 'I will not. I have lived as a beast and I must die as a beast.' Jean was to be hanged and attempted to strip naked on the gallows before the hangman hurriedly finished his job.

Their house was given a wide berth by locals for a long time and if anything remains then it's now buried beneath the Quaker Meeting House.

THE APPRENTICE PILLAR OF ROSSLYN CHAPEL

Rosslyn Chapel is one of the most intriguing buildings in Scotland, packed full of ornate stone carvings and mysteries. Everywhere you look, the chapel's walls, arches and pillars are adorned with intricate images, from biblical scenes to Sinclair family members. There's even a carved band of musical angels, playing trumpets, harps and bagpipes.

Of all the stories found on Rosslyn Chapel's walls, the most famous surrounds the Apprentice Pillar. This is one of three prominent columns standing side by side including the beautiful, but simple, Mason's Pillar. When the chapel was being constructed in the fifteenth century, the master mason carved this work of art with straight, rigid patterns.

His employer William Sinclair wasn't happy though, these columns needed to be far more impressive. The mason was struggling for inspiration, so with permission he left to tour the Continent where he could study the architecture of France and Italy.

While he was gone, his young apprentice had a vision. Fully confident in his abilities, he set to work carving the remaining column. When the master mason returned, full of enthusiasm and new ideas, he arrived at Rosslyn Chapel to be met with a perfectly finished pillar.

Its beauty is outstanding. Twisting vines and leaves reach up to a flourish of protruding plants, while writhing serpents gnaw at the base. Astonished and devastated in equal measure, the mason demanded to know which master craftsman was responsible.

When he discovered that he had been eclipsed by his own apprentice, the mason flew into a jealous rage. Picking up his hammer, he struck out and crushed the boy's skull with one blow. William Sinclair was furious, executing him for the murder, but the other craftsmen didn't think the punishment went far enough.

First, they added a replica of the apprentice's head, including the gash caused by the mason's hammer, into a corner of the chapel in his honour. Then they placed the master mason's likeness opposite the Apprentice Pillar, where he would be forced to stare at its perfection for the rest of time.

The famous Apprentice Pillar inside Rosslyn Abbey.

A DARING ESCAPE FROM DALKEITH PALACE

Dalkeith Palace has never belonged to a monarch, but it has had plenty of royal visitors over the centuries. King James VI and Queen Anne were regular guests at the older Dalkeith Castle, now absorbed by the more modern mansion.

In 1592, the King was holding court here while a young man called John Wemyss of Logie awaited his judgement in the dungeon below. John was one of James's closest friends but had been accused of plotting to kidnap the King.

To James's surprise, the prisoner confessed to everything. He shared all the details of the conspiracy, maybe hoping that the King would come to understand why people were unhappy. James wasn't the most reasonable man though and it was surely only a matter of time before John was sentenced to death.

Fortunately, the prisoner had a saviour in one of the Queen's maids. Margaret Winster had fallen in love with John and risked everything to save him. They were convinced that the King would eventually come to his senses, they just had to keep John safe until then.

Margaret told the guards that the Queen wished to see the prisoner immediately. This was Anne's most trusted servant, so no questions were asked and John was brought to the royal bedchamber. Once inside, the pair tiptoed past the sleeping royals to an open window, where John climbed down some bedsheets to a waiting horse below and his freedom.

The King was furious, but Queen Anne refused to punish her brave servant, sending her to safety with John's cousin at Wemyss Castle instead. Just as they had hoped, James did eventually calm down and forgave his friend, granting a full pardon for his part in the conspiracy.

With a royal blessing, John married the woman he owed his life to the next year, and Margaret's romantic lover's rescue would later inspire a Scots ballad known as 'The Laird o' Logie'.

HOW TO CAPTURE EDINBURGH CASTLE

How do you capture Edinburgh Castle when you don't have the firepower to storm it or the time to besiege it?

That's the question that faced Thomas Randolph in 1314 a few months before the Battle of Bannockburn. Robert the Bruce's men had been winning back castles across Scotland and Edinburgh was one of the last still held by the English. It was a hard nut to crack perched up on its rock, but when word came that James Douglas had taken the impenetrable Roxburgh, Thomas was even more determined to succeed.

The Scots had gained a reputation for cunning tactics and Piers de Lombard, the English keeper of the castle, was terrified that the Scots would find a way in. His men were much more confident of their position, locking their commander in the dungeon to stop him trying to make a deal.

They had no idea that Thomas had a secret weapon. The Scots had William Francis, the son of a former governor who had grown up inside the castle. William was a bit of a ladies' man but with a lack of eligible girls in the garrison, he had found a secret path to climb up and down the castle rock to the town below.

In the dead of night, around thirty men quietly climbed the path up the rockface, led by William. One wrong move and they would tumble to their deaths and one loose stone would alert the guards prowling above them.

With the rest of the Scots force attacking the main gate as a distraction, Thomas's force safely slipped over the walls and caught the defenders napping. They had taken Edinburgh Castle, one of the most iconic strongholds in the country, with a stroke of genius and a little bit of luck.

They wouldn't enjoy it for long though, the Scots' policy was to destroy every stronghold to prevent them from being used against them. The only building to survive the demolition, and so the oldest building still standing in Edinburgh today, was the tiny St Margaret's Chapel.

THE HERMIT & THE KING AT INCHCOLM ABBEY

The spectacular Inchcolm Abbey is just a short boat trip away from Edinburgh but remains relatively overlooked by visitors. That's just how an early inhabitant would have liked it since this island was once home to a reclusive hermit. It was the perfect place to live a simple life, as long as you didn't mind an occasional battering from the wind and rain.

It was one of these regular storms that drove King Alexander aground at Inchcolm in the twelfth century. The weather made it far too dangerous for him to set out for the nearby shore, so instead he bunked up with the hermit in his small cave.

It took three days for the storm to clear and the hermit provided the King with shellfish to eat and milk from a skinny cow to drink. For helping in his hour of need, Alexander promised to build an abbey on Inchcolm, a promise that was fulfilled after the King's death by his brother David.

Unfortunately, the island was an easy target and every summer the inhabitants of Inchcolm Abbey were forced ashore to avoid the inevitable raids that took place.

Inchcolm Abbey on an island in the Firth of Forth, said to be the Iona of the east.

In the fourteenth century, pirates attacked the abbey and carried off whatever loot they could find, including a statue of St Columba. As they tried to make their getaway, a violent storm blew up the Firth of Forth and nearly wrecked their ship on nearby Inchkeith.

Terrified that God was punishing them, they quickly sailed back to Inchcolm and put everything back just as they had found it. Muttering apologetic prayers, the sailors managed to sail back home without any further mishaps.

THE BATTLE OF ROSLIN GLEN

Located along a cycle path just outside the village of Roslin, a monument marks what may have been one of the largest and most important battles in Scottish history. Taking place in February 1303, the Battle of Roslin was once almost forgotten and is still rarely talked about in comparison to the famous victories at Bannockburn or Stirling Bridge.

Early chronicles are prone to exaggeration, but they claim that 8,000 Scots overcame the odds to defeat an English army of 30,000 men here. The invading army was so large that it was forced to split into three separate camps spread around Roslin Glen, but with no significant force nearby they felt safe and secure.

However, the much smaller force of Scots, led by John Comyn and Simon Fraser, had raced through the night from Biggar to arrive in the early hours. Catching their enemy napping, they immediately charged in and annihilated most of the first camp, the rest quickly surrendering.

The Scots probably didn't even realise that was only a third of the English army until the next 10,000 soldiers arrived to see what the commotion was. They were much better prepared and the Scots were forced to retreat to a steep bank near a stream. While the fighting lasted much longer this time, the Scots broke their opponents nonetheless.

By now the Scots had marched all night, fought two pitched battles and had no time to rest with another force on its way. Legend says that local priests used sheets to create a saltire on the Pentland Hills to encourage the weary Scots. Whether that happened or not, the depleted army roused itself to win the third battle, sending their opponents back over the border with a force a fraction of its original size.

So why wasn't the Battle of Roslin celebrated as much as Bannockburn, given the size of the victory? It's because when Robert the Bruce became King in 1306 he had just murdered John Comyn, so achievements such as Roslin were quietly swept under the carpet.

Fortunately, it wasn't completely erased from the history books and evidence can still be seen on local maps today. There's the Kill Burn, which ran red for three days, Shinbane Field, where human bones were being ploughed up years later, and Hewan Bog, where the Scots cut down their enemies.

Even though the numbers behind the Battle of Roslin might not be reliable, it's still a story that deserves to be told.

A ROYAL RESCUE ON CRAMOND BRIG

James V was one of Scotland's most interesting monarchs. Crowned King of Scots before he was 2, legend says that he loved sneaking out of his palaces in disguise so he could travel around and understand his people better. As he mingled with his subjects, he called himself the Guidman of Ballengeich.

One day, he was set upon by robbers while walking at Cramond just outside Edinburgh. The King was no weakling though and he backed himself onto the narrow Cramond Brig, where he could defend himself with his sword. Still, things were looking dangerous for James up against five men and it was only a matter of time before he slipped up.

Thankfully, a local man called John Howieson saw the fight from his cottage and raced to the stranger's aid. The two of them fought off the thieves and John sheltered James in his cottage, washing his bloody hands for him. Still in his disguise, the King asked John what he wanted more than anything as a reward.

All the farmer wanted was to own his farm for himself but he didn't see what the Guidman of Ballengeich could do about that. James revealed that he worked at Holyrood Palace and knew the King was a reasonable man. If John came to the back door, then he would happily introduce him and petition on his behalf.

A very nervous John arrived the next day and as he was guided into the great hall, he realised that he had never seen the King before. How would he know him from all the other well-dressed nobles? James explained that out of all the guests, only the King would be wearing a hat.

The farmer looked around him and said, 'I still can't see him.'

James replied, 'I told you he would be wearing a hat.'

John quipped, 'Well the King must be you or I since we're the only two wearing hats!'

James just turned and smiled at his companion, who immediately dropped to his knees in front of the laughing King.

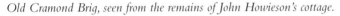

Old Cramond Brig, seen from the remains of John Howieson's cottage.

He was rewarded with ownership of his farm on the promise that he and his heirs would always be ready with a basin of water to wash the King of Scots' hands. Walter Scott told this story to George IV on his visit in 1822 and they met John's heir, who performed the ritual.

That same Cramond Brig is still there to walk across, as are the remains of John's old cottage by the side of the river.

THE VILLAGE OF THE KNIGHTS TEMPLAR

Nestled in a little wooded hollow by the River South Esk, the village of Temple and its little ruined church have an incredibly old feeling about them. Steeped in history and legend, this is Old Temple Kirk, once home to the famous Order of the Knights Templar.

Shortly after the Templars were founded in the early twelfth century, they established bases across Europe where they could gather new recruits. This fertile little spot in Midlothian was given to them by David I, originally named Balantrodach, which roughly translates as 'the Town of the Warriors'.

In the early fourteenth century, the Templars were in trouble. They had become chief financiers to the French King, but he was practically bankrupt and unable to repay what he owed. Instead, he ordered all Templars in France to be arrested and their assets seized, before forcing the Pope to encourage all Christian kings to do the same.

Any surviving Templar needed a safe place to escape to and some believe that they came to Scotland. The Pope had already excommunicated Robert the Bruce, so had a little less to threaten him with and the King was always thankful for a new band of loyal warriors.

If the last Templars did come to Scotland, then they didn't last much longer, soon being officially disbanded and their property given to the Knights Hospitaller. That included the lands at Temple and it's the Hospitallers' ruined church that stands today, replacing the original.

In recent history, the story of the Knights Templar has been linked with the mysterious Holy Grail and a rhyme local to Temple might tie in with the legend:

Twixt the oak and the elm tree, you will find buried the millions free.

The Templars were known to be incredibly wealthy, so it's possible they brought a hoard with them, burying it somewhere safe. Or maybe instead of gold or silver, the little village of Temple is the resting place of the long-lost Holy Grail.

FIFE & KINROSS

THE HIDDEN GOLD OF LARGO LAW

Rising from Fife's east coast, Largo Law is rumoured to contain a hoard of buried gold that's protected by a terrifying ghost. Everybody once knew that the treasure was there, but they were far too frightened of the treasure's guardian to even think about hunting for it.

That was until one night when a young shepherd finally plucked up the courage to approach the spectre. The boy had no trouble finding the ghost and, trembling at the knees, he approached. All it would say was a strange rhyme:

If Auchindownie cock disnae craw,
And Balmain horn disnae blaw,
I'll tell ye where the gold mine is in Largo Law.

The shepherd sprinted down the hill to prepare. First, he killed all the nearby cockerels, knowing that he could easily replace them with the fortune that would soon be his. Then he found Tammie Norrie, the cowherd of Balmain, making him promise that he wouldn't blow his horn that night under any circumstances.

Everything was working out just fine, he was going to be rich and all of his troubles would be in the past. As the sun went down, he was practically skipping up Largo Law to meet the guardian.

There it was, in the same place as before and with the Fife countryside as silent as he requested, the ghost opened its mouth to reveal the location of the treasure.

Before he could utter a single syllable, a cow horn sounded from somewhere in the darkness. The spectre screamed in rage:

Woe to the man who blew that horn,
For out of the spot he shall never be borne.

The mysterious ghost disappeared, never to be seen again, and the treasure was lost. The shepherd boy was angry enough to kill that cowherd, but he found Tammie Norrie already dead with his horn by his side.

No matter how hard they tried, the body couldn't be moved for burial. Rather than leave him lying in the open, they piled an enormous pile of rocks and soil on top until they had built the nearby Norrie's Law.

THE STAR-CROSSED LOVERS OF THE BUNNET STANE

On the quiet, west side of the Lomond Hills, along a path between the rolling fields, a very peculiar rock formation rises from the flat ground. This is the Bunnet Stane, named for its resemblance to a flat cap, but the story doesn't come from that unusual shape. Underneath there's a little man-made cave carved from the rock known as the Maiden's Bower.

The Bunnet Stane – shaped like a flat bonnet. The gate to the Maiden's Bower can just be seen on the left.

There were once two children of opposing clan chiefs who fell in love. The couple would meet at this stone every day and spend their time walking blissfully among the scenic hills and wooded dens of Fife. Eventually, the young woman's father became suspicious of where his daughter went every day and followed her out to the Bunnet Stane.

Spying his own daughter with the son of his mortal enemy, he felt betrayed. It didn't matter that she was happier than he'd ever seen her before, he had to put a stop to this, but knew the girl would never listen. Reluctant to face the boy one on one, he came up with a devious plan.

The next day, when the young man arrived at the Bunnet Stane, the girl's father and brothers leapt down from the top of the rock and attacked him together. The daughter appeared just in time to see her true love cut down by her closest family.

She was distraught at the loss and disgusted by their actions, refusing to go home willingly. They dragged her back, but every day she just ran out to the Bunnet Stane as if her partner would appear again over the horizon.

Eventually, they stopped trying to make her see reason and she carved a shelter out of the rock so that she could stay there for good. It was known ever since as the Maiden's Bower.

THE ORIGINS OF ST MONANS KIRK

In one of the many beautiful fishing villages of the East Neuk, St Monans Kirk claims to be the closest church to the sea in Scotland. Established by King David II, it's an incredible example of a traditional fourteenth-century church, but also an odd place for a monarch to invest in.

There are two stories about why David might have built a church here.

We know that the King received two arrows in the face at the Battle of Neville's Cross, where he was defeated and captured by the English. While one arrow was removed, the other was lodged too deeply and caused him headaches throughout his entire time in captivity.

After eleven years, he returned to Scotland and one of his first acts was to make a pilgrimage to the small shrine of St Monan for spiritual help with his pain. As he was deep in prayer, the arrowhead and longstanding reminder of his greatest failure miraculously fell out through his nose.

The other story claims that David was caught in an almighty storm that had appeared from nowhere along the Firth of Forth. His ship was wrecked and the King came close to drowning in the choppy water as he made his way to the nearest bit of land. David prayed for his life as he swam for all he was worth and when he washed up on the rocks, the first thing he saw was the shrine to St Monan.

No matter which story is true, the church was a fitting way for the King to show his appreciation.

THE FACE BURNED INTO ST SALVATOR'S CHAPEL

Stand outside the entrance to St Salvator's Chapel in St Andrews and you'll notice the letters PH marked in the cobbles. They stand for Patrick Hamilton, an early Protestant preacher who suffered for his faith, but there's a much more gruesome reminder of this martyr's fate nearby if you know where to look.

The Reformation in Scotland was a brutal struggle between the established Catholic Church and the new Protestant way of thinking. Before more famous characters like John Knox, it was Patrick Hamilton who stood up for the new faith.

Born into an aristocratic family, he was destined to be a churchman from a young age. Hamilton returned from studying in Paris with his head full of new ideas, publicly preaching them in St Andrews. That drew the unwanted attention of Archbishop James Deacon and in 1528 the preacher was called before a council to answer for his heresy.

Hamilton refused to deny any of the charges and was sentenced to be burnt at the stake outside St Salvator's Chapel. He had friends in powerful places though, so the burning was scheduled for the same day to avoid any chance of a rescue attempt.

Unfortunately, that meant they didn't have time to prepare properly.

It was a damp day and the freshly gathered wood burned slowly, stretching out his agony. To speed things along, somebody threw gunpowder on the fire, which exploded, but only succeeded in causing more pain without ending the torture.

Eventually, when things were too much for poor Hamilton to bear, he pled for death, crying out, 'Lord Jesus, receive my spirit!' With that, he finally died, but the excruciating pain of his six-hour burning left its mark.

When the smoke cleared, the impression of a tortured face had appeared on the wall of St Salvator's and it's still there today, directly above the entrance.

Watch out for St Andrews students hopping over the PH on the ground, it's considered terrible luck to step on the letters. If they do accidentally tread on the initials, then to avoid failing their exams they have to jump in the sea during the May Dip or run backwards, naked, around the quad.

MONUMENTS & MARTYRS IN BISHOP'S WOOD

Take a walk through Bishop's Wood near the village of Strathkinness and you'll come across some very strange monuments that tell a fascinating story. In 1679, a group of men were hiding in these woods waiting to ambush the Sheriff of Fife. He had been persecuting their fellow Covenanters and they were planning on teaching him a harsh lesson.

However, somebody had tipped the sheriff off, so he was safely hiding at home. Instead, the carriage of James Sharp, the Archbishop of St Andrews was trundling along towards them.

A pyramid dedicated to Archbishop Sharp, deep in Bishop's Wood.

The nine assassins quickly amended their plans, taking Sharp's appearance as a sign from God. It might have been the Sheriff who hunted their friends down, but it was the Archbishop who gave the orders!

Just one day before his 61st birthday, Sharp was dragged from the carriage and stabbed before eventually being put out of his misery by a shot to the chest. The killers escaped but somebody would need to be punished for killing such an influential figure.

A few months later, after the Battle of Bothwell Bridge, five captured Covenanters were brought here in chains. None had anything to do with the assassination but were executed in retaliation anyway.

The men had been offered freedom in return for signing a bond compelling them to give up their religious practices. When they refused to perjure the oaths they had already given, they were hanged and left to swing in the wind.

The Bishop's Road is no longer in use but these woods just outside St Andrews mark the spot of this brutal chapter of history. Archbishop Sharp was honoured with a small pyramid surrounded by symbolic yew trees, while the Covenanter martyrs have their large gravestone in the farmed field behind.

The monuments are barely 30m apart, showing both sides of the same story and how an eye for an eye was in danger of making everybody blind.

THE REAL ROBINSON CRUSOE FROM LOWER LARGO

Lower Largo is a quiet seaside village with a big claim to fame. A local sailor was once cast away to survive alone on a desert island with nothing but his wits and a few supplies. It wasn't Robinson Crusoe but the man who inspired the character – Alexander Selkirk.

Always a disruptive child, Selkirk had eventually run away to sea after finding himself in one violent altercation too many. Then in 1704, while serving on the privateer ship *Cinque Ports* around South America, this Fifer's lack of respect for authority got him in more trouble than he'd bargained for.

The ship was making a pitstop at a deserted island when Selkirk claimed that the *Cinque Ports* wasn't seaworthy enough to cast off again. He demanded the captain make vital repairs, claiming that he would rather stay on the island than risk travelling on such a dangerous ship.

To his surprise, the captain called his bluff.

The stubborn Alexander Selkirk was abandoned, although he initially hoped it was just a joke or harsh lesson. He waited on the shoreline, surviving on shellfish in the hope that his crewmates would soon return. They never did and that's partly because he had been right. The *Cinque Ports* sank shortly after leaving him, with the only survivors captured by the Spanish!

With his few supplies, the lonely sailor was forced to venture further inland. He hunted wild goats, fashioning clothes from their skins, and managed to build huts for cooking and living in, but soon began attracting the wrong kind of animals. Selkirk was being attacked by rats in the night, but the ever-resourceful castaway domesticated some feral cats to protect him.

Unfortunately, the only other ships Selkirk saw for years belonged to the Spanish, who would have been less than friendly to a British sailor and he was forced to hide until they left. Finally, after four years and four months, this incredible character from Lower Largo was picked up by a British vessel.

Selkirk returned to Fife a celebrity, but after spending so much time in solitude, he struggled to adapt back to regular life, even somewhere as peaceful as Lower Largo. He joined a new crew and disappeared off to sea once more, where he died during a voyage. However, fortunately, his incredible story is remembered.

Not only did he inspire the famous novel, but his castaway home was renamed Robinson Crusoe Island and its neighbour Alejandro Selkirk Island. Closer to home, the house that Alexander Selkirk grew up in, near the beach at Lower Largo, displays his statue as a proud reminder of this local legend's roots.

QUEEN MARY'S ESCAPE FROM LOCH LEVEN CASTLE

There are plenty of places dotted around Scotland with a connection to Mary, Queen of Scots, but nowhere has a story to rival Loch Leven Castle. After Mary was forced to surrender to her enemies at Carberry Hill in 1567, she was imprisoned on this island stronghold.

If it looks like a small prison now, Castle Island is about three times larger than it was in Mary's day. A tiny space for a queen used to roaming the country at will, and she was truly miserable here. Seemingly, there was no escape, but this Queen of Scots didn't give up easily.

The monarch arrived pregnant but lost her twins, then while on her sickbed she was forced to abdicate in favour of her son, James VI. Sir William Douglas, keeper of the castle, lit bonfires and fired cannon to celebrate the coronation and no doubt rub salt into the wound.

Mary was no wilting flower, she might be battered and bruised, but she still had her cunning and was very persuasive. The Queen found allies in her jailor's brother George and a boy who may have been his illegitimate son, Willie Douglas.

The trio plotted her escape and the first attempt saw Mary disguised as a washer woman, sneaking into a boat. Unfortunately, her lily-white, delicate hands were a sure giveaway of a life of pleasure rather than scrubbing, so the Queen was dragged back to the prison.

It was only a matter of weeks before the next jailbreak. The Douglases organised a May Day celebration, with lots of dances and copious amounts of booze. During young Willie's distracting performance, he managed to pick-pocket the castle keys and smuggle them to Mary.

Dressed as one of her lady companions, Mary hopped in a boat and Willie rowed with all his might towards the shore. Even if Sir William realised the Queen was gone, all he would find at the dock were holes smashed in the bottom of every sunken boat.

George Douglas met the Queen on the other side of Loch Leven, with horses and loyal supporters. They were finally ready to try and win her throne back.

THE ONLY SCOTTISH WITCH'S BURIAL AT TORRYBURN BEACH

When the tide is out at Torryburn, you might notice what looks like a random, large slab on the beach. This is the very special grave of Lilias Adie and the only known burial of a confessed Scottish 'witch' from 1704.

The first accusation of witchcraft came from a neighbour who had been drinking heavily. She awoke the next day violently ill, with a splitting head-ache, screaming that Lilias had put a curse on her. Even the zealous minister had to admit this was nothing more than a hangover.

However, it wasn't long before she was accused again and this time the authorities were determined to uncover some dark secret.

Eventually, after days of interrogation and torture, Lilias would have confessed to anything. She told them that the Devil had appeared to her wearing a hat, they had carnal relations and she had attended meetings with several other witches.

That was what the torturers liked to hear! They tried to get Lilias to impli-cate even more people, but as they pressed for information, the old lady died. Not only was it embarrassing to have their suspect die in custody, but she hadn't been put on trial and found guilty of anything yet.

The people of Torryburn were left with the body of a woman they were convinced was a witch but wasn't actually convicted of witchcraft. That meant they couldn't burn her body like usual, but there was a real fear that the Devil could reanimate her corpse.

A regular burial was out of the question. Instead, Lilias was laid to rest on the beach, between the high and low tide mark, not quite on land nor in the sea. The heavy slab was added just in case she did come back and try to dig her way free.

Once the witch trials were a thing of the past, curio hunters desecrated her grave. Walking sticks were made from the coffin and Lilias's skull was taken as a trinket. The burial was then forgotten about until recently rediscovered, still in place.

There are other burials associated with witchcraft, but they either died without confessing or were later found innocent. That makes poor Lilias Adie and her strange burial very special indeed!

The large, flat slab that marks the burial of Lilias Adie on Torryburn Beach, only visible at low tide.

A PLAY FOR POWER AT FALKLAND PALACE

Although the little village of Falkland has gained fame in recent years as a setting for the TV series *Outlander*, its real draw has always been Falkland Palace. Surrounded by woodland, with the Lomond Hills rising dramatically behind it, Falkland has always had royal connections, starting life as the King's hunting lodge.

In the early fifteenth century, this was home to the Duke of Albany, the powerful brother of the weak King Robert III. Albany was the real power behind the throne and it's safe to say that he enjoyed his role. That position was looking precarious when Robert's son David came of age, a much stronger character than his father.

It was decided by the leading Scottish nobles that as the heir to the throne, David should rule the country as Lieutenant on behalf of his father for the next three years instead of Albany. Of course, the Duke didn't like that idea one bit.

Patiently waiting until the three years were up, Albany then sent men to ambush David as he travelled past his estates on the road to St Andrews. The Prince ended up locked in a dungeon at the castle where Falkland Palace now stands.

Months later, he was dead.

Albany claimed it was natural causes, while David's supporters cried foul play, they believed the heir to the throne had been starved to death. It was a heinous crime to murder a prince, never mind your own nephew, but with David out of the way, nobody was powerful enough to stand up to the Duke.

Albany was cleared of all suspicion by public enquiry and carried on as if nothing had happened. Scotland was soon deemed too dangerous for the King's younger son James, but as he was being sent to France for protection, he was captured by English pirates. The news that his only other heir was now being held for an enormous ransom broke King Robert and he died of distress.

The Duke of Albany didn't make much of an attempt to ransom the now King James, he was much happier ruling Scotland in his absence. It leaves the enduring question – were David's death and James's capture tragic accidents or was Albany making moves to start his own royal dynasty?

A SPOOKY ENCOUNTER AT DUNFERMLINE PALACE

Scotland's newest city Dunfermline is often overlooked, but this was once the country's royal capital. First recorded in 1070 when St Margaret married King Malcolm Canmore here, she liked the area so much that she founded a new church, which her son David grew into an abbey.

Margaret was buried at Dunfermline in 1093, as were most of her children, starting a new royal tradition that would end with Robert the Bruce. The town prospered from the connection and Dunfermline Palace developed out of the royal rooms of the abbey.

This was where the ill-fated Charles I was born and initially raised, but according to legend the poor kid never really had a chance.

He was a sickly child and the sound of his crying often rang around the palace walls. One night, his father James VI was trying to read when he was interrupted once again by the sound of screaming. James stormed through but was surprised to find it was his son's nurse making the noise rather than Charles himself.

After he calmed the nurse down, she explained that while sitting in the corner of the room, the figure of an old man crept inside. He threw his cloak around the cradle and started to drag it towards the door. Understandably, that was the point she started screaming and the figure vanished!

James wasn't known to be the most patient man and replied that he wished the baby really had been taken. Not only was he a sickly child but now 'The Devil has cast his cloak over him' and nothing good would come from his reign as King.

Devil or not, James was right and Charles I had a tumultuous reign of both Scotland and England. He faced religious strife, civil war and eventually lost his head to the blade of an executioner. The once grand Dunfermline Palace was then last used very briefly by Charles's son before being abandoned to crumble into ruin.

THE SCOTTISH SEAWOLF FROM CULROSS

It's like time has stood still in the village of Culross, where you can wander the seventeenth-century cobbled streets. There are dozens of fascinating historical buildings and winding streets to explore, but the most peculiar sight is a Chilean flag flying in the main square.

Below it stands the bust of Admiral Thomas Cochrane, a man who spent much of his youth wandering Culross and would go on to be the inspiration for many fictional naval captains, including Horatio Hornblower.

Joining the Royal Navy just before the Napoleonic Wars, Cochrane made a name for himself as both a brilliant strategist and a disrespectful subordinate. If he thought that he knew better than his commanding officer then he wasn't afraid to tell him.

Unsurprisingly, he made a lot of enemies, although they couldn't deny how effective he was. Given command of the small, lightly armed

HMS *Speedy*, he captured fifty ships in a single year, including a much larger Spanish frigate. Napoleon hated Cochrane so much that he gave him the nickname 'Sea Wolf'.

Most of his victories came through cunning and subterfuge. While being chased by a much larger ship, Cochrane waited for night to fall, tied a lamp to a barrel and pushed it off in the wrong direction. The pursuer followed the lamp while his crew sailed the other way in total darkness.

Eventually, Cochrane's political enemies caught up with him and he was convicted on a false charge of fraud. He left Britain for South America to lead the newly founded Chilean Navy in their fight for independence, capturing the fortresses at Valdivia with only a few hundred troops.

Moving from Chile to Peru and then Brazil, Cochrane put his tactical genius to work for each of their national causes. Eventually, his fraud charge was pardoned and he would return to Britain with the rank of admiral and a great reputation throughout South America as the heroic Scottish Sea Wolf.

WHEN THE DEVIL BUILT A CHURCH AT CRAIL

The beautiful tower of Crail Parish Church has survived intact since the thirteenth century, but the original building didn't have the easiest of beginnings. When the church was first being built, work was slow. The master mason was struggling to find enough skilled craftsmen and so the Devil saw his chance to have a little fun.

The master of disguise appeared at the building site in the image of a young man. Strolling right up to the mason, he boldly declared that he was going to solve all his problems. The mason looked this slender boy up and down, then snorted a laugh.

The Devil wasn't put off, claiming that he was in fact the most skilled mason in Scotland but had fallen on hard times. He wasn't leaving without a job and the master mason decided that no matter how inexperienced, he could do with the help.

Work suddenly increased rapidly. The Devil wasn't lying about his skills, although he wasn't honest about his intentions. The church was growing so quickly that the locals started to whisper that the master mason wasn't what he seemed. Surely witchcraft or black magic must be involved.

The only person that suspected this newcomer was the mason's apprentice. He decided to follow the strange young boy at the end of one day. Peaking around a wall, he watched as the boy grew and twisted into a monstrous beast. The apprentice suddenly cried out for God to protect him!

At that word, a huge thunderclap sounded and the Devil leapt all the way from Crail to the Isle of May in the Firth of Forth. He wasn't happy about being banished by the apprentice though. Picking up a large boulder, he launched it at the church to destroy what he had built.

Thankfully, it split in two and both sections missed their target. One landed on the beach and the other just fell short of the church. It still sits outside the gate with a huge devilish thumb mark pressed into it.

THE LAW & THE CROSS OF CLAN MACDUFF

This pile of rocks, high on a hill overlooking Newburgh and the River Tay, is all that remains of MacDuff's Cross. Rarely visited now, it's the focal point of an old tradition that was able to get certain special people out of deep trouble.

Descended from the Scottish royal line, the MacDuffs were the early Earls (or Mormaers) of Fife. They may have missed out on sitting on the throne, but they still got their hands on the crown as they had the honour of placing it on the King of Scots' head at their coronation.

That wasn't their only benefit though. MacDuff's Cross was where desperate family members could invoke the Law of Clan MacDuff if they were ever on the run for murder in hot blood.

The remains of MacDuff's Cross in a field high above the River Tay.

All they had to do was touch the cross, wash nine times in a nearby well, prove they were related within nine degrees to the Chief of Clan MacDuff and then agree to pay nine cows and a heifer to the victim's family, tying them to hoops set into the stone. Easy, right?

This special loophole was allegedly bestowed on the MacDuffs by King Malcolm III in thanks for their help in defeating Macbeth. It was probably compensation for not pursuing their own right to the throne, too!

We don't know if the legendary Law of Clan MacDuff was ever used successfully and the cross was later smashed by followers of John Knox during the Reformation.

Legend says that the field was full of bumps and lumps from the graves of those unable to prove their MacDuff lineage. Or maybe people simply didn't respect the tradition if their family member had just been murdered.

LADY JANET'S TOWER IN ELIE

Elie is a popular seaside spot, with beautiful sandy beaches perfect for a swim. In the eighteenth century, a bold young woman called Lady Janet Anstruther loved paddling around here on warm days. That doesn't sound like it would cause too much of a stir until you learn that Janet liked swimming completely naked.

She was a famous beauty and notorious flirt but to make sure she didn't cause any real scandals, she made sure that people weren't spying on her wild swims. Any time she headed down the beach, her servant would walk through Elie ringing a bell to let everybody know to steer clear of this bit of shoreline.

On the rock above where she swam, the noblewoman had Lady Janet's Tower built; somewhere to gaze out to sea while regaining the feeling in her extremities after a chilly dip. It's a beautiful spot and directly across the water, you can spot the Bass Rock and North Berwick Law. Built into the rocks underneath the tower, a little man-made cave offered privacy for the lady to strip off before splashing around.

For a lady of high society, she sounds like a good laugh, somebody you might want on a night out or a day trip to the beach. In reality, Janet had a darker streak.

She lived with her husband, Sir John Anstruther, at Elie House, which looked over the village of Balclevie, but you won't find that place on any map these days. Allegedly, Janet wanted to improve the view from her window and convinced her husband to clear the houses away and move all the residents out!

GLASGOW & LANARKSHIRE

THE VERY ODD GRANNY KEMPOCK STONE

One of the strangest-named rocks that you'll find around Scotland is the Granny Kempock Stone in Gourock to the west of Greenock. Raised thousands of years ago for some unknown reason, it stands today like a hunched old lady, having served as an important monument for generations of locals.

Old stories refer to Granny Kempock with great respect. Local lovers would pass around the stone on their wedding day to obtain her blessing and sailors regarded her with reverence. A handful of soil from around the base was a sure way to protect your ship from storms and circling the stone seven times while carrying a basket of sand added to the power.

In 1662, a coven of alleged witches were convicted of attempting to harness the power of the Granny Kempock Stone. During a trial, Mary Lamont confessed that she danced around the stone with others, planning to throw it into the sea in order to sink ships in the River Clyde!

THE CLOCHODERICK ROCK THAT NO LONGER ROCKS

There are millions of rocks and boulders strewn across Scotland. Some have been left behind by retreating glaciers, but others were the result of supernatural occurrences.

The Clochoderick Stone, sitting not far outside Johnstone, was originally lodged in a giant's shoe. It was barely even a pebble to a creature as large as him, but as he hiked his way across the landscape, that little rock became more and more irritating. Eventually, he plucked it out and dropped it in the otherwise flat surroundings.

It originally balanced delicately on other, much smaller stones, and so, with the slightest touch, would rock back and forward. Legend says that it became a judgement stone for the ancient Celts. If anybody was accused of doing wrong, the Druids would have them sit on the rock. Depending on which direction the stone tilted, they were deemed innocent or guilty.

Unfortunately, just as with many of these rocking stones, known as 'clach bràth', the Clochoderick Stone no longer moves. Human curiosity caused their doom, with fascinated visitors moving the smaller rocks or digging around the base to see how they worked!

THE CREATION OF THE WHANGIE

There aren't many names for a rock formation as memorable as the Whangie, but then again not all rock formations have an origin story like this. Located between Glasgow and Loch Lomond, the low Auchineden hill doesn't look particularly impressive from the road. However, the real draw for hikers and climbers is hidden out of sight around the back.

An odd rock formation known as the Whangie since it looks like a whang of cheese.

It's an easy walk uphill, with fantastic views of the mountains to the north. Then as you turn a corner, you come face to face with the Whangie, named after a Scots term for a chunk of something like cheese. This huge slab of rock looks like a giant knife has sliced it open and local folklore suggests that's exactly what happened here.

Hundreds of years ago the Devil often travelled these hills, but one day he was running late on his way to meet a coven of witches. He was supposed to be one of the most cunning and powerful beings in the world, so it wouldn't look good if he was late. If the Devil can't even manage his own time, then how is he going to keep track of all the deals he has made and souls that he has to collect?

Auld Nick wasn't about to lose his reputation, so he picked up the pace and sped around Auchineden so fast that his tail was flying all over the place. That mighty tail crashed down and sliced this huge chunk out of the rock as easily as you would cut a whang of cheese.

You can climb all the way through the narrow cut in the rock and the odd formation has become a popular spot to hone rock climbing skills. Just make sure you stay well clear if the Devil is running late for his Monday morning meeting.

THE MAN WHO FOUNDED GLASGOW CATHEDRAL

At the heart of Glasgow stands its magnificent cathedral, which has come a long way from the humble chapel built here by St Mungo in the sixth century. Officially called Kentigern, he was nicknamed Mungo or 'dear one' by St Serf while growing up in Culross and has had several miracles attributed to him over the years.

As a child, he brought a pet robin back from the dead, prayed a fire into life using only a hazel branch and possessed a holy bell that he had picked up in Rome. His most famous miracle took place when he was already an established preacher, living by the River Clyde.

He had been invited here by King Roderick of Strathclyde, but neither man could have imagined how important Mungo's presence would be. One day, news reached the King that his wife was having an affair, and to make matters worse, it was with his close friend and greatest warrior.

He didn't want to believe it! The Queen seemed devoted to him and he loved his friend like a brother. That soon changed when the King saw the accused man's hand on a hunt and spied a ring that he had given his wife as a special gift. Even though he seethed with rage, Roderick decided to trick the couple into admitting their crimes rather than lash out immediately.

While the warrior slept that night, the King stole the ring from his finger and threw it into the river. When the hunting party arrived back home, Roderick asked his wife why she never wore the ring he gifted her any more. How about she put it on for the feast they had planned that evening?

The Queen rushed to her lover and asked for the ring back, but it was nowhere to be found. She began to panic and went looking for the only person who could possibly help her – St Mungo. Pleading with Mungo in his little church, she confessed her sins, begged for his forgiveness and asked for help to find the missing jewellery or her husband would surely kill her.

Wise Mungo asked one of his followers to go to the River Clyde and bring back the first fish he caught. Trusting the process, the Queen watched as he sliced into a salmon and glinting inside was the missing ring, ready to be cleaned up for the King, who had no choice but to accept it as proof.

The legend of St Mungo lives on in Glasgow's coat of arms, with a salmon holding a ring alongside the resurrected robin, burning tree and ringing bell above the words 'Let Glasgow Flourish'.

THE SIEGE OF DUMBARTON CASTLE

Guarding the confluence of the River Leven and River Clyde, Dumbarton Castle has a story that stretches back over 1,500 years. With the longest recorded history of any fortified site in Scotland, Dumbarton has seen use as a political prison, a royal refuge and a medieval castle, but before all of that, this was the mighty fortress of the Britons.

The twin-peaked Dumbarton Rock was at the heart of the independent Kingdom of Strathclyde, guarding the entrance to the River Clyde as well as access to Loch Lomond. It was thought to be an impregnable stronghold and in the year AD 870 that theory was put to the test.

A great Viking fleet had arrived in the Firth of Clyde from Ireland, led by the powerful Ivar and Olaf of Dublin. Dumbarton Rock was the only thing standing in their way. If the Vikings thought this was going to be just another speedy raid, then they had another thing coming, Dumbarton couldn't be dealt with quickly.

A direct assault was practically impossible, so the attackers were forced to practise patience for a change. They waited and waited, knowing that the Strathclyde Britons didn't have the men to risk attacking from their rock. Eventually, the well of fresh water found on the lower level of the rock ran dry and the defenders had no choice but to surrender.

It had taken them four long months to crack Dumbarton Rock, an unprecedented length of siege at the time, but it was worth it. Once let loose, the Vikings sailed into the heart of the country and the destruction that followed was terrible. It took 200 ships to carry off all the loot and the huge number of prisoners to be sold in the Dublin slave markets.

The Kingdom of Strathclyde would never be the same again and they were forced to move their capital further upriver to Govan. Now much weaker, before long they would be encompassed into the growing Kingdom of Alba, soon to be known as Scotland.

BETRAYING A NATIONAL HERO AT ROBROYSTON

Today, it's hard to believe that anybody would have betrayed Scotland's National Hero but that's exactly what happened to William Wallace at Robroyston.

Wallace had been fighting a guerrilla campaign against occupying English forces for almost ten years at this point. Myths and legends grew around him and we know more of those than we do of the real man.

The warrior had evaded his enemies by spending his life constantly on the move, avoiding being pinned down by never spending too long in the same place. One of his regular locations was said to be a barn or cottage just outside Glasgow and this is where he was resting on 5 August 1305.

His bed that night was just a few minutes' walk from a spring now known as Wallace's Well, but little did he know that when he took a drink there that evening, it would be his last as a free man. Somebody had betrayed Wallace's location and John Menteith had sent a small army to capture him.

Surprised as he slept and completely surrounded, there was little that the legendary warrior could do about the ambush. After being a

The cross marking where William Wallace was captured at Robroyston.

thorn in the side of King Edward of England for years, William Wallace had finally been captured and would soon be dragged to a sham trial in London.

Accused of being a traitor to Edward, the Scot replied that he couldn't be guilty since this wasn't his king and he had never sworn him allegiance. It didn't matter what he said, he was always going to be sentenced to death at just 35 years old. After being hanged and drawn, Wallace was cut into four quarters to be sent to Perth, Stirling, Newcastle and Berwick.

While it was John Menteith who imprisoned Wallace and sent him to his death, nobody knows for sure who betrayed his whereabouts. Legend has placed suspicion on the farmer whose cottage he was hiding in and supposedly came into a good deal of money along with ownership of his land. That man is said to be the Rab Rae who gave his name to Robroyston.

THE CURIOUS WITCH HUNTS OF POLLOK

The seventeenth century was a particularly dangerous time in Scotland with religious strife and the War of the Three Kingdoms. However, the most shameful chapter of violence is undoubtedly the ruthless hunting of witches, and Pollok Country Park to the south of Glasgow had an interesting part to play.

Pollok House in its current form was only built in 1752, but its predecessor was home to Lord George Maxwell, a dedicated witch hunter. He called himself God's pious warrior, but his religious fanaticism was a danger to those around him.

In 1676, Maxwell fell gravely ill, with a burning temperature and piercing pains in his side and shoulder. To the witch hunter and those who knew him, it seemed as if the witches were finally getting their revenge. Their confirmation came from an unlikely source.

A young mute girl called Janet Douglas had appeared in the area and, communicating through her actions, indicated that she could help Lord Maxwell. His illness wasn't medical of nature, he had been bewitched by a local named Janet Mathie. The lord had once punished Mathie's son harshly and so she had created a wax image of him, then stabbed it full of pins.

Trusting Janet, a force of armed men followed her to Mathie's home. Somehow, the girl knew exactly where to find the effigy, which had pins buried deeply in both the shoulder and the side. Mathie was arrested and after those pins were removed, Maxwell seemed to recover.

His relief didn't last long and when a new bout of illness took hold, Maxwell turned to the mysterious Janet once more. This time it was Mathie's son who was accused and just as before, the mute girl discovered an identical figure full of pins.

When both the boy and his younger sister were interrogated, several witch spots were uncovered and the pair were forced into a confession. Soon, another three women had been implicated and with Janet's evidence and the children's confession, they were all found guilty.

Unsurprisingly, the death of the falsely accused witches did nothing to save Lord George Maxwell, who died from his illness shortly after. Now famous, Janet Douglas had miraculously gained the power of speech, although she never did explain how she knew about those effigies.

With her newfound reputation, Janet attempted to make a living from condemning even more people for witchcraft, but the Privy Council in Edinburgh weren't convinced of her gift. They even attempted to exile the girl but couldn't find a ship's captain in Scotland who would agree to take her!

THE GINGER CAT THAT SAVED GOVAN

High up on the south wall of Brechin's Bar in Govan, the carving of a prowling cat immortalises the unlikely saviour of this riverside suburb of Glasgow.

Govan stands on the banks of the River Clyde and in the eighteenth century was being absorbed into the rapidly expanding Glasgow. The city had become the centre of Scotland's shipbuilding trade and the river was deepened to allow ever larger ships to dock further inland. While the industry brought plenty of jobs and wealth to Govan, it also brought something much less desirable – rats.

Hopping off the ships and heading straight for the town's middens, these unwelcome visitors had found their perfect home. They were bigger, fiercer and more dangerous than anything Govan had seen before. Rather than be scared off by the terriers and ratting dogs like most rodents, these fought back viciously.

Regardless of how much money the council offered for somebody to clear the town of the pests, it seemed that there was nobody left willing to tackle the problem. That was until a ship sailed into town one day with a specialist on board. A sailor presented his enormous, ginger cat that loved nothing more than hunting down delicious rats.

The cat was released from the ship and immediately disappeared into the streets with a hungry yowl. For days, the predator stalked the alleys, rooftops and middens of Govan, leaving a messy trail of rodents in its wake. It became a local celebrity and the sailor a rich man from the council's reward, but the fate of the ginger cat of Govan is unclear.

Some believe he lived a long, happy life of retirement in the town, while others claim his impressive purge came to a head with a showdown against the King of the Rats, where both animals died from their wounds. Regardless, thanks to this carving, the famous feline will never be forgotten!

A BETTER WAY TO WORK AT NEW LANARK

When people think of industry, they usually think of a blight on the landscape – dirty factories and ugly, rundown buildings. The mills of New Lanark couldn't be any different. The town was built in the late eighteenth century near the Falls of Clyde and there is something incredibly beautiful about it. The mill buildings and purpose-built workers' housing are now one of six UNESCO World Heritage Sites in Scotland.

New Lanark was built to take advantage of the River Clyde's power and an influx of cheap labour. Many displaced Highlanders found work here alongside dozens of orphaned children. While they might have benefited from the employment, huge cotton mills like these also put small cottage weavers out of business.

The large industrial buildings were here to stay though, and New Lanark is an example of the very best. When it opened, conditions were better than in other mills, but they were far from perfect. The children who worked there did at least have access to a little education and the food and housing were good quality.

When Robert Owen took over the mill, he initially set about making it more productive. Working hours were extended and discipline was tight. Drunk and disorderly behaviour in particular was clamped down on harshly. Then it seems Robert saw the error of his ways, starting a series of revolutionary reforms.

The picturesque mills of New Lanark alongside the Falls of Clyde.

The children's education was improved and working hours phased out. A community shop was opened where goods were bought cheaply in bulk and sold for a fair price. Sanitary conditions improved, employees received sick pay and the workforce became happier and healthier.

Robert Owens still answered to a board though and they cared nothing about improving the workers' lives. They wanted every penny to reach their pockets rather than be ploughed back into the mill, so Robert just found a new board and bought his old partners out.

New Lanark became a global success story. The ideology of the day was that to be profitable, mills had to run cheaply. That meant treating the workforce harshly and squeezing as much from them as possible. But Robert showed that a happier, healthier workforce was more productive and his accountant could prove it.

BOTHWELL CASTLE'S HALLOWEEN VISITOR

Bothwell Castle in Uddingston, with its enormous circular tower, has been described as the grandest piece of secular architecture from medieval Scotland. Sitting high above the Clyde, the castle has been an important fortification since the Wars of Independence, but it didn't just keep people out, it seems to have trapped some residents in.

One of the inhabitants of Bothwell was a beautiful girl known as Bonnie Jane. While she had a responsibility to marry for the good of the family, that was out of the question in her mind. Jane was already in love and her ideal man was just a lowly commoner from across the river in Blantyre.

With the help of a friendly monk, a plan was hatched. Jane was to sneak out of the castle the night she saw a lamp shining across the river and the monk would handle everything else.

When the agreed night came, the girl tiptoed her way out of the castle to find the monk on his own. This wasn't what she was expecting but he reassured her that her love was waiting down by the Clyde, ready to ride off to a life of blissful marriage together.

As they reached the riverbank, a barge appeared and the monk revealed he had a secret agenda. With an evil laugh, he declared that he would have Bonnie Jane all for himself! He bundled her into the vessel and ordered the boatman to take them across to Blantyre Priory.

However, it was like the River Clyde and the heavens themselves grew angry at the monk's plan. Rain lashed down and the water got choppier by the second. The boatman shouted that they were too heavy and if they didn't lighten the load now then it would be too late.

The monk cared for himself more than anything, so he shoved Jane over the side to drown in the river. Suddenly, the boatman revealed himself as none other than the Devil and grabbed the monk, delivering swift justice by dragging him down to a watery grave. Immediately, the rain stopped and the water was calm.

Bonnie Jane is now doomed to spend the rest of time trapped inside those castle walls. Every Halloween she appears at the tower, gazing out across the Clyde as if looking for that signal lamp and wondering what could have been.

INNER HEBRIDES

HOW THE CORRYVRECKAN WHIRLPOOL GOT ITS NAME

Just off the north tip of Jura, the world's third-largest whirlpool roars in the Gulf of Corryvreckan. This incredible natural feature has fascinated people for centuries, even drawing George Orwell in so close that he was almost killed when his boat was wrecked.

The unusual Corryvreckan is said to be named after a dashing Norse Prince called Breckan. He had fallen in love with the daughter of the Chieftain of Jura, but his reputation preceded him. This wasn't the first young girl Breckan had been associated with and the old chieftain didn't believe it would be his last.

However, the girl was smitten with the Norseman and pled with her father to let them be together. She couldn't possibly be happy with anybody else and over time the Chieftain relented, but on one condition. His daughter could only marry the Prince if he truly proved his love for her first.

The Chieftain set Breckan a seemingly impossible task – to anchor his ship in the whirlpool, for three whole days and nights. If the Prince survived the ordeal, then the couple would be free to marry.

The Chieftain's offer was accepted, but Breckan was no fool, he needed some specialist advice and time to prepare. Sailing back to Norway, he asked a wise woman if there was any way that he could endure the raging torrents of this legendary whirlpool. She told him that to last for three days and nights, he would need three special ropes to tie his anchor to.

One was to be of wool, one of hemp and the last made from the hair of pure, innocent maidens of Norway. Breckan was a well-loved prince and even though it meant he would be taken off the market, those maidens willingly donated their locks.

He sailed back to the Hebrides, anchored his ship with the three ropes and there he waited as the water churned around him. The woollen rope didn't last for long, snapping on the first day, but the vessel held strong. On the second day, the hemp gave up, but brave Breckan still wasn't concerned.

If there was one thing he trusted in, then it was the innocence and purity of the maidens' hair. As the third day dawned, the whirlpool spun even faster and a storm began to rock his vessel. There was little that Breckan could do but hold on tightly to save from being swept overboard but as long as the rope held, his ordeal would be worth it!

Just when his task was almost over, a single strand of hair in the rope snapped and the entire line unravelled. Somebody hadn't been quite as pure as they had claimed. Breckan was dragged to his doom, swallowed up by the swirling water, but the Prince would never be forgotten.

From then on, this churning whirlpool would be known as Corryvreckan – Gaelic for the Cauldron of Breckan.

THE OLD MAN OF STORR

The Old Man of Storr is one of Skye's most iconic landmarks. A feature this prominent deserves a fascinating myth, but the Old Man has three to choose from.

The most common story is the simplest. It's thought that Skye was once dominated by giants, something that isn't hard to believe in a landscape this dramatic. After one particularly fierce battle, a male giant lay down and died here on the Trotternish Ridge.

Over time the land swallowed most of him up apart from this one pointy part. While the Victorians altered the story to explain it as the giant's thumb, the original story is said to have featured a slightly ruder appendage.

The second legend features Skye's famous fairies and their mischievous ways. A husband and wife used to climb the hills here each and every day of their long, happy marriage. As they grew older, the wife was struggling to make the steep journey, so the man continued their tradition by carrying her up on his back.

Eventually, the fairies heard the man wishing that she would be able to keep going everywhere that he went. They appeared to the old couple and agreed to help with their request. All the husband had to do was carry his wife up the hill one more time. At the top, the devious fairies turned them both into this stone pillar, so that they would always be together.

The last story tells of a much friendlier brownie, a creature who helps people around the house as long as it's treated with respect. A farmer on Skye once saved the life of a brownie but never asked him for any help in return. The two became good friends and lived together happily for years.

Then one day, the farmer's wife passed away and the heartbroken husband followed shortly after. The brownie was devastated at losing his adopted family and he carved the Old Man of Storr in the likeness of his good friend to remember him.

The Old Man of Storr – part of a giant, an old stone couple or a brownie's monument?

Today, the rock is very unstable and has changed shape dramatically since these stories were first told. It's possible to walk around the Old Man and admire it from different angles, but not to climb it as the surface has the consistency of porridge.

If the first story is true and it's that part of a giant, do you really want to be crawling up it anyway?

THE FAIRY FLAG OF DUNVEGAN CASTLE

Dunvegan Castle on the Isle of Skye is the historic seat of the Macleods, home to their Clan Chief and a secure location for their most valuable treasure.

Visitors to the castle might not think much of a faded, battered, torn bit of cloth but this is the famous Fairy Flag. Nobody knows exactly where it came from, although some antique experts claim it's a relic from the Crusades, brought to Skye from the Middle East.

If you ask the Macleods, then they have their own, much more interesting story to explain the flag's origins.

There was once a young Macleod Chief who met a woman one day who was so beautiful, intelligent and articulate that he fell head over heels for her. The girl felt exactly the same way, but there was just one complication.

She was a Fairy Princess and if they wanted to settle down together, then they must ask her father for permission first. The Fairy King was kind, but he knew that if his immortal daughter spent a human lifetime with Macleod, she would be heartbroken when he inevitably died.

Instead, he granted them one year and one day married together, then he would arrive at the bridge by Dunvegan Castle to take her home. By the time that year was up, a son had been born who would be left behind in the mortal world.

As the Princess met her father at the bridge, she turned to Macleod and made him swear that he would never leave the child to cry. That sound would reach her ears and be far too much for her to bear.

Macleod grieved badly and his clansmen decided that the only way to cheer their Chief up was a huge celebration for his birthday and the Macleods knew how to throw a party. They went all out and the food, drink and ceilidh were starting to have the desired effect as the Chief couldn't resist tapping his feet.

However, the baby's nursemaid also couldn't resist getting involved and she left the boy sleeping soundly to watch the party for just a few minutes. Those few minutes stretched and soon the baby woke up and began to cry. The sound of the music was so loud that the nursemaid couldn't hear her ward, but even in the fairy realm, his mother could.

When Macleod went to check on his son, he found him swaddled in a strange, silken shawl. Nobody could explain where it had come from, but when the nurse admitted that she had stepped away for a few moments, the Chief knew that his wife had visited.

The shawl became the Fairy Flag of Dunvegan and if the clan were ever in need, all they had to do was wave it and the fairy folk would come to their aid. So far it has won the Macleods battles, saved Dunvegan Castle from fire and even cured a herd of sick cattle!

THE MAGICAL SLIGACHAN BRIDGE

It might just look like an old, disused bridge to nowhere, but the Sligachan Bridge on the Isle of Skye is a magical place. More specifically, the water that flows underneath has been enchanted by the fairies.

The legend starts with Scotland's greatest-ever warrior, the female fighter Scáthach, who lived at Dunscaith Castle. Her fame had spread across the water to Cú Chulainn in Ireland, who wasn't happy that somebody was considered a better swordsperson than him. The Irish demigod challenged Scáthach to prove once and for all who was strongest.

They battled fiercely for days and the fight was on a knife edge; this wasn't going to stop until one of them was dead. Scáthach's daughter Uathach began to worry that her mother would slip up and be killed. Her opponent was a demigod after all!

The girl came to the River Sligachan and begged the fairies of Skye to help her mother. Uathach wept into the water as the sound of the battle raged over the island and the fairies were moved by her sorrow. The Fairy Queen told her to wash her face and be blessed with the knowledge she needed to bring peace again to the island.

As soon as she dipped into the water, Uathach knew what to do, rushing back to Dunscaith to prepare a feast. She used the richest ingredients and the best spices, so before long a delicious smell spread to the still fighting warriors. Their stomachs began to rumble and they realised how long it had been since their last meal.

Agreeing to a truce, they entered the castle hall to sit down and eat together. At the same moment, they both realised that they had just broken bread together. As a guest in Scáthach's home, Cú Chulainn couldn't fight her now out of respect and tradition. They would have to accept the battle was a draw.

It's said that Uathach left a bit of magic behind in the water at Sligachan. Reach down to submerge your face completely in the water for seven seconds, leave it to dry naturally without wiping any off and the fairies will grant you eternal beauty.

A DOMESTIC DISAGREEMENT AT DUART CASTLE

Duart Castle on Mull is the ancestral home of Clan MacLean and everything that a castle should be. It's dramatically positioned on a crag overlooking the sea, with strong walls, an even stronger clan connection and plenty of fascinating stories.

The MacLeans took over a small tower here in the fourteenth century as part of the dowry when Lachlan Lubanach MacLean married a daughter of the Lord of the Isles. He extended Duart and cemented the clan's status on the west coast. However, not all MacLean chiefs were quite so responsible or well-liked, especially not Lachlan Cattanach, otherwise known as Lachlan the Shaggy.

He was the 11th Chief during the early sixteenth century, securing a peaceful alliance with the Campbells by marrying the Earl of Argyll's sister Catherine. Lachlan was unpopular and famously cruel, so it's safe to say this wasn't a happy marriage.

Things were so bad that Catherine decided to poison her husband during a feast at Duart Castle. Shaggy Lachlan was tougher than he looked though, surviving the poison to recognise the guilt on his wife's face.

That night, he kidnapped Catherine from her room, bundled her into a little boat and rowed out to a tiny island, now known as Lady's Rock with a little beacon on it. He dumped her there, knowing that when high tide came, the island was completely submerged and she would drown.

In the morning, there was no sign of his wife, so Lachlan wrote a sad letter to the Earl of Argyll explaining her tragic, accidental death. Argyll replied by demanding that his sister be returned for burial at Inveraray.

Lachlan was forced to travel there with a coffin full of stones and sit through dinner with Argyll, lying through his teeth. To make matters worse, Catherine suddenly appeared at the table. It turned out that she had been rescued by some fishermen from Lismore and went straight to her brother with the story.

The Chief of the Macleans had never run home so fast in his life, living the rest of his days looking over his shoulder, waiting for the Campbells to take their revenge. One night while visiting Edinburgh, Lachlan the Shaggy was found murdered in his bed, along with the knife of John Campbell of Cawdor, one of Catherine's protective brothers.

*The historic Duart Castle –
home to Clan MacLean.*

THE GHOSTS OF DUNTULM CASTLE

Perched almost at the very northernmost point of Skye, Duntulm Castle once had a reputation for being a formidable fortress, but now is more famous for its many ghosts.

The first of Duntulm's spirits is Hugh MacDonald, a man who tried and failed to seize control of the leadership of the MacDonalds of Sleat and found himself imprisoned in the dungeon. To speed up his death, Hugh was given nothing to drink and only salted beef to eat, so it's the rasping groans of his thirsty spirit that still haunt the clifftop.

Margaret Macleod has been seen weeping from her single eye among the stones of Duntulm. It was her mistreatment at the hands of the MacDonalds that started the War of the One-Eyed Woman and clearly her spirit is drawn back to the most miserable year of her life.

Donald Gorm, the 8th MacDonald Chief, is a much happier, although more aggressive, ghost. He was a famous warrior and liked nothing more than picking fights with his own clansmen for fun. You might hear him stomping around Duntulm in a loud, drunken manner trying to brawl with the other spirits.

The final ghost story is a particularly upsetting one. While Duntulm Castle might be the perfect defensive position with cliffs on every side, that also makes it a dangerous place to live. Parts of the castle have literally fallen into the sea, so this isn't a place to run around mindlessly.

A careless nursemaid once dropped the baby of a MacDonald Chief from a window ledge. It was a tragic accident, but the nurse was still killed as a punishment for her mistake. Her ghost haunts both the castle ruins and the base of the cliffs below desperately trying to find the child.

With so many ghosts packed in, it's no wonder there wasn't enough room for the MacDonalds to live here any more.

SAUCY MARY OF CAISTEAL MAOL

For all those travelling to Skye by ferry, the story of Saucy Mary from Caisteal Maol, a short walk from Kyleakin, is a particularly relevant one.

Long before the Skye Bridge was built, any ships looking to sail through the narrow strait of Kyle Akin had to pay a toll. It was a small price to pay for a shortcut that allowed them to avoid sailing all the way around the island through treacherous waters.

Tradition says that the strait was controlled by a Norwegian Princess called Mary who had married the Chief of Clan Mackinnon. To make sure that no ships tried to avoid paying their due, Mary came up with a clever idea. A huge chain was stretched across the water from Caisteal Maol, blocking the passage and only being lowered once the toll was paid.

Legend says that Saucy Mary got her nickname because once the ships' captains had paid their way, she would give them an extra treat. As the boat passed her castle, she would pull her dress down to her waist and bare all for the astonished sailors. Just a small thank you for not causing any trouble.

She was a proud Norwegian though, so often let her home nation's ships pass without paying the fee. We don't know if they still got their special treat or how her husband felt about her interesting business arrangement.

When Saucy Mary died, she was buried facing her homeland of Norway at the top of Beinn na Caillich – the Hill of the Old Woman. No doubt the Scottish sailors would have mourned her passing more than most.

ST COLUMBA'S ISLE IN THE RIVER SNIZORT

Hidden away from the busy roads of Skye, in the middle of the River Snizort, you'll find St Columba's Isle and the Snizort Cathedral. The revered Columba once preached here and the tiny island holds the ruins of small chapels, including the seat of the Bishop of the Isles. There are no soaring towers like St Andrews or Elgin Cathedral, this was a much humbler affair.

Whatever Snizort Cathedral looked like during its heyday, there are only a few walls left now. Instead, the island is better known as an ancient cemetery, full of interesting stones and fascinating stories.

When Columba first arrived on Skye, he was greeted by a group carrying a man on his deathbed. The dying man had heard stories of this remarkable Christian preacher and was clinging to life just long enough to meet the missionary.

Taking water from the River Snizort, Columba baptised the man, who then promptly died at his feet. His friends carried him to this little island, becoming the first Christian burial on Skye.

After the Reformation, St Columba's Isle fell into disuse and disappeared from regular public life. Sporadic burials still took place and the most prominent graves are for Clan Nicholson. Twenty-eight clan chiefs are said to be buried here and every so often a new stone will be uncovered, poking out from the soft ground.

St Columba's Isle is an incredibly quiet place to wander around, protected from the outside world by the river, and is to be treated with the utmost respect. There's just a small wooden bridge to cross over and this humble wee island is a welcome haven from the many packed locations on Skye.

IONA ABBEY – THE BIRTHPLACE OF SCOTTISH CHRISTIANITY

There's nowhere in Scotland quite like the Holy Isle of Iona, known as the birthplace of Scottish Christianity. It's a special place with a peaceful feeling, crammed full of history, legends and the final resting places of important Scottish figures.

This was the location of St Columba's monastery, founded after he arrived with twelve companions in 563 and intended to be the perfect example of Christian virtues. In front of the much more modern abbey, a small mound known as Torr an Aba is said to be where Columba's writing room once stood.

Pilgrims have made their way to Iona ever since, walking along the same Street of the Dead that's visible today, while admiring the intricately carved crosses lining the way. Outside the abbey, the enormous St Martin's Cross has defied the elements to stand in the same spot for 1,200 years.

It was an important journey for the dead as well as the living, with dozens of Kings of Scots buried in the Reilig Odhráin alongside legendary clan chiefs. Long after Viking attacks had made Iona a dangerous place to worship, the island monastery was revitalised by the Lords of the Isles, who formed much of the building we see today.

It was a much easier building process than St Columba's original perfect monastery, which didn't have the smoothest of beginnings.

Every day, the holy men would dig foundations, but every morning they found their work mysteriously undone. Then Columba had a vision. The only way to construct his church was to bury one of his followers beneath it and so Oran volunteered himself.

It was a tragic day, but the brave man was buried and the church finished in no time. Days passed and Columba's guilt didn't fade away. He decided to uncover his friend's face just to say goodbye once more.

Oran suddenly opened his eyes and began to scream wildly that he had seen no evidence of heaven or hell! That wasn't something Columba had been expecting, so he picked up a shovel and quickly filled the grave back in.

At least Oran is in good company with kings and chiefs, but let's just hope that he has found some peace after all that time.

A FEAST OF STORIES AT MACLEOD'S TABLES

One of the many iconic views in the north of Skye are twin hills that look as if they've had their tops sliced off. Officially called Healabhal Mhòr and Healabhal Bheag, together they're better known as Macleod's Tables.

When St Columba arrived to spread Christianity to Skye, either he wouldn't accept or was given no hospitality from the inhabitants. However, God wasn't going to abandon somebody as special as this without anywhere to sleep. The summits of these hills were flattened so that the saint had somewhere more comfortable to lie down and another place to eat.

Around 1,000 years later, the hills would come in handy again. In the sixteenth century, the Chief of Clan Macleod was visiting the court of James V. It wasn't the kind of place he enjoyed, forced to listen to all the Lowland nobles bragging.

They were trying to outdo each other with claims of their fine homes and expensive furniture. With no appreciation for what's important and even less experience outside their bubble, they saw the islands as little more than a backwater.

After days of putting up with ignorant boasting, Macleod had heard enough. Loudly, he declared that he had a table on Skye larger and more impressive than all of theirs put together. He invited them along with the King to visit him at Dunvegan to prove it.

The flat-topped hills known as Macleod's Tables with the Duirinish Stone in the foreground.

When those who had accepted his offer arrived on the island, Macleod took them to the flat top of Healabhal Mhòr. There he had laid out an enormous banquet to prove just how majestic his table really was. No doubt the Lowland nobles were far too out of breath from hiking to argue.

It's roughly a 7-mile round trip to climb both hills, but it's worth bringing a picnic so you can leave Skye claiming you've eaten at the Chief of Clan Macleod's Table!

THE DUELLING GIANT OF FINGAL'S CAVE

Sheltered by Mull, the tiny island of Staffa is a fascinating place both in geology and in legend. Reaching deep into the rock is Fingal's Cave, seemingly made up of the same enormous black columns that form the Giant's Causeway in Northern Ireland. While both locations aren't physically joined, they're forever linked by one enormous story.

This cave was originally home to the Scottish giant Benandonner, with Fingal living across the sea in Ireland. The pair had never met, but they hated each other, hurling vicious insults and threats in both directions.

Eventually, the pair built a bridge out of black columns right from Staffa to the Giant's Causeway so that they could finally decide who was strongest.

Fingal was a heroic warrior and a huge man, but not a true giant, and when he saw the size of Benandonner striding across the bridge towards him, his stomach twisted in knots. Luckily, his wife was a cunning lady and while he panicked, she formed a plan to save the day. Trusting his wife, Fingal was wrapped up in a huge sheet like a newborn baby.

Benandonner also wasn't sure what to expect when he reached the end of the causeway. Fingal had gained an impressive reputation from his many adventures, but the giant didn't think anybody could be bigger or stronger than he was. Full of bravado, Benandonner demanded to see his opponent so they could battle then and there.

Fingal's wife just shrugged. The giant was going to have to wait since his opponent was out hunting for the day, it was just her and Fingal's son left at home. Benandonner looked down and his jaw dropped at the size of the swaddled baby. If that's how big the child was, its father must be absolutely enormous!

Not taking any chances, he rushed back to his cave on Staffa, smashing up the bridge as he went so that Fingal couldn't possibly follow him. Over the years, people seem to have forgotten about poor Benandonner and as a final insult, Fingal has even managed to steal the name of his cave.

THE LORD OF THE ISLES' BASE AT FINLAGGAN

The west coast of Scotland used to be dominated by the MacDonald Lords of the Isles and Finlaggan in Islay was their base of operations. From this secluded spot, their power stretched across the Hebrides, reaching deep into Argyll's sea lochs and often much further.

This special place consists of two small islands located in Loch Finlaggan, strangely inland for a Lordship that relied on its seafaring power. Most island chiefs had their strongholds on daunting cliffs, overlooking a safe harbour for their fleet.

Finlaggan was different though. While officially these island clans paid homage to the King of Scots, in practice it was a long way to Stirling or Edinburgh, so the Lord of the Isles was the real man in charge.

Eilean Mor (Big Island) was once reached by a stone causeway and surrounded by a wooden palisade. Inside were around twenty buildings including a chapel and Great Hall, although most of the remains now visible are from a later farming township.

Just beyond this is the much smaller Eilean Na Comhairle (Council Island). In the early days it supported a stout castle but later became where the Lord of the Isles and his subordinate clan chiefs from across the Highlands and Islands could meet and talk business.

A seventeenth-century MacDonald historian described how sixteen men would meet at Finlaggan around a great stone table. Chiefs of MacGee, MacNicol, MacGillivray, MacMillan and others witnessed charters issued by their great MacDonald Lord. Complaints could be brought, controversies discussed and the next great raid planned, all while MacPhee of Colonsay kept records.

It's a hugely important, although often overlooked, location for the history of Scotland and well worth the visit.

THE SHIPWRECK OF TOBERMORY BAY

The Isle of Mull is surrounded by shipwrecks and the gentle bay of Tobermory is no exception. Below the waves lies a Spanish ship, but with two wildly different stories as to how it got there.

The more outlandish version begins with a Spanish Princess having a dream about the perfect man. She knew that this dreamy character was who she had to marry and sailed far and wide, determined to find him. Inevitably, her hunt for the perfect man brought her ship to Scotland and it anchored in Tobermory Bay.

The Chief of the MacLeans travelled out to welcome the Spaniards and as soon as the Princess set eyes on him, she recognised the man of her dreams. MacLean was already married but that didn't stop him from making regular visits to the Spanish ship.

He made so many visits that his wife was less than pleased about being ditched for this foreign beauty. She conspired with a coven of witches to destroy the ship and the Princess with it.

They dutifully obliged, overrunning the ship's crew with a horde of fierce cats. The crew were being annihilated and one man decided that he had a duty to destroy these monsters for good. Setting light to their gunpowder, the explosion dragged the ship down to the depths.

The official story of the sunken Spanish ship is a little less romantic, although equally explosive. After the Spanish Armada was defeated in 1588, one ship successfully limped around Scotland to safety at Tobermory.

Lachlan Mór MacLean agreed to provide them with the supplies needed to make their repairs if the Spanish let him borrow 100 soldiers to fight against the MacDonalds. The situation was working out well for the MacLeans until the Spanish decided it was time to go home.

As they prepared to set sail, the gunpowder mysteriously exploded and the ship sank, some say along with a hoard of Spanish gold. Among many theories, it's claimed that MacLean was responsible, unhappy that the Spanish cut their bargain short.

Maybe it was witches, maybe it was an unhappy clan chief or then again, maybe there are two Spanish ships at the bottom of Tobermory Bay. Along with that hoard of lost gold!

INVERNESS-SHIRE
& CAIRNGORMS

VISITING BEAULY PRIORY AFTER DARK

The ruin of Beauly Priory is located in such an idyllic area that the original monks named it 'Beautiful Place' in French – Beau Lieu. Tradition sometimes claims that Mary, Queen of Scots was the one to give the site its name, but it had been called Beauly for a long time before she came along. No doubt Mary was just confirming what had been suggested 300 years before.

The priory fell into disrepair after the Reformation, with lead stripped from the roof and stone reused in local buildings. The old ruins then began to gather tales of ghosts and ghouls, things going bump in the night. Nobody dared go in after dark.

That was until one night, when a tailor bragged that he wasn't afraid of anything. He'd sit in Beauly Priory and sew a pair of hose by the moonlight to prove it. Things were going well to start with, but around midnight there came a sound of scrabbling.

A skull was emerging from a tomb and peering at the tailor. It spoke to him, 'Look at my bony skull, I haven't eaten in years.'

The tailor replied shakily, 'I see you, but I'll sew this.'

Unsurprisingly, he started to work a wee bit faster.

The shoulders appeared, then the chest and every time the ghoul moved, he asked the tailor to look at his bony remains. Any time the tailor was speaking the body stopped moving, so he made his replies as long as possible.

Eventually, the strange figure was out of the tomb and crawling towards the tailor, who was working frantically in terror. The ghoul said, 'Look at my big grey paw, without blood, flesh or muscles!'

Just as it swiped for the tailor, he put the last stitch in the hose and dived for the doorway, leaving the grey paw clutching thin air.

He might have won the bet, but he wouldn't make any claims like that ever again.

Beauly Priory, where things go bump in the night.

HUNTING THE LOCH NESS MONSTER

There's no doubt that the legend of the Loch Ness Monster is one of Scotland's most famous stories. The loch holds more water than all the lakes and rivers in England and Wales combined, so there's plenty of space for a secretive creature to hide.

Descriptions vary, but the monster that's been nicknamed Nessie is often said to have a large body, sometimes with humps and usually a long neck with a small head. Many people don't see her in the flesh, just inexplicable waves on the surface or a dark mass under the water caught on sonar.

Thousands of people go looking for her every year, but this isn't just a story cooked up for tourists. When St Columba was travelling the Highlands converting Picts to Christianity in the sixth century, he came across a group of men burying somebody by the banks of the River Ness. Their friend had been swimming when a terrifying water beast had attacked and killed him.

Columba then instructed one of his trusting followers to get into the water and splash around. As the monster inevitably appeared, the saint made the sign of the cross and commanded it to leave! The beast was immediately hauled back by an invisible force, before disappearing under the surface.

While there have been scattered reports of a creature in the loch throughout history, the Loch Ness Monster really shot to fame in the 1930s. With more people travelling along the side of the loch, sightings steadily increased along with blurry photographic evidence.

People have tried to disprove the legend of the Loch Ness Monster for years, but you never know what might be down there. With so many sightings over the decades, surely something unknown is lurking in Loch Ness.

GUARDING SEATH MÓR'S GRAVE AT ROTHIEMURCHUS

Finding Rothiemurchus Old Parish Church isn't easy, down a backroad near the Doune of Rothiemurchus and hidden from view by thick woodland. Once you've arrived though, there's no mistaking the grave of the Clan Chief Seath Mór Sgorfhiaclach. A sturdy metal cage covers the burial site, not to protect the body but the stones that lie on top of it.

The Chief of Clan Shaw, Seath Mór lived in the fourteenth century, a time of turmoil when this huge warrior really came into his own. He had a fearsome reputation, with the ability to strike fear into people's hearts just with a look, whether friend or foe. That fighting spirit seems to have lived on long after the Chief passed away.

The ghost of a terrifying Highland warrior has been known to appear to wanderers passing through the forest of Rothiemurchus. With sword and shield waving violently, a challenge is yelled out to any who dare to pass.

Those who run are hunted down by the spirit, never to be seen again. However, if you keep your cool and accept the offered challenge, then Seath Mór respects you enough to leave in peace.

The ghostly Chief has company though and his grave itself is guarded by a strange creature called the Bodach an Duin. There are five oddly shaped stones, like small wheels of cheese, sitting atop the grave slab, which should never be touched.

Foolish people have tried to steal them in the past and each met a terrible fate at the hands of the Bodach. One man launched a stone in the nearby River Spey to prove the curse was nonsense. The next day, the stone was back where it belonged and the vandal was found drowned in the river instead.

To ensure that nobody comes to any more harm, the metal cage was erected to protect the stones and let the Bodach rest easy.

THE DONKEY & THE TREE OF CAWDOR CASTLE

Few buildings can boast as interesting a foundation story as Cawdor Castle, built in the fourteenth century and still lived in by the same family today. Before this tower was built, the Thane of Cawdor lived in another stronghold a short distance away but decided it was time to move.

He had received permission from the King to build a new castle, all he needed to do now was choose the location. Fortunately, the Thane of Cawdor had a dream with instructions on how to find the perfect building plot. If he followed them exactly then his family would forever prosper there.

People must have thought he was mad, but the Thane loaded a chest of gold onto a donkey and let it roam his land. Wherever it chose to stop, that was where he would build the new Cawdor Castle.

As the now wealthy donkey wandered, it sniffed a few different areas while being watched in anticipation. Finally, it chose to lie down for a nap under a holly tree and the decision had been made. Following his dream as instructed, the Thane built Cawdor Castle right on that very spot.

It seems like a bit of a ridiculous story, but on the vaulted ground floor of Cawdor, you'll find a long-dead holly tree. It's sprouting right out of the bedrock, surrounded by fourteenth-century stone walls and starved of sunlight many years ago.

Cawdor Castle, built around a tree that was chosen by a donkey.

If that hasn't convinced you of the legend, the tree has now been carbon dated and proved to have died sometime around 1372!

THE FIDDLERS OF TOMNAHURICH

It might be used as a cemetery today, but Tomnahurich Hill in the south-west of Inverness was once known to be home to the fairies.

A long time ago, there were two travelling fiddle players roaming the Highlands to make some money. They had passed through dozens of towns and villages without much luck by the time they arrived in Inverness. If they couldn't find a well-paid gig this evening, then they were sleeping on the streets.

They played in the open, busking reels, jigs and laments to drum up attention, but not many people in Inverness were impressed. Only one old man stood and watched with a big grin on his face, tapping his foot to the beat.

Eventually, he made the musicians a proposition. There was an opportunity that night to play for a remarkable group of people and he would pay double what they normally charged. All they had to do was meet him at Tomnahurich Hill at sunset.

It sounded like an excellent proposition, almost too good to be true, but the pair had barely eaten for days so it didn't take long to accept. Just as the sun was going down, they walked to Tomnahurich where the old man was waiting.

He showed them to a peculiar opening in the hillside with light, warmth and the sound of laughter blaring out. An enormous hall stretched before the fiddlers, full of people dressed in the finest of clothes around a table groaning under the weight of so much food!

A loud cheer went up from the revellers at the sight of the two men and their fiddles. A loud rumble sounded in reply from the musicians' stomachs. Their guide told them not to rush, they had all the time in the world to enjoy the food and drink before playing.

Once they were satisfied, the fiddlers tuned their instruments and announced the first song. The party was wild and the dancing lasted for hours. It was as much fun for the fiddlers as it was for the audience. They didn't think they had ever played this well before and they were certainly earning their payment!

But all good things must come to an end. When the dances were finished, the old man paid the two fiddlers before ushering them back outside into the early dawn light. One of the pair turned to ask if they needed them again, but the doorway had mysteriously disappeared.

The men walked back into Inverness, but everything seemed different. Houses had sprung up overnight and they didn't recognise any of the stores or pubs. Even the people were dressed in funny clothes.

A church bell rang out loud. Finally, something they recognised and maybe somewhere they could get a little sense, so the pair headed straight to the church. The minister started the sermon but as soon as he mentioned the Lord's name, the fiddlers of Tomnahurich crumbled into dust.

It turned out that they hadn't been playing under the hill for a single night. They had been inside Tomnahurich for 100 years after Thomas the Rhymer had lured them in to play for the fairy's party.

They should have realised that if a deal seems too good to be true, then it usually is.

THE FAIRIES OF LOCHAN UAINE

Hidden away in the Cairngorms but still very accessible is a little loch with a strange story. Lochan Uaine is the Green Lochan and is said to get its iconic, vibrant colour from the fairies washing their clothes in the water. It's not known exactly where these particular fairies come from, but Donald the King of the Fairies lives on the banks of nearby Loch Morlich.

Donald wasn't somebody you wanted to get on the wrong side of. He used to sit on the banks of the loch playing his pipes and one day he overheard somebody on the other side say that he didn't believe in fairies. That was something the Fairy King couldn't stand for.

Soon, the ignorant wanderer heard Donald's pipes getting closer and closer, but with no sign of any musician. As the sound increased, so did the wind and before he knew it the skirl was deafening, with hot gusts felt on his cheeks. Jumping aside off the path, the invisible Donald carried on piping into the distance and the man never doubted the existence of fairies again!

THE BIG GREY MAN OF BEN MACDUI

Creatures like the Yeti or Bigfoot are world famous, but Scotland has its own mysterious mountain beast known as Am Fear Liath Mòr, or the Big Grey Man of Ben Macdui.

At the heart of the Cairngorms, Ben Macdui is the second-highest peak in the UK at 1,309m and allegedly haunted by this monster. Twice the height of a regular man and covered in short hair, the Big Grey Man has a strong psychological effect on anybody he finds out on the mountain. It's said that even experienced mountaineers start to feel a sense of dread or panic when he's nearby and the fog is rolling in.

The first mention of the Grey Man was by Norman Collie, who noticed on his way down the mountain that he heard an extra footstep behind him for every three steps he took. He saw nothing around him on the slopes, continuing until eventually the panic gripped him and he sprinted down to safer ground.

On hearing his story, a Dr Kellas wrote to him and admitted that he had a similar experience with his brother near the summit where they both saw a giant figure descending on them and fled as fast as they could.

The mountains can be a sinister place when you can only see a few metres in each direction and it's easy for the mind to play tricks. However, these were well-respected climbers who were more than used to this setting and would forever hold on to the claim that something sinister was up there.

The stories continue to this day from shadowy figures in the mist and large footprints in the snow to the sound of somebody muttering Gaelic through the wind.

THE BATTLE OF CULLODEN

Just a short distance outside Inverness at Culloden Moor, one of the most infamous battles in Scottish history took place on 16 April 1746. The Battle of Culloden has been written about, romanticised and misrepresented hundreds of times and still provokes emotion hundreds of years later.

The night before the battle was the birthday of the government commander, the Duke of Cumberland, and that gave the Jacobites an idea. They were going to march through the night to surprise the drunken soldiers' merry celebrations and crush them before they could react.

Unfortunately, the creeping Jacobite columns didn't want to set off until it was pitch black, leaving far too late and only arriving a short time before sunrise. Rather than risk a disorganised attack, they just turned around and marched all the way back again.

It had been a waste of time and energy, with hundreds of exhausted men missing the upcoming battle while they looked for food or rest. When the battle lines were drawn, there were only 5,000 Jacobites left to face around 9,000 government soldiers.

Contrary to popular belief, Bonnie Prince Charlie's side was a varied mix of Highlanders, Lowlanders, Catholics and Protestants along with a small contingent of French, Irish and English.

It wasn't an ideal location for the Jacobites. The ground was too open and flat for their usual tactics, but they had to defend this spot or lose control of Inverness. The first action was a short artillery exchange, although the boggy moorland soaked up most of the damage.

Then the Jacobites decided to attack at speed because that's what usually worked. The fearsome Highland Charge consisted of rushing towards the enemy, firing a single volley just metres away before smashing in with sword and dirk swinging. It had won them every battle so far.

The Battle of Culloden Cairn, raised in 1881 by Duncan Forbes of Culloden.

That's what their opponents had been expecting and they'd trained for this very moment. Their cannon switched to canister shot – packs of hundreds of metal balls that spread out from the barrel and shredded lines of soldiers. Clan chiefs charging at the front of their men were some of the first to fall.

Even under the barrage, the Jacobite right wing still reached the government lines, causing carnage among their ranks. Unfortunately, the Jacobite left was dealing with much tougher ground and had stalled halfway. In the end, unable to push forwards, they fled and their comrades on the right were left isolated and defeated.

It was clear that the Battle of Culloden was lost, but Bonnie Prince Charlie did his best to rally the fleeing troops. He had to be physically dragged from the field by his generals and the rest is history.

Culloden is such a place of sadness that it's said no birds sing there and that every year, on the anniversary of the battle, those who lost their lives that fateful day are doomed to rise and fight once more.

REUSING RUTHVEN BARRACKS

Ruthven Barracks near Kingussie is an obvious spot for a fortification, dominating the surrounding landscape on its little mound. This isn't a traditional clan seat though, the Ruthven we see today was built to exert control by the newly formed British government.

The barracks is actually the third building on this spot, guarding the crossing of the River Spey. It replaced older castles controlled by the Comyns, Alexander Stewart, the Wolf of Badenoch, and later, the Earl of Huntly.

One popular legend claims that the Wolf was in his castle here on a stormy night when a dark, mysterious figure appeared at the door. He challenged the lord of the castle to a game of chess, an offer that was inexplicably accepted. No matter how good you are, you don't stand much chance when playing against the Devil.

Each time the visitor called check, the weather outside got worse. In the morning, the storm had broken but everybody inside the castle was found dead. Alexander Stewart himself was slumped over the table with the nails torn out of his boots.

Long after that demonic chess match took place, the government decided they needed a barracks here as a power base in the Badenoch area. Ruthven was built as one of four, connected with military roads, to try and control the Highlands after the 1715 Jacobite Rising.

There was space for 120 soldiers, which doesn't sound like a lot but in 1745 just a dozen men successfully held off around 200 Jacobites. The only defender to die was 'foolishly holding his head too high above the parapet'. Eventually, the attackers returned with artillery and the barracks surrendered peacefully.

After their defeat at the Battle of Culloden, Ruthven was an obvious rallying point for the Jacobites. Around 3,000 men gathered right here, showing they still had plenty of fight left in them!

Then a message arrived from Bonnie Prince Charlie that simply read, 'Let every man seek his safety in the best way he can.'

Their dream was over.

GUARDING THE GREAT GLEN AT URQUHART CASTLE

The impressive Urquhart Castle on the banks of Loch Ness is one of Scotland's most visited attractions. Inside the picture-perfect ruins of this once-great fortress, there are 1,500 years of tales to be told.

The castle is in a strategic position, controlling movement through the Great Glen from Inverness to Fort William, one of the few easy routes through the Highlands. That was why King Alexander II decided to build a royal castle here, on the site of an old Pictish fort.

He tasked his son-in-law Alan Durward with responsibility for keeping the peace and asserting the King of Scots' authority in the lawless Highlands. A small version of Urquhart Castle was soon constructed, but it wasn't to have a peaceful life.

Caught up in the Wars of Independence, Urquhart was passed back and forward, gaining a reputation as one of the toughest fortresses to assault. Two hundred years later, the threat from abroad was gone, but now the castle had to deal with some very unruly neighbours.

The Grants had been appointed hereditary keepers of Urquhart Castle and their main job was to keep an eye on the west coast clans who enjoyed raiding along the Great Glen. The MacDonalds were usually the worst culprits, having even captured and lived in the castle at one point.

Unfortunately, the Grants and Urquhart Castle failed their task in spectacular fashion during the Great Raid of 1545. An enormous army of clansmen led by the MacDonalds stormed the castle and carried off everything possible, including what was bolted down – around 8,000 animals, a couple of thousand bags of grain, twelve feather beds, pots, pans, boats and even the heavy doors with their iron locks.

It was an almighty show of force and disrespect, the name MacDonald became a very dirty word in the Grant household and one man to suffer for that was the bard, Domhnall Donn.

Held in a prison deep behind the castle walls, Domhnall was officially being tried for cattle theft, but legend says that he was held for another reason. This MacDonald warrior poet had fallen in love with the Chief of Clan Grant's daughter.

Even though Domhnall knew the Grants were hunting for him, he refused to run away and abandon his love. He was tracked down in the hills above Loch Ness and dragged to Urquhart Castle in chains. While the bard was imprisoned, he carried on composing heart-wrenching songs, helping to romanticise his own life's story.

Sadly, there was to be no fairy-tale ending for Domhnall, but his death earned him an eternal reputation as a local folk hero.

REFUSING A QUEEN AT INVERNESS CASTLE

The modern Inverness Castle is just the latest in a long history of fortifications dating back to at least the eleventh century. Such a strategic hinge point of the Highlands, at the end of the Great Glen and controlling the entrance to the Moray Firth, was always going to see fighting.

The latest Inverness Castle, built on the same site as many before it.

It was attacked during the Scottish Wars of Independence, several times by the Lords of the Isles, during three different Jacobite risings and even by Mary, Queen of Scots. Edinburgh Castle might claim to be the most besieged building in Britain, but it's worth Inverness calling for a recount.

When Mary arrived at Inverness in 1562, she wasn't met with the jubilation that the Queen expected. Instead, the keeper of the castle, Alexander Gordon, along with around a dozen men, locked the doors against her on the orders of the Earl of Huntly.

It's said that when the Frasers and Munros heard that their Queen was in danger, they flocked to her side. While that might have had more to do with settling a personal score against Huntly, it still had the desired effect.

The siege only lasted three days before Mary's forces swarmed the walls, captured Alexander Gordon and promptly placed his head on a spike.

Ever the romantic, when Mary watched her loyal soldiers passing by, she exclaimed how sad it was that as a woman she would never know the feeling of lying in the fields and walking the causeway with a breastplate, helmet, shield and broadsword!

RODERICK MACKENZIE'S SACRIFICE

As you travel along the A887 leading away from Loch Ness, you'll spot a raised up cairn on the left-hand side, not far from where the road joins the A87. It was placed here to remember a fascinating story from the 1745 Jacobite Rising.

Not long after the Battle of Culloden, the Duke of Cumberland triumphantly sent the head of Bonnie Prince Charlie down to London and called off the hunt for the Young Pretender. Unfortunately for the Duke, it was the wrong head.

It was actually Roderick Mackenzie, son of an Edinburgh goldsmith. He looked so similar to Charles that he became his body double, personal guard and close friend. Like most Jacobites, he was on the run after that final battle, hiding in remote locations while the government army relentlessly hunted him down.

Roderick had found a great hiding spot in a cave in Glen Moriston, but one day he was caught out while down at the river. It was clear that there was no escape for him, so to make the most of a bad situation he declared to the soldiers that their search was over. In an act of bravery and loyalty, Roderick confessed to being Bonnie Prince Charlie.

Unfortunately, Charles was wanted dead or alive and so the soldiers shot him immediately. Roderick's final words were, 'You have murdered your

Prince!' The delighted soldiers left the cumbersome body where it lay, taking only the head to Fort Augustus to claim the reward.

None of the Jacobite prisoners would confirm the identity, but Cumberland was so convinced that he followed it down to London and called off the man-hunt. By the time the ruse had been discovered, the real prince had slipped through the net and escaped to the Hebrides.

Roderick's sacrifice was crucial to the final chapter of the 1745 Rising but is still largely unknown apart from by those curious enough to stop and inspect either his cairn or his grave that's still marked down by the river!

Left: *Craigievar Castle – also known simply as the Pink Castle.*

Below: *Dunnottar Castle, where the Honours of Scotland were protected.*

The ruined kirk on the banks of Loch Lee at the end of Glen Esk, the area where the Laird of Balnamoon hid after Culloden.

Glamis Castle – still home to the Earl of Strathmore as well as dozens of stories.

Above left: *The Clachan Bridge, also known as the Bridge Over the Atlantic, with the ocean flowing through its arch.*

Above right: *Dunstaffnage Castle, which was fought over for centuries.*

Left: *The atmospheric ruins of Kilchurn Castle – built by the Black Knight of Rhodes.*

Above left: *The luxurious Culzean Castle sitting right on top of a cliff riddled with caves and stories.*

Above right: *Loudon Hill looming behind the Spirit of Scotland, depicting the outline of William Wallace.*

Below: *The three peaks of the Eildon Hill, said to be split by Michael Scott the Wizard.*

Left: *Melrose Abbey, where the heart of Robert the Bruce is buried.*

Below left: *Halfway down the 300+ Whaligoe Steps hugging the cliff to the tiny harbour among the rocks.*

Below right: *The impressive Craigmillar Castle – one of Edinburgh's best-kept secrets.*

Opposite: *Edinburgh Castle on its rock, dominating Princes Street Gardens.*

St Monans Auld Kirk founded by King David II.

Lady Janet's Tower at Elie Beach, with the Bass Rock to the left.

Above: The enormous ruined Bothwell Castle, which has a tragic annual visitor.

Right: The Sligachan Bridge with the Black Cuillin Mountains rising in the distance.

Above: *The tiny Isle of Staffa with the giant Fingal's Cave opening on the right-hand side.*

Left: *Ruthven Barracks – once home to the Wolf of Badenoch before being transformed for government soldiers.*

Opposite: *Urquhart Castle jutting out into Loch Ness, where it guards the Great Glen.*

Above: *The Glenfinnan Monument at Loch Shiel, marking the official start of the 1745 Jacobite Rising.*

Left: *Cille Choirill has an incredible view over the mountains and a bizarre origin story.*

Opposite: *The exquisite Italian Chapel interior, created by Italian PoWs during the Second World War.*

The folly on Kinnoull Hill high above Perth, where a dragon once lurked.

Creag an Tuirc marks the gathering place of Clan MacLaren above Balquhidder.

The enormous Smoo Cave – once the lair of the Wizard of Reay.

The view from Queen Margaret's Bower at Linlithgow Palace looking at the metal spire of St Michael's.

Right: *The remains of Strome Castle, once guarding an important crossing point but blown to pieces by the Mackenzies.*

Below: *Loch Maree with some of its many islands and the scene of a tragic love story.*

LOCHABER

THE BLACK FROG OF CASTLE TIORAM

Situated in an area known as the Rough Bounds, Castle Tioram is as dramatic as it is isolated. Built on the highest point of a tidal island, this simple stronghold is linked to the mainland by a causeway, only visible at low tide. It might seem remote today, but this was a perfect base of operations, with safe harbour for a fleet of warships and easy access to the islands or along the coast.

The first mention of this island comes when Christina of the Isles granted it to the Campbells in return for one ship of fighting men whenever she called. Castle Tioram's story then goes to another extraordinary lady in the form of Amie MacRuari of Gamoran, Christina's niece. She had been abandoned by her husband but held onto these lands for her children.

Amie's son became the 1st Chief of Clanranald, a group renowned for their wild ways, but their 12th Chief John was the most infamous of all. He was a downright evil man and an excellent marksman, naming his gun 'the Cuckoo' because of how quickly it could appear from nowhere and fire.

It's said that John liked to stand at the highest point of Tioram and take shots at whoever was passing, including his own clansmen. He was so hated that he even manifested a spirit believed to be sent by the Devil himself. It took the form of a terrifying black frog.

No matter where John went, this frog would be waiting for him. He once locked it in the dungeon before setting sail, only for a freak storm to overtake the boat. The sailors saw the black frog swimming among the waves and quickly let it into the boat, whereupon the winds immediately ceased.

When John's reign of terror was over and he finally died in his bed at Castle Tioram, the frog suddenly disappeared with a loud crack that sounded just like a shot from the Cuckoo.

Castle Tioram, meaning dry castle, built on an island with a causeway only accessible at low tide.

THE CHANGING SEASONS AT BEN NEVIS

The mighty Ben Nevis is the highest mountain in Scotland and according to folklore the winter throne of the Cailleach – Scotland's creator deity. This terrifying hag with icy blue skin, frosty white hair, rust-red teeth and a single piercing eye is sometimes known as Beira, the Goddess of Winter.

During the cold winter months, Beira holds a beautiful girl called Bride captive deep inside Ben Nevis. Jealous of the girl's beauty, she uses her as a slave, sending her out of the mountain on impossible chores, just to punish her for failing to complete them.

One day, while Bride was struggling to wash Beira's cloak, a kindly old man appeared and offered to help. With just a few flicks, he turned the cloak as white as snow. The stranger revealed himself as Father Winter and with a glint in his eye, gave the young girl some snowdrops with instructions to show them to her captor.

Beira was furious. The appearance of flowers showed that her strength was starting to wane and her grip on winter beginning to slip. In response, the hag rode out from Ben Nevis to every corner of Scotland, spreading more frost and keeping the land in winter for a little while longer.

At the same time, Angus, the Prince of Summer had been dreaming of the beautiful Bride and was determined to rescue the girl from her prison. Every time he tried to sail across the sea to Scotland, Beira raised huge storms to stop him.

Eventually, on the first day of spring, Angus finally reached Bride beneath the mountain but, chased by Beira, the pair were forced to flee back to his Summer Island. They longed to return to Scotland and every time they did, the sun would shine and new life would grow. However, Beira would then use her waning strength to summon cold winds and blow them away again.

Eventually, by 1 May, otherwise known as Beltane, the old hag was exhausted and unable to fight on any longer. Beira was forced to retreat to drink from the Well of Life, where she could rest and recover her strength. Come the end of October and Samhain, she's finally strong enough to return to Scotland, capture Bride and imprison her beneath Ben Nevis once more.

That battle is endless and the cycle takes place every year, but it's reassuring to spot the signs that Angus is coming to rescue Bride and know that summer is on its way.

SINGING WITH THE CAILLEACH IN GLEN NEVIS

Make the journey along the majestic Glen Nevis, through the Nevis Gorge and you're rewarded with the awesome view of Steall Falls with An Gearanach rising behind it. Keep your ears open for any strange noises while there, since this is another popular haunt of the Cailleach.

When she wasn't sculpting the hills and glens, this deity was known to protect wild animals and especially loved deer. A long time ago, a group of hunters were stalking stags in Glen Nevis when they heard a peculiar singing. That singing was accompanied by a loud tapping. The group realised this was the Cailleach keeping time while milking her herd of deer.

With the old goddess protecting her herd, the hunters knew they had no chance of catching one. They all left Glen Nevis apart from one brave soul. He needed to feed his family regardless of the Cailleach and couldn't go home empty-handed.

All day he hunted with the singing in his ears but there wasn't a single deer to be found. When he sat that night by his fire, the tune of the day inspired him and he sang:

The grizzled Cailleach, tall and stern;
Swift she glides over peak and cairn.

After a few more lines he looked across the fire, and there was the old goddess, chuckling at him. Nobody had ever been brave enough to call on her help before.

She explained to him that her herd was growing too large and that the brave young hunter could be useful. The next day, he should follow the sound of her singing and she would mark him out a deer to shoot.

From that day on, the man was blessed with incredible luck as a hunter. He never took more than he needed and the Cailleach made sure that he would succeed.

All because he had the courage and sense to call on the Cailleach for help instead of running away from her.

THE FIRST SHOTS OF THE JACOBITE RISING AT HIGHBRIDGE

The ruined pillars of Highbridge loom over the River Spean like an atmospheric monument to the past. Part of the old Military Road network, it was built to try and control the Highlands and allow government soldiers to quickly march through rough terrain. It also made their movements predictable and troops vulnerable.

In August 1745, news reached the British government that Bonnie Prince Charlie was in Scotland and busy organising an uprising. To reinforce Fort William, eighty-five soldiers were sent along the Military Road from Fort Augustus, and around 20 miles in, that involved crossing Highbridge.

The ruined pillars of High Bridge, where the first shots of the 1745 Jacobite Rising were fired.

Suddenly, they came under gunfire from across the gorge, The sound of bagpipes blared and all they could see were flashes of tartan plaid darting around the tree line. Their captain decided to send across two men to try and reason with whoever they were facing, but they were quickly captured and dragged away.

To the soldiers, it seemed as if they had stumbled upon an entire army; the rumours of a Jacobite rising were true!

In reality, it was a grand total of twelve MacDonalds of Keppoch, including a piper, that had ambushed those eighty-five soldiers. They were just making the same amount of noise as an army and that was beginning to draw more clansmen to their assistance.

The soldiers started retreating back the way they had come and the small group of MacDonalds shadowed them from a distance. By the time they reach Loch Oich, another force of Highlanders was already waiting for them. Exhausted and surrounded, the remaining soldiers surrendered and the Jacobites had won their first victory without losing a single man.

Highbridge stands in a quiet spot, practically forgotten about but not hard to find. After parking at the Commando monument, the walk heads downhill, through an adjacent field towards the trees and the ruin is reached in less than fifteen minutes.

THE SWANS OF LOCH SUNART

In a quiet corner of Scotland, near the sea loch of Sunart, an ambitious Clan Chief and his wife once lived, with high hopes for their only son. They wanted him to marry well and add to the clan's power and lands, but little did they know that their son was already in love.

She was a poor crofter's daughter, but his heart didn't care about that, he was completely mesmerised by her long, golden hair and her ivory-white skin. The lovers would sneak down to a hidden spot on the banks of Loch Sunart and spend hours together talking about their life once they were married.

Eventually, the young man plucked up the courage and went to tell his parents of his plan to marry. He didn't get the reaction he was hoping for. They were furious that he would put himself above the future of the clan and forbade him from seeing the girl ever again.

Obviously, he took no heed of his parents' instructions, as not many young people in love do, but his mother found out when and where the two would meet every day. She asked a local witch to deal with the crofter's daughter by any means necessary. Rather than simply kill the girl, the witch hid by the loch and transformed her into an elegant swan.

The Chief's son arrived soon after and waited for his partner to appear as usual. He waited and he waited. Every day he stood on the banks of Loch Sunart until sunset, but the girl never appeared. Without knowing where his love had gone he was broken hearted, so to cheer him up his friends took him hunting.

Seeing one of the many swans on the loch swim right towards him, the boy took aim and struck it with his arrow. As the bird died, it turned back into his lost love and the Chief's son immediately realised what had happened and who was responsible.

He was distraught, diving into the water next to her body before any of his friends could stop him. The boy couldn't be apart from the girl any longer and, wracked with guilt, he pulled out his knife and stabbed himself in the heart.

As the bodies of the lovers disappeared under the water, all of the swans on Loch Sunart flew away, never to return.

THE WELL OF THE SEVEN HEADS

Masked by trees along the shore of Loch Oich, a gruesome monument stands beside the road. At first glance, it looks like a regular memorial, nothing out of the ordinary, but look a little closer at the carving on top. This obelisk is topped by a hand holding a dagger and seven heads.

In 1663 Alexander and Ranald MacDonald of Keppoch, the Clan Chief and his brother, were murdered by a group of their cousins, the MacDonalds of Inverlair. There are no details of what started the fight, although Alexander had just returned from France and there's speculation that he was acting like he was too good for some of these Highland clansmen.

The government claimed that they would do something about the crime, but for two long years nobody had seen justice. The murderers had too many supporters in the area and were sensibly keeping their heads down until it all blew over.

However, the famous Gaelic poet Iain Lom MacDonald was kinsman to the victims and he refused to let the matter lie. He was eventually granted a 'letter of fire and sword' from the government, giving him the legal right to seek violent revenge.

With the help of fifty men from the MacDonalds of Sleat, Iain hunted down the seven killers at Inverlair and dealt them his own form of justice. Legend says that he cut their heads off using the same dagger that had killed his clan chief.

Before presenting the decapitated heads to Lord MacDonell of Invergarry, Iain stopped at this well at Loch Oich to wash them. From then on, it was known as the Well of the Seven Heads.

The monument was erected by Alexander MacDonell in 1812 and to prove that the story wasn't a tall tale, he had a burial mound at Inverlair excavated. Seven headless skeletons were found inside.

Once you've finished admiring the gory monument, head down the set of stairs to the left and a short tunnel leads to the well itself.

The Well of the Seven Heads, topped with a hand holding a dagger and the decapitated heads.

NESSIE'S COUSIN IN LOCH MORAR

The Loch Ness Monster seems to get all the attention, but not many people realise she has a sister called Morag who lives in Loch Morar. That's the deepest body of water in Scotland at 310m, which is 80m more than the second-placed Loch Ness!

Rather than a benevolent monster like Nessie, Morag has a reputation as an omen of death for the surrounding area. She is often heard wailing in great distress at night, terrifying those who live near the loch. This monster has been seen in broad daylight on occasion but descriptions of her range from something like a mermaid to just a great, black mass.

Most commonly, she's been described similarly to her famous sibling, with a long, thin neck and a very small head but a huge body. When large bones were discovered near the middle of Loch Morar, people began to get excited, but they turned out to just be a large deer. Clearly, Morag likes red meat.

Written records of Morag go back as far as 1887, but stories like these have usually been passed down orally for generations. One of the more famous incidents occurred in 1948 when a boat of nine people all saw a mysterious 20ft-long animal swimming in Loch Morar.

Twenty years later, two men were out in a large boat when they felt rather than saw something rise out of the water behind them. Turning around, they stood terrified as the beast sped up and bumped into their boat. One of them hit at the monster with an oar trying to scare it off but when that snapped in half, his companion fired a rifle. Morag took the hint and disappeared.

There are legends of a secret, underwater tunnel between Loch Ness and Loch Morar so maybe Nessie and Morag aren't sisters but the very same creature. When they see the research boats coming, that's when they disappear to their second home.

It's hard to know for sure what's hiding in the depths of Loch Morar, but there's no doubt that the deepest loch in Scotland has a few secrets to share.

GLENFINNAN & THE RAISING OF THE STANDARD

While many people visit Glenfinnan to see the *Jacobite Express* crossing the railway viaduct, there's a much more meaningful attraction nearby. The Glenfinnan Monument at the head of Loch Shiel remembers the unfurling of Bonnie Prince Charlie's banner and the official start of the 1745 Jacobite Rising.

Charles Edward Stuart arrived in Scotland from France with just seven companions and the dream of restoring the Stuart monarchy to the British throne. The Prince had support from the French, but the ship carrying all the men, weapons and gold they had supplied came to blows with the Royal Navy and was forced to return to port.

Without evidence of foreign help, Charles had a hard time convincing the Scots that this rising would end any differently than those that came before. He was even told by one influential chief to go back home in no uncertain terms. Travelling through the islands, the Prince used all of his famous charm and charisma to encourage the loyal clans to follow him, but he had his work cut out.

Letters had been sent to all who had previously supported Charles's father, instructing them to meet at Glenfinnan. It was the perfect location, on land controlled by the most loyal clans and with nearby mountains to protect them from unwanted visitors. Things weren't looking good though and as the scheduled meeting time of 1 p.m. passed, his grand army consisted of a meagre 200 clansmen.

Two hours later, it looked like the Prince was going to be marching south with an embarrassingly small number, but then a faint sound drifted over the hill. It was the skirling of pipes announcing that Clan Cameron had arrived with 1,000 men, soon followed by 300 MacDonalds. It might not have been the biggest army in the world, but it would have been a relief to Charles.

Climbing a small mound above the loch, the Prince addressed the assembly and his standard was raised. Rations of brandy were passed around while a MacPhee piper played in celebration and the 1745 Jacobite Rising had officially begun.

The next time that Bonnie Prince Charlie passed Glenfinnan, he was on his way to board a French frigate, fleeing from government troops and never to step foot in Scotland again.

THE LOST GOLD OF LOCH ARKAIG

Take the long road to nowhere along the edge of Loch Arkaig and you might be driving right past millions of pounds worth of lost Jacobite gold.

Only a matter of weeks after the Battle of Culloden in 1746, two French ships carrying long-awaited funds and supplies arrived on the west coast. As far as they were aware, the Jacobites were still an unbeaten force, achieving the impossible. This was the support that Prince Charles had always said was coming, but nobody believed him.

Conscious that Royal Navy ships were closing in, the crew left the Spanish gold on the beach while sailing away still holding on to the French contribution. Seven caskets of gold were unloaded, one was immediately stolen, but that still left a fortune lying on the Scottish shore.

What happened to that money is still a mystery, one that might never be solved. It's generally accepted that the gold was hidden away in the hope that it might fund another rising, but nobody knows exactly where.

Ever since the gold was landed, rumours have spread about its location. Was it all in one place or split into smaller amounts? Was there any left after the Jacobite leaders who knew about it were finished helping themselves? Fingers were pointed and people were even killed over the hunt for the Jacobite gold.

The place most associated with the treasure is Loch Arkaig and it would have been an ideal spot to hide it. It is away from main roads, close to where the ships landed and on land belonging to the staunch Jacobite, Cameron of Locheil.

The odd coin or clue has been found, but never the treasure itself and people are still hunting for it today. Maybe you'll have better luck than them.

THE SURPRISE INSIDE LOCH NAN UAMH VIADUCT

Loch nan Uamh Viaduct is the little sister of the more famous bridge at Glenfinnan and gets a fraction of the attention. Located just a short distance to the west, the same train passes here and anybody driving to the ferry at Mallaig will pass right underneath it.

For years, there was a local legend that the massive, curved Glenfinnan Viaduct had a horse entombed in one of the pillars. They were made of poured concrete and horses had been used to drag cartloads along the top of the unfinished bridge.

Loch nan Uamh Viaduct, less picturesque than Glenfinnan, but with a fascinating story.

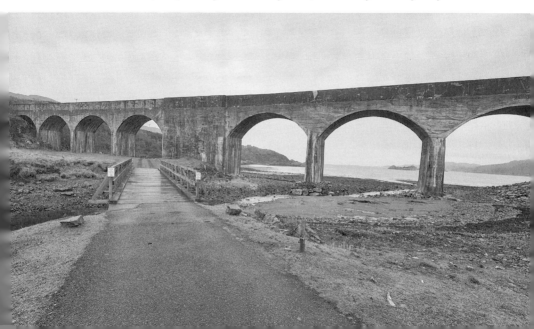

Tragedy struck when a horse and cart fell into one of the columns, but the workers didn't have the means to pull them out. Instead, concrete had to be poured over the body and the accident was hidden away.

In 1987, Dr Roland Paxton decided to test out this local legend and inspected the only pillars at Glenfinnan big enough to fit a horse in. Nothing unusual was found so everybody put it down to just a wild story, embellished by 100 years of gossip.

Then around ten years later, Paxton heard that the entombed horse may actually have been at Loch nan Uamh Viaduct instead. Eventually, with the help of advanced scanning equipment, in 2001 the remains of a horse were seen standing almost completely vertical inside the central pillar.

It wasn't good news for the horse, but it just goes to show that there's often an element of truth in local legends. Sometimes the location is warped from one viaduct to another or from one person to the next, but if you dig deep enough then you might find out what really happened.

THE MASSACRE OF GLENCOE

The Three Sisters of Glencoe make up one of Scotland's most memorable views, but this landscape is forever marred by tragedy. This area was the scene of the Glencoe Massacre, an atrocity that still stirs up emotions over 330 years later.

After the 1689 Jacobite Rising, an official government pardon was offered to any clan who swore an oath to King William by 1 January 1692. Many clan chiefs waited for permission from the exiled King James, but by the time it arrived, it was only a few days until the deadline.

MacIain, the Chief of the MacDonalds of Glencoe, set off to Fort William, arriving just in time to discover that the governor wasn't authorised to accept it. Instead, he was sent another 60 miles to Inveraray, with a letter to explain the honest mistake.

The oath was taken on 6 January and confirmation given that the clan was now protected for their part in the uprising. However, certain members of the Scottish government had been looking to make an example and they saw Glencoe as an easy target. Their oath was struck from the record.

Not long after, 120 soldiers led by Robert Campbell of Glenlyon arrived in Glencoe seeking shelter. The MacDonalds fed, watered and housed their guests for two weeks without even the soldiers knowing the real reason they were there. It's said that a local witch called Corrag tried to warn MacIain of the impending danger but was ignored.

Then late on 12 February, orders arrived. The soldiers were to slaughter the MacDonalds in their beds at 5 a.m. the next morning. It's said that many of the soldiers couldn't face their task, whispering warnings to their hosts and dropping hints that the glen wasn't safe.

Unfortunately, that wasn't all of them. MacIain was the first to be killed, along with thirty-seven others before the rest fled into the darkness. With the heavy February snow, many more may have died from the elements.

It wasn't the scale of the Glencoe Massacre that shocked people, but the betrayal of those who had lived with their victims for a fortnight before the act. Eventually, a public enquiry was ordered, but those who signed the orders, like John Dalrymple, escaped without punishment.

It's a haunting story and there are several places around Glencoe to bring it to life. In Glencoe village, the folk museum holds a wealth of information and a cross remembers the victims. Elsewhere, a short walk leads to Signal Rock, where legend says the order to attack was given and the Hidden Valley was a safe haven for those who escaped.

At the Glencoe Visitor Centre, you can find a recently reconstructed turf house made by the National Trust for Scotland. Inside you can see how the MacDonalds would have lived and where the soldiers were sheltered all those years ago.

CILLE CHOIRILL'S ODD ORIGINS

Cille Choirill at Roy Bridge is a top contender for the most picturesque church in Scotland. High up on a hillside and masked from the road, if you didn't know it was here you would easily drive right past.

This little chapel is from the fifteenth century, sensitively restored in the 1930s, but Cille Choirill has been a holy place for at least 1,400 years. It's the final resting place of famous Scottish bards like Iain Lom Macdonald and Dòmhnall mac Fhionnla' nan Dàn.

The strangest story about Cille Choirril, though, is around the man who built the church long ago. He was the Chief of Clan Cameron known as Allan nan Creach, which translates as Allan of the Forays because of his love of pillaging.

He was a ruthless warrior, somebody who wanted to win fame and fortune at any cost, but as the years passed and his sins multiplied, he started to worry about his immortal soul.

The warrior consulted a blue-eyed witch, who told him to perform a horrendous ritual known as Taghairm. It involved capturing a cat and roasting it alive over a fire. As his servant watched the fire, Allan was forced to use his sword to keep dozens of angry felines away.

Eventually, the tortured screeches summoned the legendary King of the Cats and everything else went quiet. The creature demanded that the cat be released and asked what Allan wanted in return.

All he asked was to know how he could fully atone for his sins, presumably that included just roasting a cat alive. It was a simple answer, the Chief had to build seven beautiful churches, one for each of his great raids.

We can't know for sure if Allan nan Creach's repentance truly worked, but he was right to worry, being killed shortly after completing the King of the Cat's instructions.

MORAY

THE FAIRY CUP OF DUFFUS CASTLE

Starting life as a twelfth-century motte and bailey, you can still walk along the old paved road towards Duffus Castle. You'll need to be a bit more careful than one of the previous Lairds though, unless you want to be whisked away on an unplanned holiday.

The Laird of Duffus was entirely alone on his daily stroll but could hear a loud commotion all around him. It sounded like a whirlwind full of little voices crying out, 'Horse and Hattock!'

He was a curious man, so he decided to shout the same phrase in reply. All of a sudden, he felt that whirlwind begin to pick him up, spin him around and before he knew it, he had landed in an unfamiliar cellar.

To add to his shock, he was surrounded by fairies taking their fill of the expensive wines and cheeses that lined the shelves. Not one to turn down a good party, the Laird of Duffus got stuck in and promptly drank himself to sleep.

When he finally woke up, he had some very confused and angry French soldiers pointing spears at him. Dragging him up to a great hall, it turned out that the fairies had transported him to Paris. Right into the King of France's cellar.

He was still holding a silver goblet in his hand as he did his best to explain to the French King what happened. Luckily, the King enjoyed a good story as much as anybody and let the Laird start the long and very hungover journey back to Duffus Castle. He even kept the goblet as a souvenir.

The story was passed from father to son along with the plain silver goblet, from then on known as the Fairy Cup. The family moved from Duffus Castle to Duffus House but what has happened to the silver goblet now is a mystery! Let's hope they still have that souvenir of the Laird of Duffus's wild night with the fairies.

Duffus Castle, where a laird was once whisked away with the fairies.

THE DISAPPEARANCE OF CULBIN

Today, Culbin is a beautiful beach fringed with vast woodland, but it was once a thriving community with fertile fields known as the Granary of Moray. Suddenly in 1694, during a great storm, the village of Culbin simply disappeared, swallowed up by a mountain of sand.

The devastation was likely caused by harvesting of the vegetation keeping the sand dunes in place, but that didn't stop locals from spreading their own theories. The Great Sand Drift had arrived so suddenly that it didn't feel natural. Word spread that Culbin had been cursed.

Some believed it was due to the local blacksmith's secret life – respectable member of the community by day, but evil warlock by night. He furnished fairies and other malicious creatures with special arrows known as elf bolts and his smithy is said to lie underneath the large dune known as the Armoury.

For many, it was Alexander Kinnaird, the Laird of Culbin to blame. He demanded his tenants worked the land on the Sabbath and like other foolish characters from Scottish folklore, played cards a little too late on a Saturday night. Nobody else was brave enough to continue into Sunday morning, but Alexander found a willing partner in the Devil.

As hand after hand was dealt, Alexander was so distracted by the disguised Devil that he barely noticed the storm building up outside. Sand was blowing in and by the time his game was lost, Culbin had been entirely covered by the dunes.

Whatever the truth behind the disaster, it changed people's lives forever. Residents were forced to flee with whatever they could carry, returning to find their homes had disappeared without a trace.

THE BATTLE STONE OF MORTLACH KIRK

Dufftown might be famous for its whisky distilleries these days, but this area was once better known for the ancient Mortlach Kirk. Founded by St Moluag in 566, this small church played an important part in a Scottish victory over the Vikings and there's a remnant of the battle among the gravestones.

In the year 1010, an army of Danes had landed in the north-east of Scotland and began making steady progress deeper into the country. King Malcolm and the Scots rushed to meet their enemy, catching up with them near the Dullan Water that ran past the small chapel at Mortlach.

Without any thought or battle plan, the Scots attacked immediately. The slaughter was so intense that three of the Scottish leaders fell straight away.

Malcolm was getting worried; this could be the end of a very short reign if something didn't change soon.

He turned to face the chapel on the hill above him, fell to his knees and prayed to St Moluag. He promised that he would transform the building into a cathedral if the saint helped him to victory that day.

All of a sudden, the tide started to turn. The Scots were pushing the Danes back and the King joined the fray. The invaders broke ranks and ran, with Malcolm himself catching and killing the Viking leader, Enetus.

In thanks to St Moluag, Malcolm extended the chapel by three spear lengths – roughly 12m. That doesn't sound like much, but the first Bishops of Aberdeen were based at this very church, so the King had kept his promise.

The church has been rebuilt since Malcolm's extension, but between the gravestones you can find a large standing stone allegedly carved to commemorate the victory. It doesn't stand in its original position but was moved here from a field next door for safekeeping.

If you're struggling to make out the markings, just take a closer look at the image on the church gate to see it in more detail.

ELGIN CATHEDRAL & THE WOLF OF BADENOCH

Once known as the Lantern of the North, Elgin Cathedral is a stunning location, immense even as a ruin. Established in the thirteenth century, its story will forever be linked with one of Scottish history's bogeymen – the Wolf of Badenoch.

His real name was Alexander Stewart, a younger son of King Robert II and seemingly always a troublemaker. Some of his actions were sanctioned by his father, though before he became King. The pair were even imprisoned together in Loch Leven Castle for not keeping their wild warriors in check.

On his father's ascension to the throne, Alexander gained considerable power in the north-east of Scotland. As Lord of Badenoch, he extended his lands in every direction with a collection of powerful strongholds, keeping control with roving bands of armed mercenaries known as caterans.

Alexander's marriage to Euphemia of Ross brought him even more land and now nobody in the north of Scotland could rival him. The greedy Wolf was in trouble though. His father was weakening and with it the royal protection he relied upon.

People were complaining about lawlessness in the north, and chief among them was the Bishop of Moray from Elgin Cathedral. To make matters worse, Euphemia wasn't happy about Alexander spending so much time with his

Elgin Cathedral – the Lantern of the North.

favourite mistress. It's no surprise that the bishop took her side and ordered Alexander back to his wife or the marriage would be annulled.

Then in 1390, King Robert died and Alexander finally snapped. With his 'wild, wicked Highland men,' he destroyed the town of Forres before moving on to Elgin Cathedral. The Wolf took its title of Lantern literally, setting it ablaze.

Unsurprisingly, he was excommunicated for his actions and forced to grovel at his older brother's feet while dressed in a sackcloth for forgiveness. He was absolved but spent the rest of his days hiding out in Badenoch while Elgin Cathedral was slowly rebuilt from the ashes.

The story of the Wolf rampaging through Moray, destroying churches just for the sake of violence has become a popular local legend. However, as evocative as Alexander's nickname is, there's no record of him being called the Wolf of Badenoch until years after his death.

Then again, that doesn't mean nobody whispered it behind his back.

RUNNING FROM THE DEVIL TO BIRNIE KIRK

It's not big or grand, but Birnie Kirk was the very first cathedral in Moray. Built in the mid-twelfth century, that makes it one of the oldest churches still in use today. This small church is home to an ancient bell, a hairy Bible and a dark local legend, once being sought as a sanctuary by the Wizard of Gordonstoun.

Robert Gordon lived in the late seventeenth century at nearby Gordonstoun House, before it became the private school it is today. He travelled far and wide to educate himself, scouring Europe for knowledge. The man from Moray became famous on his return to Scotland for incredible inventions and fascinating experiments.

King James was impressed with Robert's mysterious work, but the locals started to whisper. They believed he had made a deal with the Devil to gain this knowledge in exchange for his soul and payment would be claimed after thirty years.

Robert kept track of time, becoming more paranoid as the years went on. He even constructed an enormous circular building at Gordonstoun called the Round Square, making sure there were no corners for the Devil to hide behind. The night before his payment was due, he asked a priest to sit there with him in an attempt to ward off what was surely coming.

A storm whipped up and with the wind howling through the building and lightning flashing outside, the priest fled. He shouted back at Robert that the only place he would be safe was holy ground. Better head for the oldest and holiest place nearby – Birnie Kirk.

It's around a 10-mile journey so Robert raced his horse to Birnie as fast as possible. Looking back, he saw a rider on a jet-black horse behind him and heard the snarls of Hellhounds hot on his heels.

Just as Birnie Kirk was almost within touching distance, those hellhounds leapt at the horse, refusing to let their prey escape. The horse fell and Robert was thrown headfirst from the saddle, breaking his neck in the process.

The Wizard of Gordonstoun was dead, but the Devil didn't get his prize. Fortunately for Robert, his body had landed on the other side of the church wall, safely inside consecrated ground.

THE CUNNING CUMMINGS OF CARDHU

If there's one thing that Moray is known best for, it's Speyside whisky. These hills and glens were perfect for illicit distillers, making whisky anywhere with a water source that was remote enough to hide from the taxmen. Not everybody worked out in the wilds though, the founder of Cardhu Distillery relied on her cunning instead.

Helen Cumming and her husband John ran a small farm at Cardow, high in the hills above the River Spey. While John worked the land, Helen was responsible for managing the family's other business venture. She made her own whisky in the farmhouse, selling it locally to help make ends meet although it wasn't strictly legal.

Dreaded excisemen roamed the countryside, arriving unannounced to rumble illicit distillers, but they were no match for Helen. Her plan regularly outwitted the uninvited guests, while helping her neighbours out at the same time.

Any time she was running the still, Helen had fresh bread ready to bake in the oven. Sitting at the top of a hill meant that she could spot any excisemen long before they arrived, giving her time to put the buns in the oven. That explained the yeasty smell of fermentation and her apron covered in flour added to the ruse.

With her sweetest smile, Helen invited the government officials inside to rest their feet and sample the fresh baking, before sneaking out the back to raise a red flag. Now all the others near Cardow Farm knew that the excisemen were on the prowl and had plenty of time to hide their equipment.

The Cummings made so much money from their whisky side hustle that when obtaining a distillery licence became easier, they were one of the first to sign up in 1824. The story is still celebrated at Cardhu Distillery today with Helen and her red flag proudly displayed on every bottle, along with her statue outside the entrance.

BITING BACK AT BURGHEAD

The historic Pictish fort at Burghead is one of Scotland's most unique locations. Three times the size of its closest rival, spanning over 5 hectares, this was the capital of the northern Picts, but it wasn't invincible. Stormed by the Viking Earl Sigurd the Mighty in the ninth century, his harassment of Scotland would come to an end in a bizarre way.

A local Pictish leader called Máel Brigte the Tusk was constantly harassing Sigurd's attempts at securing northern Scotland. He didn't have the men to defeat the powerful Vikings, but he could make life very difficult for them.

In the end, Sigurd and Máel Brigte decided to settle things once and for all with an even, fair fight. Each leader could bring forty horses and the loser would leave for good. Sigurd bent the rules though. He brought forty horses but with two men on each of their backs. Máel Brigte only had half as many warriors and, unsurprisingly, lost the fight along with his head.

Sigurd the Mighty strapped the head of Máel Brigte the Tusk to his saddle as a trophy. Both of those men had gained their names for a reason though. Máel Brigte's 'Tusk' was a rather unclean tooth that protruded from his now decapitated head.

As Sigurd rode over the hills and along the bumpy roads, the head bounced up and down. As it moved around, that tusk rubbed into Sigurd's leg more and more, slowly creating a tiny little wound.

What Sigurd didn't realise is that this little wound on his leg was getting infected. Eventually, where hundreds of warriors had failed, that tiny infection took down Sigurd the Mighty.

Máel Brigte the Tusk had bitten him to death from beyond the grave.

ORKNEY

THE DWARF WHO MADE THE DWARFIE STANE

The Dwarfie Stane on the island of Hoy is a unique, 5,000-year-old tomb, carved out of a single, giant boulder using nothing more than antlers and stone tools. Inside, two chambers have been carefully chipped into the stone, with little ledge steps and what look like stone pillows.

The Dwarfie Stane on Hoy. That big rock in front was once used to plug the entrance.

One big rock sits outside, originally used to block up the entrance and seal the tomb. At some point, robbers smashed a hole in the roof to see what was inside, but there is another legend that might explain where the hole came from.

A long time ago, a dwarf couple lived on Hoy and were due to have a baby. Mr Dwarf couldn't have his wife sleeping outside in her condition though, so he put his hammer and chisel to good use, carving them a home in this big boulder. The pair were delighted!

But there was another dwarf on Hoy who wasn't so happy. He was jealous of how content the couple were and especially jealous of their new home. It wasn't fair that he was forced to sleep among the heather and the rain!

So late one night, once the couple had retired to bed inside the Dwarfie Stane, their angry neighbour put a rock in his sling, swung it around and launched it at the entrance. It fitted the gap perfectly, now all he had to do was wait for them to starve to death, unplug the rock and then the cosy rooms would be all his!

The crash of that plugging rock woke Mr Dwarf up. When he realised that it was stuck fast and he couldn't shove it out, he picked up his hammer and smashed a hole through the much thinner roof. Gazing around, he spotted his rival, standing and laughing on top of Ward Hill.

He wasn't laughing for long. The furious dwarf who'd had his lovely new home ruined by this vandal hopped out of the Dwarfie Stane and chased him. The pursuit carried on round and round Hoy, and for all we know they might still be running today!

KEEPING THE SEA SALTY BENEATH THE PENTLAND FIRTH

To get to Orkney from the Scottish mainland, you have to cross a treacherous stretch of water called the Pentland Firth. With powerful currents and danger-ous swells, there's a legend to explain where the turbulence comes from and it's the same reason that the sea is salty.

There was once a Danish King called Frodi who ruled during a remark-ably blissful period. In his land, there was no crime, no killing and no despair. Things seemed so perfect that these years became known as Frodi's Peace.

However, there was a reason that things were so peaceful. Frodi possessed a magical set of millstones known as Grotti that were so big, no human could move them. If you could get them to work, then the mill would grind out anything that the owner demanded.

Frodi had bought two enslaved giantesses known as Fenya and Menya from the Queen of Sweden and together the pair were strong enough to work

Grotti. Their new master's first wish was an honourable one, for the mill to grind out peace and prosperity for the land.

As so often happens, Frodi's greed eventually got the better of him. He asked Fenya and Menya to grind him gold and he watched it pile high. Even giantesses get tired, but Frodi refused to let them rest. All he would offer was as long as it takes the cuckoo to sing its song – two notes.

Fenya and Menya were getting angry.

That night, as Frodi slept, they began to sing a tune called the Grottasong. The powerful lyrics declared that they would not grind for wicked Frodi any more. An army began to appear from the magical mill, led by a sea king called Mysing.

After killing Frodi, Mysing decided to take the Grotti far away from Denmark. With the mill and the giants on board his ship, they were ordered to grind out valuable salt. As the cargo holds began to fill, they were getting steadily heavier and the ship was riding lower in the water.

Mysing ignored the shouts to stop grinding, he had been lost to the same greed as Frodi. As they reached the Pentland Firth, the ship began taking on water, sinking all the way to the bottom of the sea with everybody and everything still on board.

Every so often, a whirlpool known as the Swelkie forms on the surface, proof that Fenya and Menya are still grinding Grotti down there, keeping the ocean topped up with salt.

A RING OF GIANTS AT BRODGAR

In the heart of Neolithic Orkney, the standing stones that comprise the Ring of Brodgar stretch over 100m in diameter, making it the largest stone circle in Scotland. Thought to have been erected around 4,500 years ago by the ancient residents of that northern archipelago, local folklore claims a very different origin.

A long time ago, before humans arrived to make their mark on Orkney, it was inhabited by loud, fearsome giants. During the day, they were forced to hide from the light of the sun, which would instantly turn them to stone. However, when night fell the islands shook with the sound of their thumping footsteps.

While they might have been clumsy, aggressive beasts, they still loved to dance at any opportunity. Late one evening as they clambered into the bright moonlight, a giant fiddler pulled out his instrument and began to play. The tune caught the ear of his companions and the party was soon in full flow.

The giants joined hands and they began to dance in a ring. As the music got faster and faster, the dancers spun round and round in a perfect circle. They were all having such good fun that nobody was keeping track of the time and slowly the moon was beginning to disappear. Dawn was getting near.

Just as the first rays of sunlight shone over the horizon, the music abruptly stopped. Every giant turned its head and there they saw the fiddler had been transformed into stone. Before any of them could move a muscle, dawn reached them too and they all followed suit. Those stone giants are still standing there in a perfect circle, now known as the Ring of Brodgar.

A little down the field stands the Comet Stone, once the giant fiddler who played the music that doomed them all.

THE OLDEST HENGE OF STONES AT STENNESS

Erected around 5,400 years ago, there are four upright stones still standing at Stenness, the largest roughly 6m tall. We don't know what this henge was originally used for, but evidence suggests this was the very first one built anywhere.

From Orkney, whatever the idea was behind the Stones of Stenness spread, reaching right through Scotland, out to the Western Isles and all the way south to Stonehenge in England. This was a culture with Orkney at its centre rather than considered far-flung!

Originally there were twelve standing stones here, plus an outlier with a hole in the middle that became known as the Odin Stone – a reminder of Orkney's Viking past. Even in the nineteenth century, locals would clasp hands through the hole to make oaths or confirm their engagements.

That all stopped in December 1814, when a Captain Mackay, who had moved to Orkney and bought a farm, claimed the monuments got in the road of his plough and that all the locals visiting were damaging his land. He began by smashing the Odin Stone into pieces before starting to topple the Stones of Stenness!

Luckily, he was stopped by the law before he got to all of them and it's safe to say his neighbours weren't pleased. There were more than a few attempts to burn his house down!

Walter Scott wasn't much better for the stones after declaring one of them as being part of an altar for human sacrifice. It was just his famous imagination running away with itself, but in 1907 somebody decided to reconstruct this altar from the smaller stones.

Nobody seemed to think it looked quite right and eventually, the altar slab was pushed over and you can still see it lying where it fell.

The Standing Stones of Stenness are believed to make up the oldest stone henge in Britain, raised over 5,000 years ago.

THE SELKIE OF SULE SKERRY

Orkney is famous for stories of selkies, creatures of folklore who look just like seals but can remove their skins on certain nights to take human form and dance in the moonlight. Sometimes while ashore, they have encounters with humans that rarely end well. The rocky island of Sule Skerry, far off Orkney's shore, was one of many places known as a selkie home.

Once, a young Orcadian woman had spent a single night with a mysterious stranger and nine months later a baby son had arrived. There was no father in sight and the poor girl was distraught at how she would provide for an extra mouth.

Then one day, while trying to scrape together a meal down the beach on the west of Orkney's mainland, a large seal bull approached. To her surprise, it spoke in a deep, rich voice, telling her that he was the selkie of Sule Skerry and the father of her child. The selkie explained that the child would be well provided for and dropped a pouch of gold at her feet.

There was a catch though. When the boy reached 7 years old, he would feel an aching urge for the sea and must join his father as a selkie.

The mother raised the boy, joyful for every single day they had, but aware that she was getting closer to losing him. Not long after his 7th birthday, while down by the shore, the selkie emerged from the water again.

It was time. The selkie put a gold chain around the boy's neck so that the mother would always recognise him and before they left, told her that she would be happy again, but that his days were numbered. With that mysterious comment, the father and son disappeared among the waves.

Years passed, the woman eventually married a loving man and, although she was happy, she always kept her story about the selkies a secret in case her husband didn't understand. She always missed her son, keeping an eye out for that gold chain among the seals that regularly sunned themselves on the beach.

Then one day, her husband came home from a hunting trip with a smile on his face. He had managed to kill two seals with beautiful furs but not only that, one of them had an incredible gold chain around its neck!

To the man's surprise, his wife burst into tears as she finally understood the selkie's parting words.

THE GIANT WHO MADE HOY

There was once a giant who lived in Caithness, but he wasn't a bloodthirsty monster like many of his kind. Instead, he spent his time gardening and gazing across the Pentland Firth to Orkney, where the ground was much more lush and fertile. After toiling hard and seeing little progress, one day he came up with an idea.

He was going to bring just a little bit of Orkney soil back to Caithness, enough to at least give him a good patch of topsoil. Picking up his basket and strapping it to his back, the giant waded through the water until he reached the Orkney mainland. There, he scooped up two great handfuls of earth, leaving deep divots that filled up with water and formed the Loch of Harray and Loch of Stenness.

Now his basket was full and it was time to heave his prize back to Caithness. However, he had filled his basket just a little too much and even a giant as strong as he struggled under the weight. After taking a couple of steps into the sea, he wobbled a little and one chunk fell from his basket with a splash to become the island of Graemsay.

The giant barely made it any further before the rope that held the basket on his back broke under the strain. All of that lovely earth that he'd intended for his garden smashed down around him in an enormous pile. He was so distraught at the wasted trip and the loss of his basket that he just left it all lying there to become known as the hills of Hoy.

CREATING BEAUTY FROM HORROR AT THE ITALIAN CHAPEL

When people think of Orkney, it's usually the archipelago's ancient history that comes to mind, but there's some fascinating recent history to find here. Dating back to the Second World War, when Orkney was the main base for the Royal Navy, the Italian Chapel is a beautiful reminder of a horrific era.

Orkney's harbour at Scapa Flow was incredibly important, but with so many access points it was vulnerable. A plan was made to construct long causeways between some of the smaller islands to protect it from U-boat attacks and, as luck would have it, thousands of soldiers had just been captured in North Africa.

A number of these Italian prisoners of war were sent north to Orkney, no doubt a shock to their system after the heat of Africa, with hundreds placed on the tiny island of Lamb Holm. Living in a very basic camp was nothing new for the soldiers, but for these Italians, one important thing was missing.

The camp priest requested that the PoWs be allowed to build themselves a Catholic chapel and, thankfully, the British authorities agreed. Materials were in short supply, so the Italian Chapel was made from two bleak Nissen huts and decorated with salvaged parts. The beautifully sculpted frontage, masking its rudimentary design, was created from poured concrete – the one thing they had in abundance!

It's the interior that's most impressive though and the men were lucky to have artist Domenico Chiocchetti among them. He created the Virgin Mary mural based on a prayer card his mother had given him before heading off to war and painted the interior to look like elaborate stonework. He was so proud of his creation that he stayed behind to finish it when everybody else was transported off Orkney.

Many of the other PoWs helped, including a blacksmith, Giuseppe Palumbi, who created the iron screen and gates. While preparing the screen, Palumbi was allowed to travel to the Orkney mainland, where he met a young local woman. The pair became close friends, with the Italian even joining her family for meals.

It seems like he may have felt something a little more than friendship. When Palumbi left Orkney, he took the girl's picture with him, while leaving something of his own behind: a tiny metal heart, set into the floor of the Italian chapel, disguised as a stopper for the iron gates.

Palumbi's wife back in Italy wasn't so pleased with the lovely story, apparently burning that picture of his Orcadian friend!

OUTER HEBRIDES

THE PIRATE LAIRD OF KISIMUL CASTLE

Dominating Castlebay from its tiny rock, Kisimul Castle has been guarding the people of Barra for centuries. Protected by their fortress on the rock, the MacNeils felt more than secure enough to head out to sea and cause a little trouble themselves. They had controlled Barra since the eleventh century, but it was in the 1500s that one clan chief really put them on the map.

His name was Ruari MacNeil and he managed to cause so much trouble for the King of Scots that he became known as 'Ruari the Turbulent'. From his base at Kisimul Castle, he led raids all across the west coast as far out as Ireland, pillaging any merchant ship that crossed his path. Nobody was safe from this Pirate Laird, but he had a particular taste for English ships.

Ruari became famously rich from his exploits, decorating Kisimul with expensive silks and filling the cellar with the finest wine – none of it paid for. Not knowing what to do with all his money, even his horses were said to have golden shoes.

Eventually, Ruari the Turbulent's exploits came to the attention of Queen Elizabeth of England and she wanted him brought to justice. A price was put on his head, but with nobody willing to either betray or attack him it was pointless.

Instead, Elizabeth was forced to lean on King James of Scotland to punish his subject. There was little James could do directly, Ruari wasn't the kind of person to bow and scrape to the King. The task of bringing Ruari to Edinburgh was allocated to a much more loyal chief, Mackenzie of Kintail.

Mackenzie came up with a cunning plan, arriving at Kisimul Castle claiming to have just stolen a cargo of French wine. Ruari couldn't resist hopping aboard for a few drinks and when he awoke in the morning, the Pirate Laird was in chains.

Kisimul Castle guarding Castlebay in Barra.

Faced with execution, Ruari was asked to explain his piracy on the English ships. His excuse played to the King's heart. All he wanted to do was loyally avenge the execution of James's mother, Mary, Queen of Scots. Genuine or not, Ruari was allowed to live, although Kisimul Castle and the island of Barra were given to Mackenzie as his reward.

Mackenzie did have some honour though, leasing the island back to Ruari and his heirs for only 40 merks per year. That tradition of cheap rent continues, with Historic Scotland running Kisimul Castle on a 1,000-year lease for just a single bottle of whisky and £1 per year.

THE BLUE MEN OF THE MINCH

Most creatures of Scottish folklore can be found in multiple locations, but one odd group can only be found in a stretch of water known as the Minch. Also known as the Stream of the Blue Men, it stretches between the Isle of Lewis and the Shiant Isles and is rightly feared by many sailors.

These Blue Men are human-sized spirits with immense strength who enjoy churning up the waves with their long, powerful arms. Often spotted by sailors riding the crests of waves with their torsos half out of the water, they'll violently rock ships or pull on rudders to set them towards the rocks.

Only a skipper as skilled with words as he is with his steering board can be sure to make it through unscathed. The Chief of the Blue Men has been known to surge out of the sea and challenge a captain to a battle of rhyming couplets.

If the captain was quick-witted enough to match the Chief, then they would reluctantly let him sail through. More often than not, though, they failed and their ship would be dragged below like so many before them. We do know the exchange of one successful skipper:

Blue Man: Man of the black cap, what do you say, As your proud ship cleaves the brine?
Captain: My speedy ship takes the shortest way, And I'll follow you line by line.
Blue Man: My men are eager, my men are ready, To drag you below the waves.
Captain: My ship is speedy, my ship is steady, If it sank, it would wreck your caves.

One foolhardy group of fishermen almost managed to capture one of these mysterious Blue Men of the Minch. The strait was calm for a change and they decided to try sneaking past the sentries. Seeing one of the legendary spirits sleeping on the top of the waves, somebody had the terrible idea to make a name for themselves and capture him.

They gently wrapped the creature in every rope and chain they had spare, tying it tightly to ensure he couldn't escape. Just when they were almost out of the passage and in the clear, the sea began to churn around them. Two large blue figures were rising from the water and speeding towards them.

'Duncan will be one man,' shouted the first figure.

'Farquhar will be two!' replied the second.

The calling of his companions woke the prisoner up and he snapped his bindings like they were made of thread. Leaping to his feet, he yelled, 'Ian Mhor has no need of help!'

Then the Blue Man dived overboard, leaving the fishermen terrified at his strength and with a story to tell.

THE WHITE COW OF THE CALANAIS STONES

There are few locations in Scotland, never mind the Western Isles, that can rival the ancient Calanais Standing Stones. Around 5,000 years old, its purpose has been lost to history, but at least we have some fascinating local legends.

The Calanais (or Callanish) Standing Stones on the Isle of Lewis.

Hundreds of years ago, during a harsh winter on the Isle of Lewis, the islanders were suffering and their food was running out. All the livestock had been slaughtered for meat and fierce storms were keeping the fishermen from their boats.

One mother was getting very worried about how sickly her children looked. She was already going without so that they could eat, but it wouldn't be long before there was nothing to give them at all. In her desperation, she made her way down to the sea near the Calanais Standing Stones.

She cried out to the spirits of the water, offering to sacrifice herself if they would only help the islanders in their hour of need. Wading into the water with tears in her eyes, she saw something large moving in front of her. Rising out of the waves was a pure white cow with blood-red ears.

Looking into the cow's eyes, the woman somehow knew exactly what to do. It trudged past her to the stone circle, while she rushed home to collect her milking pail. When she returned, the white cow was waiting patiently for her. Once her bucket was filled to the brim with delicious milk, she spread the news around the other islanders.

One by one, they all filled their pails at the Calanais Stones while the cow stood quietly. Once each person had filled their bucket, the milk would stop flowing until the next stepped up. For three days the islanders were sustained by the mysterious cow, but their fortune wasn't to last.

A local witch had been enjoying watching the people suffer and she wanted rid of this cow. When her turn to milk came, she removed the bottom of her pail and fitted a sieve instead. With an evil grin, she milked and milked but her bucket would never be full.

With a weary bellow, the white cow had been milked dry. It descended from the stone circle to the shore, disappearing beneath the waves never to be seen again.

FLORA MACDONALD'S BIRTHPLACE

In a roofless, ruined cottage in South Uist, you'll find a cairn marking what is traditionally claimed to be the birthplace of Flora MacDonald, one of Scotland's most famous heroines.

Flora was the stepdaughter of Hugh MacDonald of Armadale and was living on the little island of Benbecula when Bonnie Prince Charlie arrived. By then he had been leading the government troops on a merry dance through the Highlands and Islands for months after his loss at Culloden.

Benbecula isn't a big place though, and the net was beginning to close in around Charles. He was running out of time and Flora became the Prince's last chance. She wasn't a Jacobite supporter, but after enough persuasion she agreed to play a part in helping him escape the island.

Flora obtained a permit from her stepfather to leave the island and travel to Skye with two servants and six boatmen. Charles was a little too slender to pass himself off as a boatman, so he dressed up as an Irish maid by the name of Betty Burke instead.

Somehow, the ruse worked and the unlikely group made it safely over the sea to Skye.

Once there, they travelled overland and the Prince sailed to Raasay before finally escaping to France. When the government troops caught up with the boatmen, they quickly confessed and Flora was arrested. She was taken down to London but released a year later, to be forever known as a famous Jacobite whether she liked it or not.

Flora briefly emigrated to America but lost everything during the War of Independence. Deciding to sail back to Skye and live with relatives, her ship was attacked by French pirates. The story goes that she refused to go below deck with the other passengers and was wounded in the arm while fighting alongside the men.

Without Flora's help, Charles would have struggled to escape and her risk has gone down in romantic legend. It's said that 3,000 people attended her funeral, drinking 300 gallons of whisky in the process. While Flora certainly wasn't the dedicated Jacobite that she's often made out to be, she will always be remembered thanks to the 'Skye Boat Song':

Though the waves leap, soft shall ye sleep,
Ocean's a royal bed.
Rocked in the deep, Flora will keep
Watch by your weary head.

THE REAL WHISKY GALORE ON ERISKAY

In February 1941, during harsh wartime rationing, the islanders of Eriskay received an unexpected treat from the sea. The SS *Politician* had run aground carrying over a quarter of a million bottles of whisky, a story remembered in the name of the first pub built on the island – Am Politician.

As the ship struggled with gale-force winds, it hit the rocks, ruptured its fuel tanks and the crew had to be rescued onto the island. Once the sailors were safe, the people of Eriskay set out to claim what they saw as rightfully theirs. Unofficial rules of salvage meant that anything washed up from a shipwreck could be claimed by the locals!

That didn't stop the men from taking precautions, allegedly dressing up in their wives' old dresses to avoid getting incriminating oil on their own clothes. They carried off around 24,000 bottles of whisky along with anything else they could get their hands on, including Jamaican bank notes.

Customs and Excise Officers were less convinced by the rules of salvage and set out to reclaim the bottles taken from the *Politician*. Islanders were hiding their loot anywhere they could while the police were raiding their cottages. Some were caught and charged with theft but most of the liberated liquor was never seen again.

THE BATTLE OF CARINIS OUTSIDE TRINITY CHURCH

During the legendary War of the One-Eyed Woman, the feud between the Macleods and the MacDonalds spread across the Hebrides, with every raid by one clan requiring a suitable response from the other. Nowhere was safe, not even Trinity Church (Teampull na Trionaid) on North Uist.

After the MacDonalds had devastated the Isle of Harris, it was time for the Macleods to take revenge. The islanders of North Uist knew that they were a target and had tried to hide any valuable possessions and stores of food they had inside the ruined Trinity Church.

If they thought that a sacred place meant a safe haven, then they were sorely mistaken. Once Domhnall Glas Macleod and his forty men had finished rounding up all the island's cattle, they soon arrived to discover this hoard already neatly gathered together for them. One of their new herd was slaughtered and a feast prepared to celebrate!

What Domhnall didn't realise was that word of his raid had already reached the ears of one of the most daring warriors in the Western Isles – Donald MacIain 'ic Sheumais. Without waiting for any reinforcements, MacIain sailed

The ruins of Trinity Church, where the Macleods prematurely celebrated a victory on North Uist.

to the rescue from his home on Eriskay with only fifteen men. It seemed like a suicide mission.

By the time they arrived at Trinity Church, the much larger Macleod force was a little worse for wear after all their eating and drinking. That was perfect for MacIain, who spread his men out with their powerful bows and gave them strict orders to shoot their arrows, retreat and repeat.

Taken completely by surprise, the Macleods didn't stand a chance as they stumbled out of the church but couldn't get close enough to retaliate. MacIain's seasoned and sober clansmen won such a complete victory at the Battle of Caranish that thirty-eight out of the forty raiders perished. That included Domhnall Glas Macleod himself and the area is still known as Feith na Fala – the Ditch of Blood.

LIVING WITH THE LOIREAG OF SOUTH UIST

As the highest point on South Uist, the mountain of Beinn Mhor appropriately translates as Big Mountain. At 620m it towers over most of the surrounding islands and was once believed to be home to a strange creature known as the loireag.

The loireag is a small fairy woman who was known to be as stubborn as she is cunning and who loved the taste of milk. Any animals left to graze on the slopes of Beinn Mhor would be preyed upon by her, often found to be completely dry when the time came to milk them.

A girl once caught the loireag in the act, sucking on the teat of a cow, ignoring the shouts and curses to leave it be. Driving her away failed and so did pulling the animal, which seemed to be magically stuck in place.

The girl ran to tell her father what was happening and he rushed to Beinn Mhor to deal with the supernatural terror himself. First, he tried to throw stones at her but only succeeded in hitting his own livestock.

In a rage, he grabbed the cow by the horn and screamed to leave it be in the name of Columba. With the mention of the saint's name, the loireag immediately leapt away and scurried away up the mountain!

The only thing that the loireag loved as much as milk was a well-made woollen garment. She watched over the women of Uist who weaved and waulked the wool back and forward on a table to soften it.

The ladies sang songs as they went to keep the rhythm and the loireag was known to lash out if she wasn't happy. If anybody sang out of tune or the same song was repeated more than once then they would find their fabric had been mysteriously ruined.

ALCOHOLIC RITUALS AT ST MOLUAG'S CHURCH

Close to the Butt of Lewis at the very northern tip of the Outer Hebrides stands the solitary St Moluag's Church. The saint is said to have established a chapel here almost 1,500 years ago, but at some point around the 1600s it was involved in a very strange local ritual.

Every 1 November, the traditional first day of winter, the islanders of Lewis would gather at St Moluag's to brew ale, each family contributing a little bit of their grain from that year's harvest. One person was then chosen to wade into the sea up to their waist with a full cup and offer it to a sea spirit called Seonaidh.

In return, Seonaidh would grant them a bountiful harvest of seaweed over the next year, an essential source of fertiliser for the islanders. Once the offering had been made, everybody retired back to St Moluag's, where a single candle on the altar was snuffed out.

That was the signal for everybody to head out to the fields surrounding the church and enjoy the rest of the ale they had made, celebrating until morning. It's thought that similar ceremonies once took place across the Western Isles, with the islanders of Lewis holding on the longest until the tradition was finally discouraged.

PERTHSHIRE

MCCOMIE MÒR & THE STONE OF THE COCKEREL

The Clach na Coileach is a large lump of rock, with its own car park, sitting just off the Old Military Road through Glen Shee. Translated from Gaelic as the Stone of the Cockerel or simply the Cockstane, it doesn't look like much, but this is the traditional gathering place of Clan MacThomas.

The stone has been important to the clan since an event in the seventeenth century involving their legendary Chief McComie Mòr, who had a fierce temper and a hatred of tax collectors.

Clach na Coileach or the Stone of the Cockerel, traditional gathering place of Clan MacThomas.

These lands were owned by the Earl of Atholl and one day his taxmen came to collect from an old widow. All this lady had to keep her going through the approaching winter was a handful of hens and a single cockerel. If she handed those over there was no way that she would see spring, but ignoring her protests, the tax collectors took the lot.

There was only one person who could help her now and she ran to plead with McComie Mòr. Nobody picked on his people and got away with it, no matter if they were employed by the Earl himself. It was time to deal his own form of justice and, gathering a handful of men, the Chief raced after the chicken thieves.

They found them and their loot resting against this large stone and McComie gave them a chance to return what they had taken if they knew what was good for them. It seems that they had no idea what was good for them, because they laughed in McComie's face.

Calmly, he drew his sword and cut the head off the closest taxman in one swift movement. His men jumped into action and three more fell before the rest turned and ran.

The sack carrying the poultry was dropped as they tried to escape and the cockerel leapt up onto the rock, crowing loudly in celebration. From then on, the rock was known as Clach na Coileach and became the perfect place for the clan to gather and remember the heroic exploits of McComie Mòr!

THE SPIRITS IN THE HILLS BEHIND BLAIR CASTLE

If you wander the hills around Blair Castle, there's every chance you'll bump into one of two mysterious entities. The first resides in Glen Tilt, known as the Whistler on account of the strange noise that accompanies its presence. Nobody has ever seen its form, only ever heard it whistling and barking the odd command.

Many thought the Whistler of Glen Tilt was the spirit of a shepherd since he was known to herd sheep with his strange noises. This was no malevolent being though, it enjoyed watching the flock so much that it even told the farmer just to leave them on the hills under his care. When an opportunistic thief tied up a sheep and tried to carry it off, the booming voice of the Whistler demanded he leave it, before knocking the man off his feet!

High above Glen Tilt rises Beinn a' Ghlò, a soaring ridge of mountain peaks where the weather can turn dangerous in minutes. Two hunters were once sent to bring down a stag for the Duke of Atholl's table but found themselves caught in a freak snowstorm. Even experienced men such as these lost their sense of direction and were forced to blunder on in the hopes of finding shelter.

Thankfully, they came to a small hut with welcoming smoke drifting from the chimney. Nobody answered their frozen knocking so the braver of the pair slowly opened the door. The only occupant was an old lady by the fire, with her back turned to them while bent over her weaving. She made no noise or sign of distress, so the hunters approached with apologies for the intrusion.

Now they could see her by the firelight, a chill colder than the blizzard went down their spines. Her arms were far too long and spindly, her eyes as black as night and she spoke a language neither man recognised. Eventually, one cleared his throat and asked if she could spare any food.

Without a word, the old woman disappeared before bringing them a perfectly cooked salmon, with vegetables on the side and something strong to drink. Then finally she addressed the men, 'Little you thought I would be the one to give you dinner today and what a dinner it is!'

She told them that the snow had been her doing, she had called the weather down in order to bring them to her but would explain no further. Soon, they fell into a deep sleep and by morning the weather had returned to normal. As the two hunters left, they asked who or what the woman was and she simply replied, 'I'm the Wife of Beinn a' Ghlò.'

It seems she was a part of the mountain itself.

SCHIEHALLION: THE FAIRY HILL OF THE CALEDONIANS

The lonely peak of Schiehallion is one of the most iconic mountains in Scotland, an almost perfect pyramid near the heart of the country. Its accessibility has made it a popular hiking route, but this is much more than just a summit to conquer. This is a mountain with stories to tell.

The name has been translated as 'The Fairy Hill of the Caledonians' and one of its many caves was believed to hide a gateway to the Fairy Kingdom.

There were once two old men who lived on opposite sides of Schiehallion, one at the Braes of Foss and the other near Tempar. They both struggled with the aches and pains of several years of hard labour, but that didn't stop them from taking turns walking around the mountain to visit each other every Sunday.

During one weekly walk, one of the men heard the faint sound of music floating on the slopes of Schiehallion. Following his ears, he soon spotted light and laughter pouring from a cave entrance. He passed this way every fortnight and it was always empty. It was clear that this was no mortal gathering.

Quietly peeking inside, he saw dozens of fairies feasting, dancing and singing, not paying him the slightest bit of attention. The sight was so enchanting that the old man couldn't help but join in with a song. Fortunately, his voice was one of the best in Perthshire and the fairies seemed delighted to share their revelry with him.

They rewarded his contribution by mending his old, broken back and tired muscles, granting him perfect health. When he finally arrived at his friend's home, the other man couldn't believe his eyes. After listening to the story, he rushed out to the cave to see what the fairies could do for him.

The only problem was that he couldn't carry a tune to save his life. In fact, his voice was so offensive that the fairies cursed him to stoop even lower than before and twisted his face into a horrible grimace. Sheepishly returning home to face his friend, the old man had learned the hard way never to risk offending the fairies of Schiehallion.

WHO WAS MAGGIE WALL?

Just outside Dunning, a large cross clearly marks the spot where Maggie Wall was burned as a witch in 1657. The strange thing is that there are detailed records of accused witches and warlocks in the area, but none with that name, leading some to believe that Maggie never existed.

The monument itself is a mystery, nobody knows who built it or why. When many innocents were being tortured and killed across the country, something must have been special about Maggie to deserve this. Sadly, she wasn't the first and definitely not the last to be burned as a witch.

Of course, there are local stories. The prime suspect is local landowner Andrew Rollo, who is rumoured to have built the monument shortly after the event. Interestingly, he died in 1659, so was Rollo suddenly overcome by guilt at Maggie's fate as he knew his time was almost up?

Or did his heir erect the monument after Rollo's death, having never agreed with what took place that day?

We will probably never know the truth behind the Maggie Wall Memorial, but there is one last mystery. Who keeps painting the writing on the stones, so it stays looking so fresh?

The Maggie Wall monument near Dunning, stating that 'Maggie Wall was burnt here 1657 as a Witch'.

THE BATTLE OF KILLIECRANKIE

The steep-sided Pass of Killiecrankie, carved by the flowing River Garry, is a beautiful woodland spot to wander while appreciating Scotland's changing seasons. This perfect chunk of Perthshire wasn't quite so peaceful on 27 July 1689 when the first Jacobite rising made itself known.

While the Battle of Killiecrankie is fascinating enough, the legends that followed it make for even more interesting reading.

The Jacobite leader was John Graham of Claverhouse, also known as Bonnie Dundee, and he had a reputation as a devil in a fight. People said that was because he had made a pact with the actual Devil and couldn't be killed by steel swords or lead bullets. As with all servants of hell, silver was his only vulnerability.

It was a straightforward battle. The Jacobite commander waited until the sun was just setting, then ordered his 2,500 men into a Highland Charge. They raced down the slopes towards the 4,000 inexperienced government soldiers, fired a single musket volley while just yards away and then quickly smashed into the chaos.

It was a complete rout and the remaining soldiers fled from the wild clansmen. Many were cut down, but one man called Donald MacBean grabbed a horse, trying to ride alongside the river to safety. He was caught and knocked out of the saddle by a group of Jacobites, who had him pinned against the crashing river.

It was a long way to the rocks on the other side of the water, but Donald realised that standing his ground was certain death. At least this way, he had a chance. In a daring feat, he successfully jumped an 18ft gap over a waterfall, at a spot now marked as Soldier's Leap.

It had been a famous Jacobite victory, but their commander had been mortally wounded in the charge. While lead shot couldn't possibly have killed him, it's said that a musket ball hit one of Bonnie Dundee's silver buttons, lodging it in his torso like an enchanted bullet.

THE LADY OF OLD LAWERS

Follow a rough path near the village of Lawers down to the edge of Loch Tay and you'll come across a small collection of ruined buildings. This is Old Lawers, once home to Mary Campbell, a famous Scottish seer who foretold plenty of unfortunate events.

Better known as the Lady of Lawers, Mary lived in the seventeenth century, first making a name for herself after warning locals that the ridging stones for the new church would never be fitted into place. People scoffed, the stones were sitting there ready to be hoisted up the next day, but overnight a great storm washed them into the depths of Loch Tay.

Nevertheless, the church was eventually built and an ash tree was planted in its grounds. The ever-gloomy Lady of Lawers, who was now taken a little more seriously, had another prophecy to tell. When the tree reached the height of the gable, the church would split in two and when it reached the roof, the House of Balloch would be left with no heir.

Chopping the tree down wasn't an option, Mary claimed that whoever tried would be struck by evil. Nerves grew as fast as the tree did, and when its highest branch reached the gable, a lightning strike smashed the church roof in half. Around twenty years later, with the tree now the height of the remaining roof, the House of Balloch was indeed left without an heir.

Even after the Lady of Lawers was long gone, the seer's words lived on. Refusing to believe silly superstitions, one farmer took his axe to that famous ash tree. Shortly after, the horse used to drag it away dropped dead, the worker who helped had gone mad and the farmer himself was killed by a bull.

Among the many other prophecies foretold by the Lady of Lawers that came true, there are others waiting to be fulfilled:

A ship driven by smoke will sink in the Loch with a great loss of life.
A strange heir will come to Balloch when the Boar's Stone at Fearnan topples over.
The time will come when Ben Lawers will be so cold that it will chill and waste the land for 7 miles.

Maybe a visit to Old Lawers will help you draw inspiration to decipher exactly what they mean, but remember to leave any ash trees well alone!

ABERFELDY'S TROUBLESOME URISK

The Birks of Aberfeldy make a lovely woodland walk around a series of tumbling waterfalls but keep your eyes open and you might spot a little more than you bargained for. Tradition says that Aberfeldy comes from the Gaelic – Obair Pheallaidh or 'the Work of Peallaidh', a shaggy little water spirit called a urisk.

Urisks live for a very long time, so even though Peallaidh had created the waterfalls centuries ago, he was still around long after humans had moved to Aberfeldy. He wasn't aggressive or threatening, but he wasn't exactly somebody you wanted hanging around your home.

The tumbling Moness Burn at the Birks of Aberfeldy, haunted by a urisk known as Peallaidh.

A housewife was baking one day when she spied the urisk sneaking through her door and snatching up the first batch of bannocks off the table. He boldly sat munching away in the corner, clearly waiting for more. The baker wasn't happy but didn't want to risk offending this supernatural creature.

She continued to bake, watching the cooled bannocks being snatched up as soon as the last batch was eaten, hoping that he would leave once full. However, the urisk showed no signs of being satisfied and she was almost completely out of flour.

Worried that her family would starve, the housewife took longer with the next batch, waiting until Peallaidh was finished eating. Then she turned with a bannock fresh from the fire and dropped it straight into his outstretched hand. The urisk screamed with pain, bolting through the door to plunge himself into the cool waters of the Moness Burn.

While the baker was pleased that she'd got rid of the pest, she felt terrible about hurting him. Up in his waterfall, the scalded Peallaidh was feeling just as guilty about eating the woman out of house and home.

The next day, the urisk found a glass of milk and fresh bannocks waiting on a rock near his home – a peace offering. In response, the woman's husband soon found that a dry, barren patch in his field was suddenly moist and fertile.

Both were making amends.

A GAELIC LEGEND'S GRAVE IN GLEN SHEE

Down in the valley of Glen Shee, well away from the road near the Spittal of Glenshee, there's a large mound supporting four standing stones. That wouldn't normally be unusual in Scotland, but these are said to mark a special place. This is known as the grave of Diarmuid, companion of the legendary Gaelic hero Fingal and part of a story with many different versions that cross the Irish Sea.

Diarmuid was famously handsome and found himself sought after by a beautiful young woman called Grainne. The problem was that she was Fingal's bride-to-be and despite his best efforts, Diarmuid fell madly in love with her too. He tried to turn her down and run away, but Grainne just followed him.

Eventually, the illicit lovers gave in to their urges and accepted a life on the run together. Fleeing across the water from Ireland to Kintyre, they moved from place to place, until they finally felt safe, hidden away in Glen Shee.

Fingal was both furious and devastated. Not only had he lost his beautiful bride but his best friend as well. Instead of immediately hunting them down, he tried to forget them. As long as the runaways were out of sight, they were out of mind.

Inevitably that all changed when he travelled to Scotland to hunt a legendary boar that was prowling around Glen Shee. Fingal felt a searing rage as he came face to face with Diarmuid once again but still couldn't bring himself to kill him in cold blood.

Instead, he issued a challenge for Diarmuid to take on this enormous boar alone to earn his forgiveness. This was no little pig, it was bigger than a man, with long sharp tusks and a back covered in spikes.

The battle was fierce and the beast charged straight for Diarmuid, churning huge chunks of earth out of the ground. With his life on the line and a monster bearing down on him, the warrior didn't flinch. He levelled his spear, stared into the boar's eyes and struck true. Down the monster fell, sliding to a stop at Diarmuid's feet.

Fingal wasn't pleased, he'd hoped that the boar would have made life easy for him. Then he remembered that the bristles on its back were deadly poisonous. He asked the oblivious Diarmuid to measure out how big this gigantic beast really was.

Up the young man hopped, walking along the boars back from snout to tail calling how many paces as he went. Fingal snorted, 'There's no way it was as large as that, measure it again!' As Diarmuid turned and counted his way back, one of those poisonous bristles sunk deep into his foot.

There was no joy in Fingal's eyes as he wrestled with his guilt and, finally, he couldn't take any more. He had a magical gift, that any wound could be healed by drinking from his cupped hands, so he raced to the river.

Hurrying back to Diarmuid, it was too late, his friend had taken his last breath. No amount of magical water could bring him back now, so he was buried where he had fallen and marked by these stones.

THE DRAGON OF KINNOULL HILL

Hundreds of years ago, Kinnoull Hill above the city of Perth was an especially dangerous place to explore. Not just due to the sheer cliffs but because this was home to a ferocious dragon.

This terrifying beast had made its base in a cave deep inside Kinnoull Hill. From here it would torment the local countryside, snatching up livestock in its powerful jaws and carrying off bonnie young lassies.

The people of Perth were in a panic. They knew where the dragon's cave was but none of them were brave enough or strong enough to fight it. Fortunately, they had the help of St Serf, who had no problem at all slaying the mighty creature with the help of his trusty staff.

The source of the dragon's power was a diamond-like stone, set in the middle of its head, but somehow in the excitement around the monster's demise, the stone was forgotten about and lost. Not that the people cared, they were just happy to be free of terror, starting a new festival in celebration.

Every 1 May, otherwise known as Beltane, the fiery Festival of the Dragon was held on Kinnoull Hill. Young men and women would march through the town, beating drums and playing pipes on their way to the hill. There, they would attempt to climb up to the dragon's cave as a spectacularly dressed figure looked on, with only a handful ever succeeding.

It was far from a Christian festival, but the crowd was allegedly still full of monks enjoying a break from their usual solemn activities. After the Scottish Reformation, the Festival of the Dragon was banned and the cave mostly ignored.

Around this time, a local man was said to have found the lost stone in the dragon's cave. It gave him the power of invisibility and he used it innocently to play pranks on his friends. Unfortunately, he lost it once again and, while the cave isn't accessible, the invisibility stone may still be hiding around the slopes of Kinnoull Hill today.

THE FAIRIES OF GLENSHEE KIRK

Glen Shee translates as Glen of the Fairies, so it's no surprise that this is a place full of magic and folklore. It's been an important route through the mountains for thousands of years and nowhere makes this long history more obvious than Glenshee Kirk.

At first glance, it might just look like a small, simple church built in a picturesque location, and Scotland has hundreds of those. But take a peek around the back and you'll see it was built right next to a fairy mound that's topped with a 4,000-year-old standing stone.

Nobody really knows why a 6ft stone like this was placed here, but if it was just a marker for people to gather at, then it's fitting that the kirk carries on that tradition. Don't worry about the building infringing on the fairy hill though, this is exactly where the wee folk wanted it.

There had been people worshipping in a makeshift church by the standing stone for generations until it was decided they needed a sturdier place to pray. A new spot for the church was picked further along the glen, but the fairies took offence.

Every morning, the builders would arrive on site to find any work they had completed the previous day pulled down and their tools scattered. After several mornings of despair, they realised it wasn't bored kids or vandals, it was a message from the fairies.

Glenshee Kirk with an ancient standing stone on a low mound to its left.

They took the hint, built the new church where it stands today and the fairies left them alone to finish their work!

THE BATTLE OF NORTH INCH

Today it's one of Perth's main public parks, but in 1396 the North Inch saw one of the strangest battles in Scottish history. Exactly who was involved is still debated, but one side is accepted as Clan Chattan and they were involved in a feud that was spiralling out of control.

King Robert III had to put an end to things, but he couldn't negotiate a suitable peace; both sides wanted blood. Robert agreed to give it to them, but with a fair trial by combat, known as the Battle of North Inch.

Barriers and seating were constructed to keep the public safely out of harm's way, as well as give the King a good view of the spectacle. There were to be thirty men on each side and with everything organised and ready to go, one of the Chattan fighters went missing on the morning of the fight.

There wasn't another suitable clan member there to take his place and their opponents refused to drop anybody to even the odds. Rather than leave Clan Chattan at a disadvantage, a brave local blacksmith called Henry Gow volunteered himself.

The fight may have been staged but it wasn't just for show. It was a bloodbath and by the time Clan Chattan were victorious, nineteen of them had been killed and only one of their opponents was left alive. With his fellow warriors all dead or dying, he leapt over the barrier and swam across the River Tay to fight another day.

Thankfully, Henry the blacksmith was one of the survivors and many claimed that it was his strength that tipped the scales. He was rewarded with membership of the Chattan confederation, starting his own Clan Gow within their ranks.

THE FORTINGALL YEW – OLDEST TREE IN SCOTLAND

Situated on a quiet road in Glen Lyon, Fortingall is a picturesque little village, home to the oldest living thing in Scotland. All yew trees are notoriously difficult to age, but the famous Fortingall Yew has been placed somewhere between 3,000 and 9,000 years old.

It's certainly been around a lot longer than the church and may have been a focal point of this community for millennia. The regenerative power of yew trees made them a sacred symbol since long before Christianity and this ancient tree has quietly watched through all the incredible events in Scotland's history.

There is even a legend that Pontius Pilate, the Roman involved in the sentencing of Jesus Christ, was born here and played under the Fortingall Yew's branches. Most will put this down to a local joke, but the story is that a Roman envoy was once sent to visit the local tribe's chieftain, subsequently having a child with a native woman. That would make Pontius Pilate half Scottish!

At its largest, the trunk of the Fortingall Yew had a diameter of 18ft, but unfortunately, a long time ago people began snapping pieces as souvenirs and chunks were turned into cups and bowls to sell as mementoes.

In the field across the road, you can find a small mound with a stone marker, known as the Cairn of the Dead. In the fourteenth century, the plague was sweeping across Europe, but for a while, Scotland seemed to be spared from the curse. People believed it was divine intervention.

Seeing how badly England had been laid low by the hand of God, the Scots took the opportunity to raid Durham, managing to bring the disease back home among the loot. Now the plague was in, there was no stopping it and quiet little Fortingall paid a high price.

Legend says that every person in the community succumbed to the disease, apart from a single old lady. She was then left to deal with the aftermath on her own. Helped by her horse, she dragged every single body into this field, away from the church so as not to contaminate holy ground, and buried them under this mound.

THE STONE OF SCONE

Outside Scone Palace, atop the tiny Moot Hill, you'll find a replica of the Stone of Scone where dozens of Kings of Scots sat to be crowned. There's plenty of history attached to the Stone. Legend says it was originally Jacob's Pillow from the Bible, taken to Ireland and then Dunadd in Argyll to be used by the Kings of Dàl Riata.

When Dàl Riata merged with the Picts to form Scotland, the Stone was moved here to Scone. Like a symbolic gesture of the new union, kings were crowned on a relic from Dàl Riata at an important Pictish site.

Every King of Scots from Kenneth Macalpine, through Macbeth, up to John Balliol was crowned on this spot, sitting firmly on the Stone. That all stopped when Edward I of England raided Scone Abbey and stole this icon of Scotland for himself.

However, there's a chance that he was duped.

The Stone we have today doesn't match early descriptions of a dark, probably meteoric rock covered in carvings. It's even been tested and seems to be quarried Perthshire sandstone, which has led to some convincing theories.

The abbot at Scone knew that Edward was coming, so he had plenty of time to hide the Stone and fashion a fake. Just two years after taking his prize away, Edward came north to ransack the abbey again. It seems like he was still looking for something.

There are tales of Templars guarding the real Stone, or that it's lying hidden in the River Tay just a few hundred metres away. There's even a story that workmen found it in an underground chamber 200 years ago, although after it was sent away for inspection, the trail went cold.

In 1950, four students from Glasgow University managed to pull off a daring heist, sneaking the Stone out of Westminster Abbey where it had sat for centuries. They smuggled it back to Scotland before eventually allowing it to be found at Arbroath Abbey, but some think that was just a copy they had commissioned.

If all of these stories are true, then that makes the stone found at Scone Palace today a replica of a copy of a fake!

SHETLAND

THE SHETLAND BUS

Shetland might be more famous for its Viking connections and unique folk-lore, but a small monument in Scalloway tells a true story of bravery and determination from the Second World War. This inspirational operation was known as the Shetland Bus.

When the Nazis invaded Norway in 1940, they took the country by surprise. Thousands fled in little fishing boats across the North Sea, but many more were left behind. Some formed into resistance groups, but they needed external support and that was where Shetland came in.

Young Norwegian fishermen who had found refuge here volunteered to sail back and become a link between their old and new homes. They were tasked with smuggling in weapons and agents to carry out sabotage, before picking up more refugees to bring back to Shetland.

They didn't have the weapons to take on the Nazis, so they had to use deception instead. The battered, old Norwegian fishing boats they had escaped in were perfect for inconspicuously appearing on the coastline. However, the most difficult part of the operation was getting there.

It was a long voyage across open sea, so to remain undetected the brave sailors operated out of Scalloway during the long, dark Shetland winters. They might have been safer from enemy eyes, but these tiny vessels weren't designed for the extreme North Sea winter.

There were many close calls and daring escapes, but sadly forty-four of the volunteer crewmen lost their lives to storms or attacks. That doesn't count any of the soldiers or refugees on board as passengers.

Eventually, the Nazis grew suspicious of the fishing boats lurking around the shore and their stealthy tactics were scuppered. Fortunately, the Americans

The Shetland Bus Memorial at Scalloway.

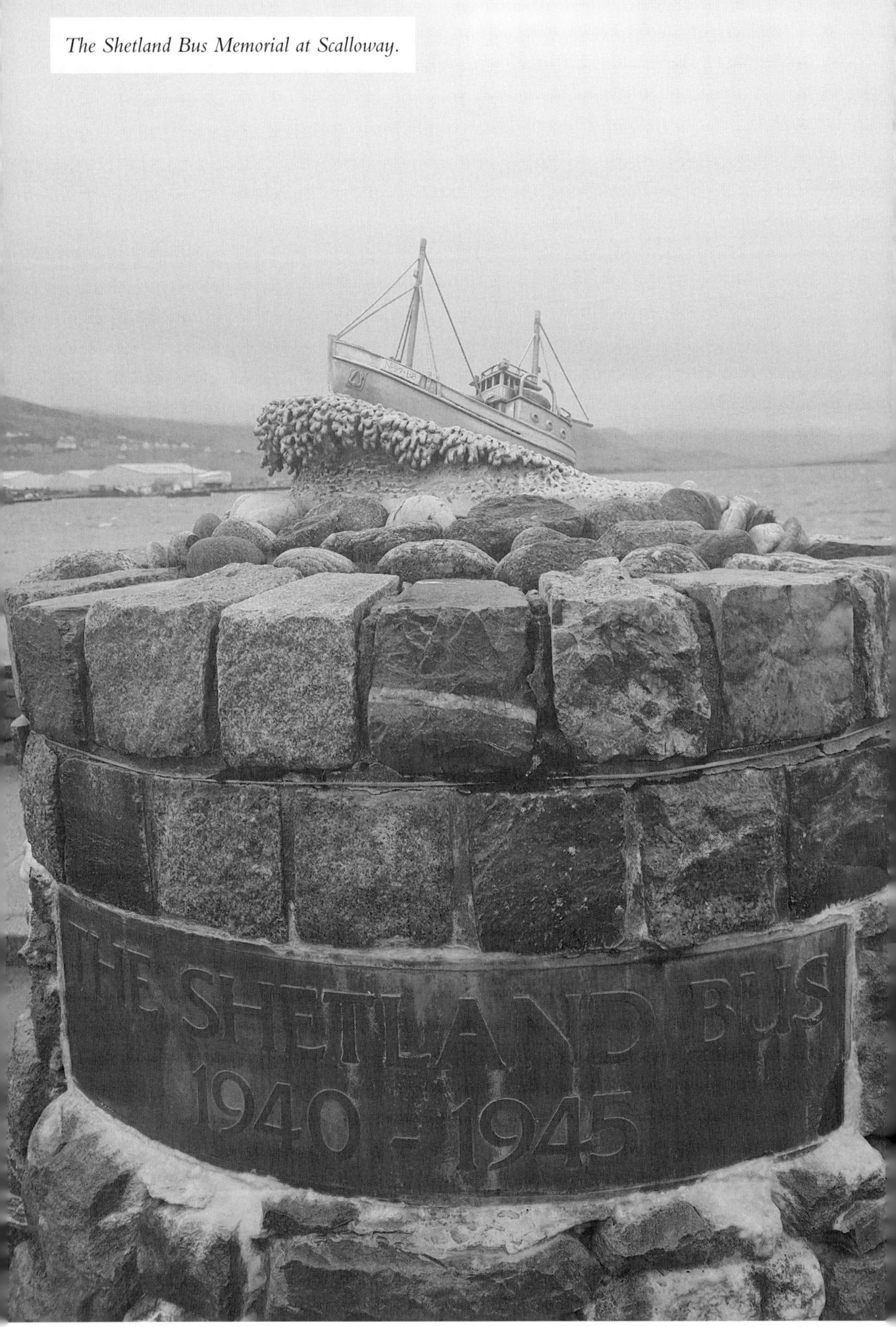

had joined the war and supplied small sub-chaser warships and the operation didn't need to worry about deception any more.

They soon carried out missions with such clockwork that it was just like a Shetland Bus to Norway. Not a single life was lost after that, which just goes to show how dangerous those fishing boats truly were.

After the war, several films were made about the Shetland Bus and amazingly some of the heroes even played themselves on screen!

THE BATTLING GIANTS OF UNST

Among many other incredible creatures, Shetland was once home to enormous giants. With egos large enough to match their size, these creatures rarely got along with each other, usually choosing to live in solitude. However, on the island of Unst, two giants had their homes a little too close together.

Saxa lived on Saxa Vord and Herman on Hermaness, two fingers of land separated by one small stretch of water. Typically, the pair hated each other and spent their days launching boulders across the water. Giants might be strong, but their accuracy isn't great and many of the large rocks lying around Unst are attributed to this pair.

Most of Saxa and Herman's arguments were about a woman. Not a regular woman though, the pair were both in love with a mermaid. She would never have settled down with a giant, but this beautiful creature egged the two on, enjoying watching them fight over her.

Then one day, the giants were spitting insults across the water and the whole island of Unst shook with the sound. That little mermaid popped out of the water and Saxa and Herman immediately fell silent. She issued the pair a challenge to win her heart forever.

Instead of fighting, they would compete by racing to the North Pole. She would swim on ahead and whoever was first to meet her there would have her.

Both giants were terrified of water, but they would do anything for the mermaid. Saxa stepped a foot into the sea, so Herman was quick to follow. Neither was going to let the other win despite the fact they couldn't swim!

The people of Unst waited quietly to see which would return victorious, but in the end, the mermaid appeared alone laughing to herself. Both giants had drowned in the sea and Unst would be a much quieter island from then on.

The welcoming entrance
of Busta House Hotel.

THE UNPOPULAR LAIRD OF SCALLOWAY CASTLE

Shetland doesn't have many castles, but what it lacks in quantity, it makes up for with the quality of stories. Scalloway Castle dates from the very end of the sixteenth century, built by Patrick Stewart, probably the most wicked man in Shetland's history.

His father Robert was the first Lord of Shetland and a very unpopular figure with the islanders. It must have seemed like things couldn't get any worse, but when he died in 1593, the son successfully outshone his father.

Known by locals as Black Patie, he made his mark with cruelty and oppression, leaving behind the wrong kind of legacy. Nothing signifies that better than the remains of Scalloway Castle.

Tower houses simply weren't a thing around Shetland, but Patie wanted something especially grand to show off his power here in Scalloway. Legend says the castle was built using forced labour and the mortar holding everything together was made from those workers' hair and blood mixed with eggs!

To keep his lavish lifestyle going, taxes were increased and the Shetlanders made to cut huge quantities of peat to fuel the fires in Scalloway Castle. Eventually, like most vile characters, Black Patie's deeds finally caught up with him.

The landowners had finally had enough of this jumped-up tyrant and reported him to the authorities in Edinburgh. Eventually, a party of men were sent north to chase the Earl around the islands. There weren't many sympathetic locals willing to help smuggle him to safety.

It's said that being aware of the risks faced by running away, Patie decided to stay put in his grand Scalloway Castle, secretly hiding right under his hunters' noses in a turret. It's easy to get bored spending hours tucked up in a place like that, but luckily the Earl had his tobacco pipe with him.

As he puffed away quietly, the men searching for the missing villain spotted the pipe smoke wafting from his hiding place! Black Patie was soon dragged away to face punishment in Edinburgh.

His execution was allegedly delayed to give him enough time to learn the Lord's Prayer. Then he met the very sharp end of the Maiden, Scotland's famous early guillotine!

GHOSTLY GOINGS-ON IN BUSTA HOUSE HOTEL

Not everybody relishes the thought of spending the night in a haunted hotel, but for those who do, Busta House Hotel is the perfect destination. Built in the sixteenth century, the most intriguing story from this small mansion took place in the 1700s when it was home to Thomas Gifford, his wife Lady Busta and their fourteen children.

Tragically, things started to go wrong for the Giffords when five of their children were taken by smallpox. Not long after that, their remaining four sons took a boat trip across the bay together one evening to enjoy some drinks with friends. They had made this trip dozens of times and arrived without any problems. Unfortunately, they weren't so lucky on the way back.

The boat was found floating on its own and after a mass search, the body of the eldest son John was eventually recovered. That evening had been calm and the water still, so naturally people began to tell stories of a supernatural cause of death. The brothers had been out seal hunting the day before they died so maybe selkies had come to get their revenge!

The story doesn't end with their demise, especially since the Giffords were now without a male heir. Seemingly out of nowhere, Lady Busta's niece Barbara Pitcairn came forward to say she had secretly married John and was even carrying his child.

Lady Busta wasn't happy with being replaced as mistress of the house by Barbara. She refused to acknowledge the marriage and it's claimed that she hid the legal documents that proved it. Barbara was allowed to stay at Busta to have her son Gideon and he grew into a fine lad. Thomas Gifford must have recognised his likeness in the boy since he made him legal heir to his estate.

Lady Busta hated Barbara though and made her time at Busta House a nightmare. When Gideon was 6 years old, his mother was kicked out of the big house and forced to live in Lerwick. The poor woman died ten years later, having only ever seen her son one more time.

No wonder Barbara's spirit returned to Busta House after her death, searching for any sign of her lost son.

THE FINNMAN OF FETLAR

The inhabitants of Shetland have always depended on the dangerous whims of the sea and that was even more true for those who lived on the smaller islands like Fetlar.

There was a young fisherman from Fetlar called Ertie and he had no fear of the waves though. Some said he was far too headstrong and overconfident, believing that he was the best fisherman in all of Shetland.

Then one stormy day, a tall, dark stranger approached Ertie with a mischievous smile on his face. Even before he spoke, Ertie guessed this was a Finnman, a mysterious creature who lived in the sea and could control the waves.

The stranger offered Ertie a challenge to prove that he was as great a fisherman as he claimed. He wagered that the man couldn't catch anything before Yule had passed and, without thinking, Ertie accepted.

For days the wind howled and the waves around Fetlar crashed against the rocks. Even the usually confident Ertie decided not to risk going to sea, but his time was beginning to run out. With only a few days to Yule, the weather began to ease so the fisherman ran to his boat.

In his hurry, he hadn't prepared any bait so only had strips of linen on his hooks and a flask of oil in case of emergencies. Heading out to the best fishing ground, Ertie pricked his finger, doused the linen in blood and cast his line out. The macabre method worked and he quickly reeled in a tiny fish – enough to win his bet – so he turned straight for home.

That was when he saw them.

Three enormous waves had appeared from nowhere. He crested the first wave safely but had to hold on for dear life when the second crashed in. Ertie knew he didn't stand a chance against the third wave.

He poured some oil onto the water, but the old ritual had little effect. Not knowing what to do and seeing his life flash before his eyes, Ertie threw the rest of the oil, including the flask itself, right into the teeth of the wave.

Suddenly, the wave fell flat with a crash.

Once safely at home, the fisherman enjoyed his miniature meal more than any fish he had ever caught, but he wondered what happened to the Finnman. It was a few days later when they met again.

He was in a bad way, with a broken nose, and two black eyes. When Ertie brought up the wager, the Finnman yelled, 'You'll be getting nothing from me after you doused me in oil and threw a jar in my face!'

Thankfully for Ertie, he never saw the Finnman again.

DANCING WITH THE TROWS OF SHETLAND

One creature unique to the Northern Isles are trows, similar to Scottish fairies but mixed in with the Scandinavian troll, who live underground and love music. They're mischievous at best and malicious at worst but rarely seem worried about how their antics might impact humans.

One Tulyas E'en, a magical night seven days before Yule, a fisherman called Sigurd had just finished filling his nets in St Magnus Bay at a place near Sandness called Gord. As he headed home with his catch, he passed an infamous trow hill and to his surprise, he could swear he heard music.

Sigurd was tired but as a fiddler himself, curiosity got the better of him, so he crept around the edge of some rocks. Right enough, light was shining through a crack in the hill and a host of trows were dancing inside! Captivated by the sight, the man forgot all about heading home to his hungry family.

Instead, he walked inside the trow hill and picked up a fiddle.

The fisherman played, the trows danced and he was the life and soul of the party! After what seemed like a couple hours of fun, the celebration came to an end. Sigurd was lucky enough to escape back out into the open and onto the road home again, but even better, he was still carrying the fiddle.

Nothing looked quite as he thought it should but, then again, maybe he was just tired. Those thoughts went from his mind when he opened his front door and found a strange family inside. Shocked and then angry, he roared at the intruders to get out!

The group inside seemed just as surprised as Sigurd, but an old man in the corner calmed things down. He asked the fiddle-holding fisherman for his name, nodding sagely at the answer.

'There was a man called Sigurd of Gord who lived in this house once, but he vanished without a trace 100 years ago.'

When the fisherman realised his family were long dead, he walked outside, lifted his fiddle and played a slow lament. Just as he finished the final note, his body crumbled into dust.

STIRLING, CLACKMANNAN & LOCH LOMOND

THE BEHEADING STONE OF STIRLING

A short distance behind Stirling Castle, the Mote Hill (also know as Heiding Hill) holds a fascinating showpiece. A big lump of rock protected by an iron cage is proudly displayed as the Beheading Stone.

Some claim it's nothing more than a regular rock, dug out of a field, and that the 'axe marks' on the top come from wayward ploughs. However, one thing that can't be denied is that executions took place on this spot. With Stirling Castle being the most important royal stronghold for centuries, it was a natural place to dish out royal justice.

The most famous person to lose their head here was Murdoch Stewart, the Duke of Albany, in the fifteenth century. He was a cousin to King James I and had once been captured while fighting against the English. During his time as a prisoner, the young King James was also abducted and Murdoch's father Robert swept in to control Scotland.

Robert ruled with an iron fist as a cunning and capable man, but one thing he didn't try hard to achieve was the ransom of his nephew, the King. After twelve years, Robert did manage to secure the release of his own son and James never forgot it.

By the time the King returned to Scotland, Robert had died and Murdoch was now in control. James must have been furious that he couldn't get revenge on his uncle, but he was more than capable of taking that rage out on his cousin.

Murdoch, two of his sons and his father-in-law were all arrested and placed on trial for treason. Whether they were guilty or not didn't matter. The assembled nobles had an anointed king on the throne for the first time in years and they weren't about to get on his bad side.

The Beheading Stone on Heiding Hill outside Stirling Castle.

THE BEHEADING STONE

If there wasn't already enough evidence, Murdoch's remaining free son started a revolt and burned Dumbarton. That was the final nail in the coffin and the men were all found guilty.

Brought to Mote Hill, it's said they were executed on this stone with a wooden plank placed on top. James had only been back for one year and the most powerful family in Scotland and the biggest threat to his authority had been completely destroyed.

THE BATTLE OF STIRLING BRIDGE

Stirling is in such an important tactical position that it's seen more than its fair share of conflict and turmoil. Holding this town and its castle meant controlling access to the north of Scotland and so during the Wars of Independence the English army was determined to hold on to it.

In 1297, the Battle of Stirling Bridge catapulted William Wallace's name into the history books, but he wasn't alone. While he had been building a following with fearless determination in the south, Andrew de Moray had been showing his tactical brilliance in the north-east. Stirling was where both of their campaigns combined.

The Earl of Surrey had camped his army next to the old wooden bridge, just a little upstream from the fifteenth-century replacement that stands today. Watching from Abbey Craig where the Wallace Monument stands today, the Scots army made their plan.

The bridge was so narrow that only two horses could cross together and the Scots used that to their advantage. Surrey was nervous about how long it would take to form up on the other side of the river, but Hugh de Cressingham was impatient. Overconfident that they would mow down the lightly armoured Scots, he convinced the Earl to attack.

When almost half of the English army were across the bridge, the Scots charged into the troops forming up on their side of the river. The reinforcements on the bridge were just adding to the mayhem by pushing those in front onto long Scottish spears.

In the end, it was a slaughter. Knights were cut to pieces or drowned trying to swim to safety and Cressingham was killed, with Wallace allegedly making a sword belt from his skin. The Earl of Surrey cut his losses and gave up, destroying the bridge and running away with what was left of his army.

The English war machine turned out not to be invincible and while Wallace's name would go down in history, it's thought that Andrew de Moray was the real mastermind of Stirling Bridge. Wounded during the battle and dying soon after meant that he became Scotland's forgotten hero.

THE LOCH OF THE LOST SWORD AT DALRIGH

Not far from Tyndrum, next to the West Highland Way, there's a tiny pool of water known as the Lochan of the Lost Sword. With a name like that, this wee pool of water must have a good story and thankfully, it doesn't disappoint.

Following Robert the Bruce's defeat at the Battle of Methven in 1306, he was forced to retreat westwards in search of safety on the other side of the mountains. Unfortunately, all the King found was a large force of rival MacDougall clansmen blocking his path.

With just a small force, still reeling from their earlier defeat, Robert was forced to try and fight his way out of the trap. The Battle of Dalrigh was short and brutal, with the King right at the heart of the conflict and almost hauled from his horse by the cloak. As that MacDougall attacker was struck down, he was left with just a bejewelled brooch in his hand, still treasured by the clan to this day.

The legend goes that Robert knew their only option was to outrun their attackers, but they were too weighed down by their heavy weapons. As they fled, the King ordered everybody to throw their swords into a nearby lochan to lighten the load while ensuring their enemies couldn't reuse them.

Nobody has ever found the weapons, so Robert Bruce's large claymore may still be hiding somewhere in the depths. Before you dive in, there is debate as to whether the Lochan of the Lost Sword is the right location or if Lochan nan Arm to the south is a more likely candidate!

THE BATTLE OF BANNOCKBURN

June 1314 saw one of Scotland's most significant victories on the battlefield, an event that has shaped national pride ever since. The Battle of Bannockburn pitched an enormous English army led by King Edward II against King Robert the Bruce's force of Scots to fight over control of Stirling Castle.

The 6,000 Scots were outnumbered around three to one, but if Edward thought that they would run away at the sight of his enormous army, he was badly mistaken. As the English arrived, the only thing between the two sides was the small Bannockburn stream.

Robert the Bruce on his horse at Bannockburn Battlefield.

A group of cavalry rushed ahead, reaching the other side and going straight on the offensive, hoping to crush the Scots early on. Robert the Bruce was out in front of his troops, giving orders and words of encouragement, when he was recognised by an English knight.

Henry de Bohun saw Bruce on his light pony, with little armour and just an axe at his side. He saw his moment of glory.

The knight charged at the King. On his huge warhorse, with full armour and his lance lowered, Bohun must have been feeling confident. The Scots army may have been worried, but knew Bruce was no easy target.

With Bohun just metres away, Bruce sidestepped his pony, stood up in his stirrups and struck down with his axe so hard that it split his opponent's skull in half. The rest of the English cavalry were quickly defeated and at the end of the first day morale was high in the Scottish camp.

The only Scot not happy was Robert the Bruce after breaking his favourite axe.

When dawn broke on the second day, the Scots army was already wide awake, kneeling in front of priests. Edward scoffed that they were praying for mercy and one of his advisors replied that if they were, it was only from God for what they were about to do. They were there for a fight.

Without warning, King Robert did what was least expected and ordered his outnumbered army to attack. Four huge schiltrons, bristling with spears like deadly hedgehogs, descended on the English, who barely had time to get into order. The attack had come so quickly that their longbowmen were now useless.

When those archers broke out to the flank, the small group of Scots cavalry sprang to action, scattering the opponent's greatest weapon. With the main force hemmed in by the contours of the river, numbers didn't matter any more, just grit, determination and very long spears.

The English were already wavering when the Scottish 'small folk' charged onto the field. These were untrained commoners, farmers and locals without real weapons who rushed towards the fight with no orders.

To the tired and battered soldiers, it looked as if another army had suddenly appeared and that was enough for them to panic and flee. Bruce wasn't finished fighting for Scotland, but this was a day that would live forever in Scottish memory.

CLACKMANNAN TOWER'S ECCENTRIC OWNER

The simple, sturdy Clackmannan Tower sits high above the town on the majestically named King's Seat Hill. There aren't many early details, but with a name like that it was probably the site of a royal hunting lodge. We know that in 1359 King David II decided to keep it in the family by gifting it to his relation, Robert Bruce (not the famous one).

It was most likely Robert who built the core of this castle, although it later doubled in height and had an additional small wing bolted on. Eventually, the power of the Bruce family started to wane and they were forced to sell much of the estate, keeping hold of just Clackmannan Tower.

The last Bruce to live here was the eccentric and fiery Lady Catherine Bruce. She was a staunch Jacobite, holding on to her strong beliefs up to the day she died at the grand age of 95. Lady Catherine also knew how to throw a party, holding extravagant ceremonies at Clackmannan Tower, where she would knight special guests with a sword once owned by King Robert the Bruce.

She claimed that as a Bruce she had a better right to bestow a knighthood than anybody in the current royal family. The most famous person to receive one of Lady Catherine's honours was the poet Robert Burns in 1787.

Today, the building has a very slight lean on it after mining beneath the hill caused subsidence, but thankfully it's still standing. While Clackmannan Tower is only open for visitors on special days, the short climb is worth it for views over the River Forth and the Ochil Hills alone.

No wonder the King wanted a seat up here!

THE GLOOMY CASTLE CAMPBELL

Perched above the Burn of Care and the Burn of Sorrow in Dollar Glen stands a tower once known as Castle Gloom, but today better known as Castle Campbell! As descriptive as the word Gloom sounds, it comes from the nearby gorge rather than the tower's moody atmosphere. However, there is a local story that might explain the name a little better.

There's a small pool of water a little way up into the hills behind the castle called the Maiden Well, said to be haunted by the spirit of a beautiful girl. It's thought that this was a Pictish princess who had been a prisoner in an ancient fort here, long before the castle was built.

She would only appear at night and was so striking that all who laid eyes on her were captivated. Many even tried to carry her off home to keep for themselves, but this princess wouldn't be held captive again. Every single man was struck down where they stood.

Edwin, son of the McCallum Chief who once lived in the castle, decided on his 21st birthday that he would win over this maiden. Women always fell for his charms so after boasting to his pals, he set out up the hill path in the dark, stumbling towards the well.

It took three attempts before he could summon the spirit and when she finally appeared, he was stunned. She was indeed so beautiful that he was lost for words, but when he looked a little closer, there was only pain and anger in her eyes.

As a deep feeling of foreboding came over Edwin, he panicked and tried reaching for his sword, but found he couldn't move. All he could do was watch as the maiden placed one hand on his shoulder and he slowly collapsed into the well, sinking to his doom.

Castle Campbell and the surrounding gorge is a beautiful place to visit, just be careful not to invoke any spirits and remember to always keep your hands to yourself!

THE BIRDMAN OF STIRLING CASTLE

The famous Stirling Castle has dozens of tales to tell of ghosts and violence, but one story stands well above the rest. High up on its rock, the castle once witnessed an attempt at the first human flight.

The oppressive entrance to Stirling Castle.

King James IV was known as a Renaissance King, attempting to push forward learning and culture in Scotland. He surrounded himself with leading artists and famous intellectuals, which is how an eccentric alchemist by the name of John Damien came on the scene.

John was an Italian who had spent time plying his trade in France without much success. King James must have seen something in the man because he threw money at him and his experiments, trying to create both the elusive fifth element as well as valuable gold.

Constant failures were testing the King's patience, so John had to try and impress him in another way. To everybody's surprise, in 1507 he declared that he would create a pair of wings and fly himself from Stirling Castle to France.

John confidently climbed up to the battlements with his home-made wings and promptly threw himself into the sky. The crowd gasped and then groaned as he plummeted to the ground, fortunately landing in a dung heap, breaking his leg but surviving.

Trying to salvage a little bit of pride, John explained to the King that his failure was because he had used chicken feathers instead of eagles'. With hindsight, he realised that chickens spend more time scratching in the dirt than soaring in the sky.

John Damien never attempted to fly again and his alchemy didn't take off either. At the very least, he was a colourful character who must have livened up the sixteenth-century court a little.

He became the butt of jokes and satires but his legacy lives on as the Birdman of Stirling Castle.

BALQUHIDDER'S BATTLE OF THE WET FISH

Looming above Balquhidder and Rob Roy's Grave is Creag an Tuirc, which translates as Boar Rock. It's both the traditional gathering place and war cry of the Clan MacLaren, and while the cairn is relatively modern, the stories surrounding it are much older.

When the MacLarens needed to assemble for any reason, this was where they would meet. They might have been joining the King of Scots for a great battle or maybe planning on a lightning raid against their neighbours.

Or maybe it was because a MacLaren had been slapped with a wet fish.

In the fifteenth century, the MacLarens were constantly fighting with the Buchanans of Leny. Even minor altercations would spill over into violence. When one of the MacLarens was returning from a fair at Kilmahog carrying a fresh salmon and bumped into a few Buchanans, trouble was in the air.

Badly outnumbered, the poor MacLaren boy was being pushed around. Suddenly, one of the bullies grabbed the fish out of his hands and slapped the boy across the face with it!

Seething with rage at being assaulted with his own dinner, he challenged the Buchanans to try that again at Balquhidder. Let's see if they were so brave in a fair fight! The day of the meeting arrived and the entire clan turned out at Creag an Tuirc to take revenge for the insult.

The Buchanans were no fools though. They had brought all the support they could muster and the MacLarens could see from their vantage point that they were outnumbered. A runner was sent to ask the MacGregors to come to their aid and offer them anything in return.

The Buchanans climbed the hill and attacked, seeing that they had the advantage. The fight looked bleak for the defenders until the MacGregors arrived to save the day. The MacLaren Chief cried, 'Creag an Tuirc!' and his men rallied forward. Legend claims that not a single fighting Buchanan survived the battle.

All that the MacGregors had demanded in return was the right to enter Balquhidder church before anybody else. It might seem like a small thing, but before long the MacGregors had taken over the whole glen.

The MacLarens were pushed out of their home, all because one of them was slapped with a wet fish!

THE FAIRY MINISTER OF ABERFOYLE

The small Doon Hill, rising among the woods behind Aberfoyle, is believed to be a fairy hill. One man was so sure of this fact that the fairies had to get rid of him before he could share their secrets.

The Reverend Robert Kirk was minister of Aberfoyle in the seventeenth century, but as well as his Christian belief, he was fascinated by folklore. Being a seventh son is said to have given him an insight into the otherworld and, rather than scold his parishioners for old-fashioned beliefs, he became convinced they were right.

Kirk collected oral folk stories and could often be found wandering Doon Hill, where he claimed the fairies lived. The minister compiled everything he knew about these secretive, supernatural beings into a book that would become known as *The Secret Commonwealth*. Unfortunately, he would never see his work published.

At 47 years old and apparently in good health, the body of Robert Kirk was found on the side of Doon Hill in mysterious circumstances. There were no marks nor an evident cause of death, so people began to whisper. News spread that he had angered the fairies, who had taken him into their realm before he could do any more damage.

His grave lies in Aberfoyle Old Parish Church, but it's thought that part of him lives on still. On Doon Hill, there's a tree covered in old rags that some people believe holds the spirit of Robert Kirk, the Fairy Minister.

The story is entirely true and Robert's book was eventually published. Read it at your peril though: who knows if that's enough to invoke the wrath of the fairies.

ROB ROY'S GRAVE IN BALQUHIDDER

Rob Roy MacGregor – the Highland Rogue sounds like a fictional character but he was a living, breathing clansman who became a legend within his own lifetime. He was born in Glengyle near Loch Katrine in 1671, was buried at Balquhidder in 1734 and lived a life of adventure that is hard to separate from myth.

Known as Red Rob due to his fiery hair, his uncle was the Chief of the MacGregors, a clan who were still being persecuted by the Crown for previous misdeeds. All that did was steer people like Rob to operate outside the law.

Officially, he worked as a very successful cattle drover, but this rogue's real business was a protection racket, extorting blackmail from local landowners. One popular story saw James Campbell refuse to pay up, just to have Rob round up all of his cattle while the Laird was at a party and demand the money for their safe return.

Those who did pay their dues could at least rely on their animals' safety. Rob had a fierce reputation as a fighter (often said to be due to his long arms), so anybody foolish enough to steal from his protected herds was soon hunted down and dealt with.

This reputation meant that Rob was trusted to buy cattle for the very wealthy, driving them through the glens to sell at Lowland markets. That all changed when a large sum of money that Rob had borrowed from the Duke of Montrose went missing.

Declared an outlaw, Rob fled into the hills to avoid soldiers sent by Montrose and waged a private war against the Duke and his factor, Killearn. Stories began to emerge making him appear as a Scottish Robin Hood. When one old widow was due to pay rent that she couldn't afford, Rob gave her the money to pay before ambushing the factor to take his cash back.

There are many locations associated with the folk hero's days on the run, such as the Falls of Falloch, otherwise known as Rob Roy's Bathtub. In Loch

Katrine, you'll find Factor's Isle, where Rob allegedly held Killearn captive as he negotiated a ransom from Montrose. When the Duke refused to pay, the factor was released after promising to stop collecting rent on MacGregor land.

Seen as the people's champion, they helped Rob hide when soldiers came looking, although he was captured a few times. He had a habit of breaking out of captivity either by daring escape or simply bribing the guards, who were in awe of his legend.

An anonymous novel about his exploits titled *The Highland Rogue* was written in 1723 and impressed King George so much that he granted Rob a pardon. Now in his 50s, the former outlaw was able to finally settle down to a quiet farmer's life.

While it's often claimed that Daniel Defoe was the author of the novel, that's no longer believed to be the case. Nobody knows who it was, but it's not too far-fetched to think that Rob himself either wrote or commissioned it in an attempt to spread his fame further!

Balquhidder Kirk, where Rob Roy MacGregor – the Highland Rogue – is buried.

SUTHERLAND

HOW LOCH MA NAIRE GOT ITS POWER

Just a few miles short of Scotland's northern coast, Loch ma Naire is a small body of water. This wee loch would be completely unremarkable if it wasn't for its alleged magical power, gained due to the actions of a wise old lady from Strathnaver.

Using a strange, white pebble, this healer could turn any water into a cure for all manner of illnesses. People would travel from miles around to be healed by her and they paid handsomely for the service.

Unfortunately, a member of the neighbouring Gordon family caught wind of how lucrative a business this old lady had made out of her power and he wanted it for himself. Motivated by his greed, the Gordon man travelled to Strathnaver and knocked on the old lady's door feigning an illness.

Always happy to help, the healer sat him down and began to discuss his symptoms. Something wasn't adding up and the Gordon's shifty eyes and vague answers gave him away.

Now he was rumbled, he demanded to know how much the old lady wanted for the stone. When she told her visitor it wasn't for sale, he began to get angry and the bargaining turned violent. He lunged at his host, but she was quick and ducked her way through the door, pebble in hand.

No matter how fit she was for her age, there was no way she could outrun the young man, so her mind raced for another answer. Before she could be caught, the old lady waded out into a nearby loch and turned to face her pursuer. As he screamed at her to give up, she just laughed.

Throwing the magic pebble far out into the depths of the water, she declared that from then on it would possess healing qualities for all but those by the name of Gordon. Furious at being denied, the man rushed into the water and attacked the old lady, who cried out the word shame in Gaelic over and over – 'Naire! Naire! Naire!'

It's said that the powers of Loch ma Naire are most effective at midnight on the first Monday of February, May, August or November. Those wishing to be healed have to strip off, plunge into the water three times, take a small drink and then throw in silver coins as payment. Then it's a race to be out of sight of the loch by sunrise or it will all have been in vain.

HOW THE PEOPLE OF CEANNABEINNE DEFENDED THEIR HOME

Located on the high ground above one of the most beautiful beaches in Scotland, the ruined township of Ceannabeinne is an emotional place to explore. In 1841 there were fifty people living and working here together, then by 1842 there were none.

This community was on Clan Mackay land, part of the Rispond Estate that had been rented to a man called James Anderson. By this point, the people of Ceannabeinne must have hoped that the worst of the dreaded Highland Clearances were a thing of the past. They wouldn't be so lucky.

Anderson had decided that he wanted them off his land. Rather than risk the full wrath of the township, he waited until all of the men were cutting grass a few miles away before serving the eviction notice.

This landlord clearly underestimated the women of Ceannabeinne. When the sheriff officer arrived and informed those women that they had forty-eight hours to leave, they grabbed hold of him and forced him to burn the writ.

A few days later, the police superintendent tried to stamp his authority on the situation, but only managed to lose his coat before being chased off with stones. More force was needed so the superintendent was sent to gather together enough men to evict the tenants. He scoured the north coast and only found three men willing to turf the people of Ceannabeinne out of their homes. They didn't even bother trying.

Eventually, on the evening of 17 September, a larger police force arrived in Durness to inform the community they had to leave the next day. That group of fifty from Ceannabeinne swelled to around 300 angry locals who sympathised with their neighbours. They chased the police out of the parish, but they knew this was a fight that would never end.

Unfortunately, the law wasn't on their side and while Anderson was morally wrong, he was still legally within his rights. The strong statement from the crofters had gained them a positive public opinion and they were allowed until May to find somewhere else to go, leaving behind only these tumbled-down walls.

Ceannabeinne Beach on the far north coast, seen from the ruins of the cleared village.

THE HERO & VILLAIN OF BALNAKEIL CHURCH

The ruins of Balnakeil Church are the final resting place of two very different men. One was a local folk hero, the other a local villain.

An impressive obelisk marks the hero, a man called Rob Donn Mackay, otherwise known as the Robert Burns of the North or the Reay Gaelic Bard. He lived in the eighteenth century, throughout a time when the Gaelic language was coming under attack, but he never saw the use in learning any English.

Rob was a bard, a poet, a cowherd, a poacher turned gamekeeper and somebody who stood up for social justice in both his words and actions. He was even forcefully removed from his home to a planned township after refusing to stop hunting deer in the forest, something that people had been doing for generations.

His poetry was a social commentary on this turbulent time, considered a work of genius and something we can be grateful that local ministers insisted was written down so we can read them still today.

Somebody much less respected was a man called Duncan MacMorrach, sometimes known as MacMurdo and definitely considered a villain. He was a hired thug for the local Mackay lairds and a downright nasty guy.

If somebody was causing trouble, then MacMurdo would be sent to knock some heads together or just make them quietly disappear. He often did it by dumping their body down the waterfall at Smoo Cave.

After he died, it's said that the locals refused to have somebody so evil buried in their churchyard. He had to go somewhere though, and the Laird always had the final say, so a compromise was reached.

The thug was buried into the church wall, where you can still make out this inscription with only a slight translation:

Duncan MacMorrach here lies low. Was ill to his friend, worse to his foe.
True to his master in wealth and woe.

Spare a thought for the locals who had to walk past a reminder of the man every single Sunday.

THE DISASTROUS DINNER OF HELMSDALE CASTLE

Sadly, Helmsdale doesn't have a castle any more; it was demolished to make way for a new bridge in 1970. The small fortress that once guarded the mouth of the River Helmsdale was a stronghold of the Sutherlands – a powerful but not always happy family.

In 1567, Helmsdale Castle was home to Isobel Sinclair, who graciously invited her nephew John Gordon, the Earl of Sutherland along with his wife and son over for a feast. However, things weren't what they seemed and if the Earl wasn't suspicious of the invitation, he should have been.

Isobel was one of those overprotective, pushy mothers who wanted her son to rise to the top and achieve great things. In fact, she was convinced that her boy would make an excellent Earl of Sutherland if only she could get rid of the current incumbent and his heir.

As her guests enjoyed their lavish dinner in Helmsdale Castle, oblivious to Isobel's scheming, they enjoyed their fill of expensive wine. Then slowly, something began to feel wrong for the Earl and his wife. At the look on their faces, the hostess couldn't help but let out a wee smile.

The Earl immediately realised the entire evening had been a trap; they had been poisoned. Even through the choking, he saw his 15-year-old son was about to help himself to a goblet and quickly slapped it out of his hand. It was too late for his parents, but that quick thinking saved the boy's life.

While all of this had been taking place in the Great Hall, Isobel thought her own son was safely away finishing a long list of tasks she'd prepared. Either he was faster than she thought or lazier than he looked because the boy had returned home early.

Maybe he just didn't want to miss out on the feast since he was picking through dishes in the kitchen, avoiding the commotion around the dinner table. He came upon a half-full pitcher and washed his dinner down with the remains of the poisoned wine.

Not only had Isobel failed to murder the heir to the Earl of Sutherland, but she'd accidentally murdered her son! She was tried for the crime and condemned to death, but mysteriously died in custody. Sounds like she had kept the last of the poison for herself.

THE MERMAID OF ARDVRECK CASTLE

The ruins of Ardvreck Castle make a lonely sentinel keeping watch over the icy waters of Loch Assynt. Every so often, you might spot a strange splash or hear a supernatural sob while wandering around the shore here, because this dark loch has a tragic tale to tell.

It's said that the Chief of the Macleods of Assynt couldn't afford to build Ardvreck Castle on his own, so the Devil, disguised as a tall, dark, handsome man, offered to help finance the operation. All he wanted in return was the Chief's immortal soul.

It was a steep price and Macleod was reluctant to pay, so the Devil changed his offer to the Chief's beautiful daughter's hand in marriage instead. To the man's eternal shame, he agreed.

Ardvreck Castle was built in a matter of days and now it was time to pay the Devil. The poor girl had no idea what she was getting into, until her father, overcome with guilt, came clean about his terrible bargain.

Distraught, but with no way of escaping the castle before the ceremony the next day, the girl decided there was only one thing to do. Rather than marry the Devil, she would end her life, throwing herself from the top tower of Ardvreck Castle and plunging into Loch Assynt below.

The groom was furious to discover he'd been cheated out of his prize. He threw hundreds of rocks from the sky to destroy Macleod's land, the remains of which can still be seen, before disappearing in a big huff.

However, the story isn't over. People soon started hearing a gentle, heart-breaking crying around Loch Assynt and even caught glimpses of a large, flicking tail disappearing under the water. Instead of drowning, the girl had transformed into a mermaid, keeping herself hidden from the Devil in caves deep below the surface.

The water level often rises and falls in Loch Assynt and that's said to be the lonely mermaid, filling the loch with tears, shed for a life that she was never able to live.

Ardvreck Castle and Loch Assynt, where a weeping mermaid lurks.

THE LEGENDS OF SANDWOOD BAY

Situated in a remote north-west corner of Sutherland, Sandwood Bay isn't an easy place to get to. Those looking to enjoy its beautiful, sandy beach need to endure a 4-mile hike, but the effort ensures plenty of peace and quiet. That's as long as the ghosts don't make an appearance.

Sandwood is just around the corner from the dangerous Cape Wrath, and so this seemingly serene bay has seen many shipwrecks over the centuries. Viking longboats, Spanish galleons and Scottish merchants have all washed up on this beach, with the evidence buried somewhere in the sand.

People gathering driftwood on the beach have been bellowed at by disembodied voices, while a group in old-fashioned clothes have been seen crying into their hands as they wander the dunes. Surprisingly for a remote beach, the sound of ghostly horses has even been heard galloping past.

An abandoned cottage near the adjacent loch once offered some shelter, although many visitors reported ghostly activity from a spectral sailor, wearing heavy boots, an old coat with brass buttons and a peaked hat. His crunching footsteps could be heard around the cottage, followed by a loud knocking on the windows and occasionally a bearded face peering through the glass.

There are other supernatural creatures who enjoy the solitude of Sandwood Bay though. In January 1900, local crofter Sandy Gunn was walking his dog along the beach when it started barking towards something among the rocks. It was no seal or washed-up whale, but something with golden hair and piercing eyes that looked almost human.

There was no doubt in Sandy's mind that he had witnessed a real-life mermaid. No matter how much he was ridiculed, this straight-talking crofter didn't change a word of his story up to the day he died over forty years later.

THE WIZARD OF REAY & SMOO CAVE

The enormous Smoo Cave, complete with its waterfall pouring through the roof, is one of the highlights of the north coast of Scotland. Long before it was a popular stop on driving routes like the North Coast 500, this secluded spot was the perfect hidden retreat for Donald Mackay – the Wizard of Reay.

Like many other sorcerers, he had trained in the dark arts under the Devil in Italy, but when the time came to pay his teacher, the price was set at Donald's soul. The quick-thinking Scotsman yelled, 'de'il tak the hindmost!' and shot out the door, leaving only his shadow in the Devil's grasp.

The shadowless wizard terrorised the north coast from his base at Smoo Cave but eventually his old master came calling.

When Donald returned to the cave one day, his hound ran on ahead and suddenly gave a loud yelp from the next chamber. The poor wee dog ran back without a hair on its body, followed by the distinct smell of brimstone. It was a sure sign that the Devil was in there.

Donald knew he couldn't run, so he decided to face his fate. Inside Smoo Cave, the Devil was waiting, along with two witch companions, but dawn wasn't far away and with it the wizard's salvation. He kept them talking, happy to let them gloat about how he was cornered with nowhere left to run.

When a cockerel crowed to announce the first light of day, the hellish figures had no option but to flee. They shot up through the roof leaving three holes, including where the waterfall flows today.

When the waterfall isn't too wild, there are boat trips that travel deeper along the river inside the cave. A long time ago, two excisemen were hunting for illegal whisky distillers along the north coast and a local boatman had been hired to help them access Smoo Cave.

Being close friends with the culprits and a particularly strong swimmer, the boatman deliberately rowed into the torrent of water, capsizing the boat. The bodies of the government taxmen were never found, but their ghosts have been known to make the occasional appearance.

WEST LOTHIAN

THE PRISONERS OF BLACKNESS CASTLE

The Ship that Never Sailed, otherwise known as Blackness Castle, juts out into the Firth of Forth in a domineering fashion. Built in the fifteenth century, this was an important stronghold halfway between the royal centres of Stirling and Edinburgh, guarding the port that served nearby Linlithgow Palace.

It's shaped like a ship, ready to leap out into the water with a central tower like a giant, stone mast, angular curtain walls and even the hint of a prow and stern. Although intended to be a comfortable nobleman's residence, Blackness ended up spending most of its working life as a state prison.

The central tower was for those of higher rank, albeit still unwilling guests, while the north tower by the sea had a special pit for less-fortunate souls. Twice a day, while the tide was high, their cell would slowly fill up with sea-water. It's unclear which of these inner prisons held James Kirkcaldy in 1573, a man with terrible timing.

After Mary, Queen of Scots was forced to abdicate, the garrison of Blackness had stayed loyal to her with Alexander Stewart in charge. Or at least that's what James Kirkcaldy thought when he sailed up to the walls on his return from France carrying weapons, ammunition and money for the Queen's cause.

It turned out that Alexander had recently swapped sides, coming to favourable terms with Mary's opponent, Regent Morton. James was welcomed in as a returning hero, but it was all a ploy and he found himself led straight to a cell instead of a bedroom. He was clapped in chains, his cargo confiscated and the keeper of Blackness trotted off to Edinburgh with the good news.

Unfortunately for Alexander, James was a very persuasive character. From his cell, he managed to bend the ear of the guards and successfully converted the entire garrison back to supporting Mary.

When Alexander returned, he had no idea that Blackness Castle was now under the control of his former prisoner. It was almost a carbon copy of James's arrest, with the keeper of the castle walking straight into his own jail cell.

DODGING THE DEVIL AT THE HOUSE OF THE BINNS

The House of the Binns is an odd-looking turreted mansion house with one of the most interesting tales of the Devil. While there are plenty of similar stories around Scotland, this one might actually have some proof!

The mansion's most famous resident was General Tom Dalyell, who had a colourful military career, escaping imprisonment in the Tower of London and fleeing to Russia. He returned to Scotland with the nickname Muscovite Devil and died an old man in 1685.

That doesn't sound too exciting, but his servants claimed that they often witnessed the Muscovite Devil playing cards in the evening with the real Devil on his marble-topped table. Like most mortals, Tom was never able to beat his foe, until one night he decided to cheat.

He placed a mirror behind his opponent's seat and for the first time he succeeded in winning a game. The Devil knew it wasn't down to luck or skill and he wasn't happy when he discovered the trick.

In a rage, he stood up and stamped down hard on the marble table with his hoof, but it didn't break, so he kicked it right at Tom. The general managed to dive out of the way and the table landed with a splash in the pond.

The House of the Binns, once home to General Tom Dalyell, who regularly played cards with the Devil.

Around 200 years later, during a drought, the pond level dropped and a beautiful, marble-topped table began to poke out of the water. To make things even more interesting, it had a bizarre burn mark in the corner that looks suspiciously like a hoof. That table is still there inside the house, available for visitors to inspect a little closer and decide how much truth there is in the tale.

Maybe those dalliances with the Devil are the reason that Tom's spirit hasn't been able to rest. His ghost is sometimes seen riding a white horse along the driveway to the house and in those moments his spurred boots disappear from their display case inside.

THE COMPLETELY USELESS BINNS TOWER

On top of the hill above the House of the Binns stands a curious little folly called Binns Tower that looks as if it's been plucked straight off the side of the main house. Lots of estates have a decorative folly, but this is one with a difference.

It was built in the 1820s as the result of a drunken dinner wager between the 5th Baronet, Sir James Dalyell, and his friends. The bet was to see who could come up with the best way to waste £100 on something completely useless, with the other gamblers forking out the cash.

Sir James won the bet with his idea of building a tower up here to gaze over the land of the Hope family, people he looked down upon for being 'new money'. Even though James won the £100 wager, he spent less than £30 building his project and pocketed the rest for himself.

Then in the 1930s, a wind turbine was added to the top of Binns Tower to produce electricity for the house, but that meant it was no longer a useless folly. The conditions of the bet had been breached and locals claimed that the sails spinning on the tower represented the Laird of Duddingston chasing Sir James around hell trying to get his lost money back.

That wind turbine has now been removed, so hopefully Sir James and the Laird of Duddingston can rest easy again.

IGNORING THE SIGNS AT LINLITHGOW PALACE

The enormous Linlithgow Palace was once the favourite countryside retreat of the Stewart monarchs. Almost every king from James I made their own mark here, although it's most famous as the birthplace of Mary, Queen of Scots. While the palace itself is fascinating, its history is intertwined with St Michael's Church, right next door.

It was here in 1513 that James IV received a prophetic warning from a mysterious figure. The King was in the church praying before marching off to battle when an ancient-looking man in strange robes approached.

The stranger told him he had been sent to warn the King to delay his expedition and proceed no further. No matter what he thought, he wouldn't prosper from this campaign and all of Scotland would suffer. Obviously, the strange man was hauled away while the King finished his devotions, but James couldn't get those words out of his head and demanded to speak to him again.

Nobody could find him anywhere around the church, palace or town, as he had vanished as quickly as he had appeared. Queen Margaret begged her husband to heed the warning, but the King had already called the summons, he couldn't back out now.

Off James marched with the Scottish army to the Battle of Flodden and his doom. It was one of the country's greatest military disasters and very few members of the Scottish nobility came home again.

The Queen was ever hopeful, climbing up to the tallest tower in Linlithgow Palace every day and gazing south for a sign of the King, who would never return.

Some say she's still up there, watching and waiting from Queen Margaret's Bower.

THE TOMB OF JOHN DE GRAHAM OF THE BRIGHT SWORD

Outside Falkirk Trinity Church stands the elaborate tomb of Sir John de Graham, one of Scotland's greatest freedom fighters, although most have never heard of him.

He was William Wallace's right-hand man, but the Guardian of Scotland has cast such a large shadow that people like Graham have been forced to live in it. Known as Sir Graham of the Bright Sword, he was known for his courage, his wit and his skill with a blade.

Most of what we know about this hero comes from Blind Harry's epic, but often exaggerated, poem known as *The Wallace*. One of Graham's first acts was to rescue his famous friend from a fierce fight with English soldiers near Queensferry on the banks of the River Forth. Just as things were looking dire and Wallace was looking for a way to escape, Sir Graham appeared with thirty men to win the day.

Everywhere Wallace went, Graham wasn't far behind and the two of them narrowly escaped an ambush in the narrow streets of Lanark. They hid in the home of Wallace's wife Marion until the coast was clear, before leaving the town in darkness.

The sheriff was furious and executed Marion, burning her house down to provoke the fugitives. In an act of vengeance, Wallace dealt with the sheriff and his son personally, while Graham led the attack that defeated the rest of the garrison.

These two best friends shared the joy of victory after the Battle of Stirling Bridge, but their great partnership was to be cut short. Sir Graham of the Bright Sword fell ten months later during the Scottish defeat at the Battle of Falkirk. It's said that his armour hadn't been fitted properly and an English knight took advantage of the weak spot.

Wallace risked his life to return to the battlefield and take the body of his friend away, carrying him to Falkirk Parish Church for burial. After recently being restored, the tomb of Sir John de Graham is now protected by an ornate cage with a replica of his Bright Sword on top.

The Tomb of Sir John de Graham of the Bright Sword.

THE BATTLE OF FALKIRK MUIR

On a backroad in the south of Falkirk, a monument that looks like a giant pencil commemorates one of the lesser-known, but largest, battles of the 1745 Jacobite Rising. In January 1746, Bonnie Prince Charlie's men were returning north after reaching as far south as Derby. Things hadn't gone to plan, but this was still an army that had never lost a battle.

They were in the process of besieging Stirling Castle when a government army of 7,000 soldiers led by Henry Hawley approached, making camp near Falkirk. With Jacobite reinforcements arriving all the time, they now had 8,000 men available to take the battle to their English opponents.

Hawley was overconfident and underinformed. He thought that he was facing a disorganised rabble and that his cavalry would sweep them away. When scouts informed the commander that Jacobites were approaching, he didn't believe that they would dare attack and began a boozy lunch in Callendar House.

He couldn't have been more wrong.

It was late in the day, but the Jacobites formed up and forced the government army to engage. The MacDonalds under George Murray led the way against Hawley's treasured cavalry, waiting until the very last moment as the horses thundered towards them before firing one devastating shot.

Any horses that didn't fall immediately were in a panic from the noise and smoke. They turned and trampled their own infantry marching behind. The clansmen charged after them and the government left side broke and fled.

Over on the Jacobite left flank, things weren't going so well, but with a snowstorm blowing, Murray and his men couldn't see what was happening. Instead of sweeping around to relieve the pressure there, the MacDonalds ran towards the government camp to fill their sporrans with loot.

By the time the government army retreated, nobody was sure who had won. It wasn't until the next day that it was clear the Jacobites had lost around fifty men to their opponent's 300.

Unfortunately, there was one last, tragic fatality. The Jacobites were ransacking everything left behind in Falkirk when one Highlander found a good-quality pistol. To make it safe, he took the lead ball out before firing out the window to get rid of the loaded powder.

He hadn't realised there was a second ball inside. The young son of the Glengarry Chief, Aeneas MacDonell, was in the wrong place at the wrong time and was hit by the wayward shot. His death, along with the punishment for the culprit, caused rifts that the Jacobites could have done without on their long march to Culloden.

THE BLACK DOG OF LINLITHGOW LOCH

At some point in Linlithgow's distant past, a man had been tried by his peers and found guilty of an unknown, heinous crime. The sentence was death, but not by a quick execution or even a slow hanging. He was to be chained to a tree on an island in Linlithgow Loch and left to starve.

Days passed and the sight and sounds of the man crying out while wasting away should have served as an excellent warning to other troublemakers. The only problem was, he didn't seem to be in any distress at all. A wee bit bored maybe but not exactly wasting away.

A closer watch was put on the island and the riddle was solved. The man's black dog was swimming out to the island every night with food for her master and keeping him alive.

Sadly, the answer to this problem was to chain the black dog to the same tree and both master and faithful pet died together. However, the brave, loyal dog lived on in the hearts of those living in Linlithgow as they made her image chained to an oak tree their town's coat of arms.

WESTER ROSS

THE LONELY GHILLIE DHU NEAR GAIRLOCH

Only found in one specific birch wood around Loch an Draing near Gairloch, the Ghillie Dhu is a unique fairy. Dhu comes from the Gaelic for black and so the Ghillie Dhu had dark hair and clothed himself in leaves and moss. It's thought that there may once have been many of these solitary creatures, but their numbers dwindled until there was only one left.

The Ghillie Dhu could be wild and aggressive to adult humans who trespassed in his woodland but was known to be very kind and protective of children. In the eighteenth century, a young girl called Jessie Macrae became lost while wandering among the trees.

Thinking her situation hopeless, she sat down and started to cry. That was when the Ghillie Dhu appeared. He calmed her and guarded her through the night, before leading her back home in the morning, safe and sound.

He was supposedly seen on numerous occasions but would speak to nobody but Jessie. When she was a grown woman, for some unknown reason the Laird of the area, Sir Hector Mackenzie, gathered a party of men to hunt down the Ghillie Dhu.

Jessie's husband was stuck with hosting the men on the night before the hunt, but somehow the next day they couldn't find a trace of the fairy. It's not hard to imagine that once Jessie got wind of what was planned, she would have sneaked off to warn her fairy friend.

The Ghillie Dhu hasn't been seen since then so maybe Jessie's friend was the last of his kind. Not many people wander through the woodland by Loch an Draing any more, so if he is still around then that's probably just how he likes it.

EILEAN DONAN CASTLE'S BIRD-LOVING BUILDER

Eilean Donan Castle may well be the most photographed building in Scotland, with hundreds of thousands of visitors stopping here every year. While it was reconstructed in the early twentieth century, many don't know that the original castle is said to have been built by a warrior with a special power.

There's an old Scottish legend that a baby who has their first drink from the skull of a raven will be granted a special power. A particularly pompous clan chief from Kintail decided to prove this was superstitious nonsense by using his firstborn son as the test subject.

Then one day, to his father's surprise, the boy was found conversing with the birds around their home in a strange language. The Chief tried to ignore his son's gift out of stubbornness but eventually, when the screeching around the great hall was too much, he demanded to know what the birds were saying.

The son replied that he wouldn't like the answer but if he had to know, the birds were repeating a prophecy that the father would wait on the son in this very hall. Furious, the arrogant Chief cast the boy out and told him to never come back.

Eilean Donan Castle – built by a man who could talk to birds.

The gifted young man took a small boat and travelled Europe, using his gift to make a name for himself and was handsomely rewarded for his deeds. He helped the King of France bring peace to a noisy flock of sparrows tormenting his sleep, and was gifted a ship in return. Then by giving his ship's cat to deal with the rats plaguing a powerful noble, the boy gained a chest full of gold.

Years later, now a wealthy and powerful man, he returned to his father's home, barely recognisable as the boy who had left. Ever eager to impress somebody of importance, the old Chief welcomed the newcomer with food and drink. He had fulfilled the very prophecy that had enraged him, but the old man was just happy to have his son home.

The story of the man who could talk with birds spread. When King Alexander heard about this traveller's wisdom, he granted him the Isle of Donan, where he could build a castle and use his gift to protect Kintail.

DESTROYING STROME CASTLE

Guarding an old crossing point of Loch Carron, the ruined Strome Castle was once part of the wide network of sea-based strongholds reporting to the MacDonald Lords of the Isles. As royal authority increased, the strength of that Lordship began to fall apart. Those clans who tried to cling on to the old ways soon found themselves in a dangerous situation.

By the sixteenth century, Strome Castle was in the hands of the MacDonells, who had a long-running feud with their neighbours, the Mackenzies. Unfortunately, Kenneth Mackenzie was a royal teacher's pet, successfully gaining power and territory by subduing his neighbours as the King's representative in the north-west.

Some MacDonells would be killed, then a few Mackenzies slain in retaliation. Back and forward it went. Eventually, the two clan chiefs both went to the King to complain about each other. Mackenzie showed his experience in navigating the Scottish court, along with some dramatic flair, by producing the bloody shirt of a clansman to the council.

When MacDonell saw the way things were going, he fled back north and refused to be summoned to Edinburgh. Declared an outlaw, Strome Castle was now fair game and the Mackenzies were only too happy to lay siege in 1602.

The story goes that no matter how hard the Mackenzies tried, they just couldn't break down Strome's strong walls. Every time they tried an assault, the MacDonell guns successfully fought them off. The besiegers were ready to give up and head home when they had a stroke of luck.

One of the castle servants was filling up barrels with water inside the walls when in the darkness they accidentally poured the buckets into the last barrel of gunpowder. A Mackenzie prisoner overheard the servant getting an earful and shouted to his clansmen outside that the castle was now defenceless!

The MacDonells had no choice but to surrender and the Mackenzies used their gunpowder to blow the castle up. You can still see huge chunks of masonry right where they landed during the blast 400 years ago.

THE TRAGIC LOVE STORY OF LOCH MAREE

Loch Maree is one of the largest in the country, containing sixty-six islands including the mysterious Holy Isle Maree – the setting for a very tragic love story.

Around 1,000 years ago, a Norwegian Prince called Olaf ruled here, sailing out on raids from Loch Ewe, a sea loch connected to Maree by a short river. This tough Viking warrior soon fell in love with a local girl, building a small tower for his Scottish Princess on an island in Loch Maree.

They were blissfully happy, but Olaf still longed for the sea air and clash of battle. His men were even beginning to think he'd gone soft, so to keep them satisfied he planned an audaciously daring raid.

His wife wasn't happy now. Was he not content staying at home with her? What if he never came back again?

They came up with a plan to ease her nerves. When the ship sailed back into Loch Maree, Olaf would fly a white flag to show that he was safe and would be there soon. If he was dead, his men were instructed to fly a black flag instead but, of course, he assured her that wouldn't happen.

The Princess waited for days; with her eyes constantly fixed towards the passage into Loch Maree. Her active imagination was running wild and she conjured up all kinds of ideas in her head. Maybe he loved raiding more than her or maybe this was all an excuse to see another woman!

Mad with worry, Olaf's wife decided to test him. His ship sailed into Loch Maree with the white flag happily flying away. The girl raised a black flag from a boat left behind and lay inside, pretending to be dead.

When Olaf saw it, his men rowed double time to reach the boat. Seeing his beloved wife lying there, the Prince blamed himself for leaving her alone and in one swift action, pulled out his knife, stabbing it into his chest.

The girl watched helplessly as she realised too late that her Prince really did love her. Unable to live with the guilt, she took the same knife and plunged it into her own heart. The pair are buried together on Isle Maree, under stones carved with crosses that are still visible today.

THE BATTLE OF GLEN SHIEL

Surrounded by soaring mountains, the road through Glen Shiel is one of Scotland's most stunning drives. These slopes are more than just scenic though, they're also a battlefield from the smallest and often forgotten Jacobite rising.

The 1719 Rising came just four short years after the previous well-supported, but ultimately disastrous, campaign. Many of those who had joined that cause were still suffering from harsh repercussions and were in no position to fight.

The real catalyst in 1719 was support from the Spanish, who were locked in war with Britain and planned to use the grumbling dissent in the north as a foothold for an invasion. Even without a lot of commitment in Scotland, the Spanish set sail with an army and plenty of gold.

The majority of the fleet was wrecked in a storm, although a very small force did eventually make its way to Eilean Donan Castle. Three hundred Spaniards joined around 1,000 Highlanders and headed inland to face the government army marching to intercept them.

With a bit of time to prepare, the Jacobites built defences with rocks on the steep slopes around Glen Shiel. With height advantage and now well protected, it would be no easy job for regular muskets to dislodge them now.

What the combined Jacobite–Spaniard force hadn't counted on were the introduction of new government mortars. Rather than cannonballs fired up the slope towards them, shells were raining down behind their temporary fortifications. While they didn't cause many injuries, the mortars had the desired effect – they caused sheer terror.

The defenders put up a good fight against the redcoats marching up the hill but the mortars created panic. With darkness falling, they retreated into the fog and the rising was as good as finished after just a matter of weeks.

Fortunately for the Spanish, they were regular soldiers so they could surrender and be shipped home, but their assistance wouldn't be forgotten. The hill where they fought is now named Sgurr nan Spainteach – the Peak of the Spaniards.

THRIM'S REVENGE AT APPLECROSS

While you might think that you've never met any Norse giants, if you've visited Scotland in summer then there's a very good chance that you have!

This particular giant was called Thrim and he had been exiled from Norway for being a terror to society, coming down from the icy mountains to wreak havoc, biting off heads and drinking villagers' blood. It's not like exile bothered him, he was large enough to wade through the sea towards Scotland.

The giant slowly moved from Caithness to the west coast, spreading chaos and misery as he went. Refugees fled before the monster, screaming warnings that it was after blood. Eventually, the people of Scotland realised they couldn't keep running and as Thrim headed towards Applecross, they decided to make their stand.

There was only one way to get to Applecross, over the Bealach na Ba, and so there the locals laid their trap. On one side of the narrow pass, they dug a deep pit filled with sharp spikes. Then a huge rope was strung from mountain to mountain, tied onto the largest boulders they could find.

The ground shook as their tormentor stomped his way towards them and the sound of his voice filled the air, 'I'm going to find you and I'm going to eat you!'

Intent on finding some prey, the giant didn't spot the rope and tripped directly into the enormous pit, impaling himself on hundreds of spikes. However, still Thrim shouted the same threat!

The terrified Scots ran out to finish the giant off, hacking away at him until he was in a thousand pieces. It was time for a celebration and of course, they all went to the pub.

The Bealach na Ba on the road to Applecross, where the infamous midge was created.

But they could still hear it. Back in the pit, a thousand little voices were coming from the remains in a low murmur, 'I'm going to find you and I'm going to eat you.'

A huge pyre was built over the body, burning fiercely for hours until eventually there was nothing left but fine ash. Surely, he was gone for good now!

Then a light breeze picked up, as it often does in the Highlands, and the ash was lifted on the wind. Then the trembling villagers heard millions, if not billions, of tiny voices whispering, 'I'm going to find you and I'm going to eat you.'

Suddenly they started to feel dozens of little bites on their arms, faces and any exposed bit of body. The Scots ran from Thrim's revenge, realising too late that they had cursed the entire country with the creation of the bloodthirsty midge!

THE FRIENDLY FISHERMAN OF LOCH TORRIDON

Long before the plush Torridon Hotel existed, a poor fisherman lived on the banks of Loch Torridon. One night, he was cooking a salmon over an open fire along with some potatoes and the delicious smell wafted over the loch. The man was so engrossed in his dinner that he didn't notice three strange cats appear.

He got a bit of a fright, but they were the strangest, most miserable creatures he'd ever witnessed. They were soaking wet, one was a fiery red colour, another only had one eye and they were all meowing pitifully.

The man welcomed them around his fire to warm up and he started tossing little chunks of salmon at them. More and more salmon followed and the cats were purring happily now until the man realised there was no fish left for him. With a sigh, he realised it was going to be just potatoes for dinner.

Now that the salmon was gone, the three cats stood up and stretched, then to the man's surprise, they walked to the loch and disappeared under the surface.

A couple of days had passed when word reached Loch Torridon that there was a boom of herring fishing around Lewis. The fisherman jumped in his wee boat and made his way out to the islands.

A storm was brewing overhead but news of the herring had spread and every possible accommodation to hire was full on Lewis. It looked like the fisherman was going to be spending a very cold and wet night under the stars until a woman approached him on the path.

She seemed delighted and escorted him back to her home to meet her two companions, one with fiery red hair, the other with one eye. These witches were the three cats he had fed that night around his fire.

They had been rounding up shoals of herring and chasing them along to Lewis but ended up exhausting themselves. Without the man's kindness (and salmon) they would surely have died, so he was welcome in their home for as long as he liked.

WHERE DO I FIND
MY STORIES?

That's probably the most common question I get asked and the simple answer is – everywhere!

These are all true, traditional stories, and when I say true, that doesn't necessarily mean that the events played out exactly as the tale is told. It means that it's not a story from my imagination, but one that has been passed down through the generations, making it a firm part of that local culture.

Whether you believe that a giant is truly trapped under that hill, a ghost is haunting those halls or a kelpie is lurking in that loch is entirely up to you.

Some stories were gathered on-site, through chatting with local guides or reading information panels installed by heritage groups that are always a great source of knowledge, even if it's just one throwaway comment that gives me a reason to research further. I highly recommend reading everything you can, especially Historic Environment Scotland's online 'Statement of Significance' for each site they maintain.

In many of Scotland's regions, there's no substitute for local knowledge and I'm fortunate to benefit from reading stories collected by people like Tom Muir (Orkney) or Lawrence Tulloch (Shetland). There are tales here that were once shared by storytellers with whom many will be familiar, such as Walter Scott or Robert Burns, who did a great service in increasing the popularity of Scotland's stories.

Following in their footsteps, the later 1800s and early 1900s saw a drive from some to travel around Scotland gathering oral stories directly from locals. The collections that were published as a result were invaluable sources for this book, such as:

Popular Tales of the West Highlands by John F. Campbell.
Superstitions of the Highlands & Islands of Scotland by John G. Campbell.
Wonder Tales from Scottish Myth & Legend by Donald A. Mackenzie.

Without the work of all these people, many of Scotland's stories would have been lost forever as people stopped telling them around the fire. I see it as my responsibility to keep that legacy going by now sharing them with you here, as well as through my website (www.scotlands-stories.com), which has lots of extra information!